Sociology

as Political

Education

Karl Mannheim

Sociology as Political Education

David Kettler & Colin Loader
editors

Transaction Publishers
New Brunswick (U.S.A.) and London (U.K.)

Library of Congress Catalog Number: 00-053258
ISBN: 0-7658-0054-3
Printed in the United States of America

Library of Congress Cataloging-in-Publication Data

Mannheim, Karl, 1893-1947.
  [Selections. English. 2001]
  Sociology as political education / Karl Mannheim ; edited and translated by David Kettler and Colin Loader.
    p. cm.
  Includes bibliographical references and index.
  ISBN 0-7658-0054-3 (alk. paper)
  1. Sociology. 2. Sociology—Study and teaching. 3. Sociology—Political aspects. 4. Sociology—Germany. I. Kettler, David. II. Loader, Colin, 1941- III. Title.

HM447 .M36213 2001
301—dc21   00-053258

Contents

Preface

This volume of translations, like its companion work by the present editors Colin Loader and David Kettler, *Sociology as Political Education: Mannheim in the University*, originated at a conference organized by Martin Endreß of the University of Konstanz and Ilja Srubar of the University of Erlangen to discuss Karl Mannheim's first lecture course at the University of Frankfurt in 1930, a transcript of which had recently been discovered in the papers of Mannheim's one-time student and assistant, Hans Gerth. The supplementary materials derive from published and unpublished German texts accumuated by the editors from various sources over their years of research. Credits are noted in appropriate places. Special thanks are due to Professors Endreß and Srubar, as well as to Gabriela B. Christmann, who edited the original German version of the transcript and supplied it with helpful notes. Generous access to additional materials was provided by Eberhard Demm and Reinhard Laube. Bard College and the University of Nevada at Las Vegas supported the research. David Kettler wishes to express appreciation as well to his good friend and long-time collaborator, Volker Meja, without whose schooling during many past joint ventures these translations would be more pedantic and even less in the spirit of Mannheim's own hopes for colloquial transparency.

Introduction

David Kettler and Colin Loader

The history of sociology during its first century as a separate inquiry is simultaneously a struggle for definition and recognition. Its proponents have fought, first, to delimit their work from the mere elaboration of one or another political ideology, and, second, to establish their place in the prime legitimating agency for truth-seeking intellectual activity, the university. A recent survey of "classics of sociology," for example, opens with chapters on Comte, Marx, Spencer, Pareto, Tönnies, Simmel, Durkheim, Mead, Max Weber, and Robert Park.[1] The relationships to the world of political brochures and journalism are major themes in the biographies of almost all, with the issue of specifying the "scientific" nature of their own enterprises a major feature, something to be argued in detail rather than tacitly presupposed. Except for Spencer, as it seems, the lives and works of all are no less strongly marked by the places they sought or attained in the disciplinary and pedagogical undertakings of the university. These genealogical circumstances entered into the structure of sociology, at least in its classical writings.

The earliest articles by Karl Mannheim included in the present volume were published one hundred years after Auguste Comte's *Plan de traveaux scientifiques nécessaires pour réorganiser la société* of 1822, and the 1930 lecture course that comprises our primary documentation coincided with the centennial of the first volume of Comte's *Cours*. Mannheim's treatment of the issues of ideology and pedagogy in the texts translated here testifies to his conscientious but innovative engagement with the history of sociology. The mode is reflexive. While acknowledging the indispensability of separating sociology from political ideology, he considers it no less essential to find ways of drawing on the cognitive resources generated by direct political interest and conflict. That this is the point of Mannheim's renowned sociology of knowledge, most familiar from *Ideology and Utopia,* is made nowhere as clear as in these hitherto unpublished or untranslated texts. The point is to let sociological inquiry and ideological confrontation learn from one another, inform one another. This civic "mission" of sociology, to use a term increasingly important to Mannheim, has vital consequences for sociology as a university subject, just as the opportunities offered to sociologists by their pedagogical work in the university affect the questions they must address in sociology and the manner in which the discipline must communicate. Above all, sociology cannot become scholastic, its method constrained by the exigencies of systematic instruction. Mannheim's effort can be encapsulated in the formula, "sociology as political education," but only if it is understood that such education is the modern counterpart of the transcendent idealism of the older classical or liberal arts education, what the German discourse of the time called *"Bildung."*[2]

In Weimar Germany, the question of sociology was intimately tied to the standing of the republic. The principal advocate for the extension of sociology as a university subject was Carl H. Becker in the Prussian Ministry of Higher Education, an ardent supporter of the constitution, and the opponents of the new discipline were almost all opponents as well of the new dispensation. Sociology, the opponents said, politicized the university, notably by infusing socialist doctrine, and sociology lacked scientific detachment or discipline. In rebuttal, Max Weber was put forward by the members of the German Sociological Association he had helped to found before his death, as the embodiment of a social-scientific attitude detached from politics and dedicated to rigorous and neutral study; but his asceticism was given a barren turn by Leopold von Wiese and others who claimed the succession, and younger sociologists had to find a way of encompassing more of the intensity and scope of contemporary social thought than von Wiese's kind of disciplinary institutionalization permitted. From the publication of *Ideology and Utopia* in 1929 until the end of 1932, Mannheim was widely recognized as the representative figure among these sociologists . His major, translated published writings during the few years of his Frankfurt professorship, however, notably his study of economic ambition and his handbook article on sociology of knowledge,[3] were mainly designed to overcome suspicion among established professionals in the field. The present collection balances this interest with documents that derive primarily from Mannheim's work as charismatic teacher.

Taken in chronological order, the translations include four items from Mannheim's years as independent scholar and *Privatdozent* in Heidelberg, six documents of the Frankfurt years, including the major text, and one retrospective epistolary exchange written in exile. Strictly speaking, Heidelberg was already a place of exile for Karl Mannheim, since he settled there in 1921 only after the establishment of a counter-revolutionary regime in his native Hungary made it an unsafe home for a Jewish intellectual broadly on the Left, especially a former close associate of Georg Lukács, who had been cultural commissar in the short-lived Soviet regime.[4] Mannheim arrived in Heidelberg as a philosopher, hoping to prepare his habilitation under the noted Heinrich Rickert, but he soon reoriented his studies to the cultural sociology of Alfred Weber and Emil Lederer.

The earliest of our supplementary translations, printed here after the primary document, date from the year of transition. The first of these indicates that Mannheim is undergoing more than one transition. In two literary letters published in the Hungarian emigré journal Tüz, Mannheim treats Heidelberg as a synecdoche of German culture, contrasting it with the dispersed and damaged Hungarian intellectual life which had been centered in the Budapest metropolis. The articles pose a choice between the worlds of Max Weber and Stefan George, and explain Mannheim's regretful rejection of the latter. These are not the times, he concludes, for exalted communities. The second of these early pieces show Mannheim increasingly at home in Heidelberg. A sparkling newspaper article on the cultural pages of the liberal *Frankfurter Zeitung*, the brief paper expresses Mannheim's basic conviction that the interests generated by the intense political, religious, or artistic engagements of youth must be addressed by academic disciplines, even while the popular articulation of those interests in the myths that captivated youth had to be corrected by the critical methods of the university. That remained Mannheim's lifelong program, undoubtedly comprehending his self-understanding of his own development as well as his design for sociology as a university subject.

Our chronological sequence jumps forward seven years to another contribution to the *Frankfurter Zeitung*, where Mannheim takes up the same basic themes, this time with reference to the academic study of newspaper work, where the immediate effects of human experience register less in the enthusiasms of youth than in the distillations of opinion found in the press. Again, the aim is not simply to objectify this social activity but to engage and enhance it as communication. Mannheim's writing on the subject, moreover, is reflection on the work he is himself doing as an instructor in the Institute for the Journalistic Medium associated with Alfred Weber's institute in Heidelberg. The third text in this order is a protocol of two joint meetings of their seminars organized in 1929 by Weber and Mannheim in order to argue through some of the intellectual issues that divided them. Taking as their point of departure two student papers on *History and Class-Consciousness* by Georg Lukács, Weber and Mannheim end up with the unresolved question whether sociological cultivation should aspire first of all to a transcendent and spiritual self-experience, as Weber maintained, or whether it should aim to enhance the capacity for practical mastery in a world shaped by power and material interest, as Mannheim cautiously proposed.

Thanks to the active support of Carl H. Becker, the still youthful Mannheim was designated in 1930 to be the professor of sociology at the University of Frankfurt, a dynamic municipal foundation that attained standing as a state university only in the late years of the war. The principal document in our collection, then, is an almost complete transcript of the first lecture course he taught in his new appointment, in which Mannheim works out an account of sociology's relations to both ideology and academic study that is unmatched in his published writings and in the unpublished writings published heretofore. Sociology, he says, is the activity that articulates and comprehends the distance between modern actors and the contexts of meaning that seemed self-evident to earlier generations. It is a way of encountering as well as understanding the world. Yet while sociological thinkers experiment with their lives and are anything but passive, their mode of action seems irresolute to practical organizers, and they must cope with a world where the urgency of perceived needs and the bitterness bred of complexity fosters utopian and "reprimitivized" strategies of theory and practice. Mannheim hopes to help his students to remain true to their personal social knowledge under these conditions and to attain to a higher platform of realistic judgment. Mannheim's efforts to connect the questions originating in his students' life experiences to sociological instruction receive a methodological expression in two excerpts translated here from Mannheim's own lecture notes for courses he taught in 1931 and 1932. He speaks of a sociological method grounded in "life"–literally, a method of life-science,—and he cautions against pursuing questions that are not in fact pressing and thus once more against a purely scholastic sociology.

An excerpt translated here from a transcript of a conversation on religion organized in the summer of 1931 by Paul Tillich shows Mannheim addressing the limits of sociology and of the rational attitude that sociology epitomizes. There is a purely personal space of religiosity and spiritual need, he insists against Horkheimer, Pollock, and Wiesengrund [Adorno], although this cannot countermand the need to be socially efficacious in the domain that functional knowledge can master. A letter to the psychologist Max Wertheimer a few weeks after this occasion, referring to discussions at a lecture by Max Horkheimer, tilts the balance back in the direction of scientific appraisal, if also with a keen sense of the historical location of both science and that which it studies. Like the translated excerpt from the Tillich conversation, this item illuminates the limiting context of Mannheim's strictly sociological enterprise.

In 1932, Mannheim organized his thoughts about the multi-dimensional and open field of sociology in a long lecture on the sociological curriculum, setting himself off from both Leopold von Wiese, the proponent of a rigorously formalistic and specialized sociology, and Hans Freyer, the advocate of an activist sociology understood as a volitionist intervention to constitute a militant people. We include a translation of about a third of this text, highlighting the theme of political education as a characterization of the practical core, a return for Mannheim to an argument already evident in the central essay of *Ideology and Utopia*. The publication of this work at the time signaled the highwater mark of Mannheim as a leading force in the emerging profession.

Our last inclusion is a translation of searching letters exchanged in exile between Mannheim and Eduard Heimann, a colleague from Frankfurt and an intimate collaborator of Paul Tillich. Heimann reproaches Mannheim for having abandoned the search for the pre-rational ultimate grounding of knowledge and Mannheim replies uncompromisingly as a proponent of the instrumental uses of knowledge to counter the evils we can know. Some commentators have agreed with Heimann's assessment that Mannheim in effect reverts to the engineering illusions of the first fathers of sociology, but we present his agonized analysis as proof that Mannheim never abandoned the hopes that fueled his pedagogical project at its inception. The letter is a document of pain, but not of surrender.

One of Mannheim's themes in this correspondence is that German intellectuals were too narcissistically involved in their personal stories and therefore insufficiently attentive to the world as it must be understood for effective action. In this spirit, we propose these texts not simply as artifacts of Mannheim's biography or as documents of a bygone era, however fascinating, but as serious contributions to our continuing attempts to make disciplined thought serve human practice without reducing the latter to a congeries of technical problems. Our own questions too must include political education for the sake of practical political knowledge.

1

An Introduction to Sociology

Johann Wolfgang Goethe University,
Frankfurt a. M. Summer Semester 1930

The lecture course documented here, offered in the summer semes-
ter of 1930, was Mannheim's first as professor of sociology in Frank-
furt. The transcript was recently discovered among the papers of Hans
Gerth, who was one of Mannheim's assistants in Frankfurt and subse-
quently became a well-known American sociologist. It is unclear who
transcribed the lectures, but there are several indications in the tran-
script that this was done by a listener and not by Mannheim himself.
These technical matters have been well discussed by the German edi-
tors.[5] It would not have been unusual for Mannheim to have hired a
stenographer, especially for his inaugural course, where the question
of publication may have been in his mind. Freyer's introduction to
sociology primer, for example may well have originated in such a
transcript. As the nearly stenographic protocol of the joint seminars
and the stenogram of the "Frankfurt Discussions" indicate, and as we
know from other historical sources, notably the lengthy stenographic
reports of speeches that filled the newspapers of the time, it would
have been quite common, in any case, for an assistant or other student
to have had stenographic skills. Mannheim did prepare very detailed
hand-written lecture notes for his courses, highlighted as for a read-
ing script, throughout his career. Many are available in the archive at
the University of Keele in North Staffordshire. The difference between
the present manuscript and those others, apart from its having been

1

*typewritten, is the absence in the others of the direct address, from
first to second person, so striking in the present transcripts.*

*The transcript is complemented by a set of abbreviated student
notes on the lectures that also cover introductory remarks and a final,
eleventh lecture not in the transcript. The notes on segments not otherwise transcribed are included below. They were taken by Kurt H.
Wolff, a younger student in Mannheim's classes during Mannheim's
years at Frankfurt and later the foremost continuator of Mannheim's
more philosophical sociological inquiries, and a prominent American
sociological theorist in his own right. The detailed and accurate correspondence between the lecture transcript and the summary account
in these notes, where there is overlap, leaves no doubt about the
reliability of the text.*

Mannheim titled these lectures "General Sociology" (Allgemeine
Soziologie). *We have amended this because Mannheim did not further
develop this concept in the lectures and it therefore remains uninfor-
mative and obscure. In his posthumously published 1921 treatise "The
Distinctive Character of Cultural-Sociological Knowledge (Mannheim
1982)," the term is reserved for sociology in the manner of Max
Weber, which he there characterizes as comprising empirical gener-
alizations based on historical studies. It is contrasted with "pure sociology" in the manner of Simmel and "dynamic" sociology with Marxist features, and all three varieties, each with its range of justifiable
application, are said to have corresponding cultural sociologies. This
is clearly not the present sense.*

*In addition to inserting a new set of descriptive lecture titles, we
have departed from the published German edition in two ways. First,
we have silently adopted almost all of the German editors' changes.
They have corrected spelling and grammatical mistakes and have added
paragraph breaks and words and phrases in order to make the manuscript read more smoothly without changing its meaning. In their text,
these insertions are indicated by either footnotes or brackets. Second,
the German edition is heavily annotated with references to works the
editors believe inspired or elucidate Mannheim's ideas. From these,
we have kept only those references that Mannheim himself made,
supplemented by occasional contextual remarks by the present editors.
We have done this because our study of issues raised by the text would
make many of these annotations redundant.*

The lectures include several significant terms that Mannheim either

introduced here, e.g. "reprimitivization," or raised to special impor-
tance here, e.g. "enactment." We have discussed these terms in our
study of these lectures,[6] and, more briefly, in footnotes to the transla-
tion. Because of the difficulty of translating many German terms into
exact English equivalents, we urge readers to consult our discussions
of the terms.

Lecture 1
The Subject Matter, Method and Attitude of Sociology[7]

Our first question is "what is sociology?" This question requires us
to carry out a preliminary intellectual maneuver. We must often take
such preparatory steps, because our thoughts and reflections are loaded
down with preconceptions that lie so deep that they become manifest
only in a crisis, notably when we are not ready to deal with something
new. The rise of sociology is just such a new object, and it is at first
burdened by the preconception that sociology must be exactly like the
other sciences and academic disciplines (*Wissenschaften*). In our view,
the point of methodology is not to destroy a newly emerging object
like sociology, something that is first being existentially enacted
(*Vollziehendes*). The need is, rather, to work out a methodological
apparatus as intricate as we may require to grasp and to understand the
novelty. First, accordingly, note our caution about the functions of
methodology.

The second preliminary move is the recognition that the human
sciences are not originally products of university work (*Univer-
sitätsbetrieb*). What is most important for science originates in life, in
distinctive forms of attitude and comprehension for both material and
spiritual (*geistigen*)[8] objects. The overall configuration of emergent
problems and systematizations is grounded in the contexture
(*Zusammenhang*) of life.

We tend to think that the human sciences, the social sciences—to
name just a few—have their birth at the scholar's desk, and that they
can be classified according to principles appropriate to the teaching
enterprise. Max Weber, however, has shown in his legal sociology
how legal science arises out of the contexture of life and how systematization only begins when a guild takes over. The impulse to
traditionalization, stabilization, rendering-teachable comes from the
scholastic element common to both the pedagogical enterprise

(*Schulbetrieb*) and system—making. This is not to condemn systematization. But its roots are in the pedagogical enterprise. It is very difficult to distinguish between systematization that is genuine and that which arises simply from an arbitrary: "I want order."

The second of our preliminary points, then, is that sociology has arisen in life and from life before our own eyes, just as philosophy and legal science once did. We ourselves have witnessed its entry into academic life. What is forgotten about other disciplines—that they arose from the contexture of life—is manifest in the case of sociology.

We want to avoid the source of error that besets the earlier systematized disciplines. Most are affected by it, notably those that should be keeping up with newly developing life. To be sure, there are subjects, [like formal logic and mathematics], that are distanced and thus independent of the process of social emergence. The newly emergent, nevertheless, takes precedence over principles that are already systematized and grounded in earlier systems.

The third element I want to introduce is the sociological category of limitation (*Beschränktheit*). The essence of limitation, in its deepest sense, consists less of limits on the wealth of what can be and is in fact known than of limits within the apparatus of conceptualization, of categorization. We try to grasp the whole of life through paradigms—models—appropriate to a specific narrow sphere of life. In this sense, everyone is limited. This limitation can only be overcome by means of a constant movement. This entails an attunement (*Einstellen*) to what is coming into being, using the apparatus of thought and everything that a person can bring to bear on things, a process of self-expansion, situating oneself in the center of what is happening. The present is marked by conflict through particularistic political tensions and disputes among countries, it is a time when particularistic attitudes are forced to take one another's measure. If it is impossible to overcome (*aufhebbar*) these tensions, we will see more clearly in such a situation if we undertake a self-audit (*Selbstrevision*) at every confrontation and conduct ourselves in the spirit of Goethe's words, that every well-observed new object calls forth a new organ in us.[9] That is a decisive statement. If you want to know what essential learning is, note the following: to let such new organs take shape within ourselves and, never to rest until one has, in a new contexture of life, generated such a new organ. This is the self-expansion whose agent is above all sociology. Not every object is new. In many areas life simply repeats itself. There are, however, new spheres where one cannot simply apply old categories. For example, if one comes to biology from mechanics, one cannot but see the mechanistic aspects alone. Here we have the problem of limitation. The distinctive did not constitute itself until a new attitude came into being, a standpoint from which this object was capable of being comprehended as well.[10] This object was simply not present in mechanics. The case is the same in sociology. It is a matter of a new objectification (*Gegenständlichkeit*). This was the way towards opening up the problematic (*Problematik*), thereby making the new attitude possible. The essential thing is not that one becomes acquainted with five new pieces of information and gets to know them, but that one appropriates the distinctive movement of thought through which one works up an object sociologically. Such understanding cannot be conveyed by direct transfer but only on occasions where we are faced with new objects and where a process of opening-up becomes necessary.

Sociology has been criticized for failing to fit the pattern of the specialized sciences. I will here anticipate my response to that charge. I think, taken all together, what we address as sociological is multiform. Three layers can be uncovered. Although these layers tend to divide, they are nevertheless held together by something. We must, on the one hand, isolate them, in order to unravel the confusing overlap of things by distinguishing their inner essences; then we can ask ourselves whether the comprehensive concept of sociology still retains a meaning and how the three layers may be interconnected. I assert that sociology, at a certain level, is without a doubt a *specialized discipline*. In the scientific account of society (*Gesellschaftslehre*), it has a clearly delimited subject matter. It has a subject matter like any other science as long as it limits itself to addressing such questions as what is a class, a state, or a nation—in a word, as long as it explicates social formations or asks about the social processes that give shape to the movements of society. It analyzes the forms of human coexistence (*Zusammenleben*). When a sociologist looks at a war, for example, he searches for the general factor that determines this social formation. Limited to such themes, sociology is without question an unassailable specialized science. Since it first aspired to become a specialized science, sociology has been occupied with the question of how it must present itself in order to fulfill this objective. In order to have a teachable subject matter correct by academic standards, sociologists have abandoned the social theory of ideas, as well as cultural sociology—precisely the matters that life demanded and that originally led to sociology.[11] In the academic setting and for the instructional enterprise, however, something has counted as science only if it possessed an unambiguously delimited subject matter.

There is also, however, sociology as *method* within all the specialized human sciences. It is possible to treat the history of love or the idea of freedom or any historical theme in a sociological manner. Sociology is accordingly also a method applicable in all human sciences. Perhaps not in the natural sciences, because those sciences cannot be so directly traced to the social process; although the question must remain open. It is certain that philosophy, literature, and the other human sciences can be treated sociologically. In this class of cases, the essential common factor is not the object but the method. We shall later define this method more precisely. It is a specifiable method that operates without any ambiguity.

Sociology is, finally, also a posture of consciousness (*Bewußtseinshaltung*), a specific attitude. Not only that. The new discipline that renders society visible and makes this new method possible is ultimately rooted in the emergence of a specific new posture of consciousness. In the end, that is the foundation for the spiritual possibility (*Geistig-Möglich-Werdens*) of the new discipline. If we want to grasp sociology more deeply, we must begin with man, with man who has become sociological. What is unsettling about the situation is that the whole man must undergo the most profound transformation in order to have access to the sociological way of seeing. It is a matter of a new phase of consciousness, as understood in the philosophy of history. We are experiencing the transition to the sociological stage, and it does not really matter whether this clash between philosophy and sociology is the ultimate conflict. Sociology is a new kind of philosophy, I think. In its actual origins, it is a secularized philosophy. This process of emergence is the most important developmental process in the history of the human spirit. A science can be characterized by its subject matter, by its method, or by the spiritual posture (or attitude) which mark its emergence. Among the natural sciences, chemistry and physics can be unambiguously characterized by their subject matter. There are other sciences where method dominates. And there are some which can be characterized only by taking spiritual posture into consideration, disciplines which relate to the human being. The question of spiritual bearing, which we shall have to discuss further, can be put aside in the case of attitude to external nature, the attitude towards a nature which is simply there to be investigated for its lawful regularities. In contrast to this are the disciplines in which man has himself as subject matter.

Literature: The thought that knowledge of humans arises through a certain attitude (in the sense of *Einstellung)* is first hinted at by Simmel, who spoke of an *Attitude.*[12] In his essay, "On the essence of philosophy and the moral precondition of philosophical knowledge" in *On the Eternal in Man* Scheler used attitude as basis *(Prinzip)* in a cognate field.[13] The concept of attitude gains a profound significance in Husserl's *Ideas towards a Pure Phenomenology.*[14] Another reference is Jaspers' *Psychology of Weltanschauung.*[15] Finally, I have myself attempted to indicate the importance of these matters for sociology in two writings: "The Ideological and Sociological Interpretation of Intellectual Phenomena," *Jahrbuch für Soziologie,* and "On the Interpretation of *Weltanschauung.*"[16]

What is at issue in the discovery of attitude *(Einstellung)*? That in the human sciences the scientific subject matter under discussion somehow constitutes itself in human life, that it is conditioned by the subject. I want to face up directly to the question whether this does not subjectivize the whole of science, whether we do not end up with nothing but relativizations. That is not what we mean. Quite the contrary. The more we see of these factors, the more we can allow for them. We are rendering the sources subject to control. One attends to things quite differently if one views them from this point. As a rule, man thinks as from a remote objective and comprehends things in relation to that goal. It was Dilthey who saw clearly that the inquirer in the human sciences must himself arrive at the historical stage where a given study is important. He said that the human sciences must be carried on by the whole man. The whole man is implicated.[17] Only when we possess the whole man in his historical form can we begin to understand the science proper to this entity.

That follows from the thought, present in Hegel and Marx, that in history we have to do with an identity of subject and object. In history we do not gain knowledge of a nature external to our inner world; history is recognition of self, not other. This has a number of consequences. Changes accompany the act of cognition *(Erkenntnis).* I change myself as a man at the moment that I come to know myself. Similarly, an act of cognition puts us in a position to change history. Because of the rise of a new posture of consciousness (*Bewußtseinshaltung*), one that can no longer be contained within the old form. The tension between theory and activity that can be tolerated when faced with a house, for example, ceases when it comes to human history. Cognition has its origins in a way of conducting oneself towards the world, a way of relating to the world, a certain attitude. That is, however, not a theoretical but an existential act, something in being. It takes place between two entities in being. In short, what is essential is that the constitution of the subject matter turns into a subject matter of science when we establish a relationship (*Verhältnis*) to the things, and that cognition only takes place in the medium of this relationship.

If one looks at history it will become evident that the objectifications of the human sciences are empirically subject to variation. Take art, for example. Here you have an picture. You may approach this picture with various attitudes. The attitude of a merely receptive, merely attentive person, who lets an overall effect radiate towards himself. Quite a different attitude is that of the creative person, who is himself situated in the flow of a new activity, a new creation. He appropriates the picture from this standpoint and may consequently allow himself to be addressed by no more than one point, perhaps, in order to let something grow in himself. This is a completely different relationship. And it is something altogether different again when an art historian takes a stand on the picture. In the case of the art historian we find an attitude quite different from that of the creative genius or the aesthete. It is a completely different existential relationship, as is that of the collector.

Consider a concrete example. Writing about Saint-Simon—this French nobleman who escapes from his social enclosure (*Gehäuse*), becomes an adventurer, etc.—Lorenz von Stein quotes a French author: "Silent in the midst of all this noise, judging others without being himself judged, both mondaine and spendthrift, more by system than inclination, he lived fifty years in the span of one. He plunged into life, instead of stepping in. He used and abused everything in order to be able to allow for everything in his calculations. A completely experimental life." Most important is the word experimental. It is a new factor. That a man experiments with his life, that a man has a relationship of experimentation towards himself and the world. When is such a thing possible, and what is it? Why does it exist and is it an evil or not?

This is the point at which a phenomenological and sociological interpretation of the sociological way of relating should begin. The human type would have to be reconstructed from here. The how is more important than the what.[18]

Lecture 2
The "Experimental Life" and Distantiation from Life (*Lebensdistanzierung*)

In the previous lecture we attempted to analyze the sociologist as social human type. At the same time, we sought to work out the specific attitude from which sociological knowledge grows. We reached this topic in the context of defining the essence of sociology, and we claimed that it seems ever more evident that the human sciences, those that concern themselves with man, somehow develop in the element of the whole man and that the whole man stands behind them (Dilthey). One cannot understand their emergence (*Werden*) if one does not also keep in view as background the emergence of this whole man. Accordingly we next want to understand the objectifications as well as the methods that characterize sociology by beginning with this human type, this sociological attitude.

We chose a concrete example in order to exemplify and to recognize sociology by addressing this particular case. We chose an attribute of Saint-Simon which seemed to reveal what was essential. As we now turn to the analysis, I want to make a preliminary point. We will treat this analysis in some breadth and expand it, because I am convinced that the foregoing thoughts imply that you can only know and recognize what sociology is in the process of doing it.

The analysis will be sociological. The manner in which we will examine this phenomenon assumes a definite form. The manner of examination is very specific. We do not simply accept the nature of the experimenting man but ask ourselves how it is possible that such a human type comes into being. What had to happen earlier to make it possible for such a type to emerge? We examine this spiritual-psychic phenomenon,[19] "the experimenting man," just as a geologist examines a cross sectional core of earth, as if it contained all the layers of past happenings that have escaped us but that we can again bring into view. We speak of layers only in a metaphorical sense. Nevertheless a human type if examined closely is to a certain extent a representative of what went before. The past is not stored up in experience as if occupying space, but by way of a dimension, by way of an intensity in a sense first depicted by Hegel. He coined the expression *aufgehoben*.[20] In the synthesis, he said, thesis and antithesis are *aufgehoben* in a threefold sense.

First, inasmuch as the thesis, the first positing, is destroyed. *Aufhebung* can mean destruction. On the other hand the thesis is also *aufgehoben* in the second sense, in the sense of retention. And third, in the sense of the being-taken-along (*Mitgenommenseins*) of the entire process.

At the instance of the [Saint-Simon] example we want to analyze this being-taken-along of the past. We want first to approach the quotation again quite directly, and then to question it more deeply. "He plunged into life, instead of stepping in." This brings an interesting phenomenon into view. As if one could enter upon the enactment of life in two ways, by plunging or by stepping. One might think at first that it is a matter of the modern, accelerated tempo of life. That is certainly a part of it. One can either live like a peasant, who ages in wisdom and does everything with equanimity and patience—or one can plunge in. It is a difference in mentality. One can appropriate phenomena in different ways. One must keep these things in mind if one wants to grasp what is going on.

"He used and abused everything." An excellent observation. One has the feeling that life is actually not there to be used. *Things* exist to be used, but not the *contents of life*. He used and abused them at the same time. A very subtle observation. Converting a subject into an object. We have here a special kind of attitude towards an object. One shifts things that should be present in a thou-relationship to an it-relationship. A very nuanced characterization. There has been discussion of the reification of modern life. "He infected himself with the illnesses of the century."[21] The problem of an experimental life. He who wants to see everything must also infect himself with all the illnesses in order to be able to cope with them. This human type believes that it is possible to settle with life only if one has gone through all the possibilities of this existence. The prophet must sin with the others in order to be able to help them. "A completely experimental life." At the center is the expression "experimental life." What must have come before? What is *aufgehoben* in this attitude to life? How does such a person live, and at what historical stage does such a thing appear?

Bringing out the elements of an answer to these questions must be effected (*vollzogen*) in several stages. Now to the first step, the enactment (*Vollzug*).[22] A most elementary reflection on antecedents shows clearly that a religious attitude must first be destroyed. Experimenting with life is impossible for a religious attitude. One is not allowed to experiment with one's own life or that of others because this is perhaps the gravest sin for religion. Life does not exist to be made the object of experimentation. Life exists to achieve salvation. From the standpoint of this plan of salvation, everything must be taken as absolute and serious. Nothing is possible for the religious attitude except dedicating one's life unconditionally to the plan of salvation. It is the absolute submission to a world that is given. There are only two possibilities: either to fail in this world or to prove oneself in it—or perhaps also to despair. Never is it possible to distance oneself from the objects and tasks of this world. Such a problem can simply never arise in such a context of life. That is the immanent explanation.

Sociological analysis must always move towards the structural and attempt to grasp it. What is structurally characteristic of experimental life (in contrast to the religious)? I have already pointed it out. The structural difference consists in a difference in attitude. Experimental life presupposes a distantiation from life, while the pre-sociological and religious life is neither inclined to nor capable of such distantiation.

This distantiation of inner life is the culmination of a process that begins with taking distance from the rest of the life-world that is different from oneself.

What makes up this distantiation? Can it be more precisely specified? Distantiation consists of the fact that when we take distance we cease to live in an unambiguous alignment of meanings (*Bedeutungsrichtung*). Distantiation becomes possible for the individual only when the unambiguous alignment of meanings has fallen apart for some concrete group. I can take distance from my own life only when I no longer find unambiguous for me the unambiguous alignment of meanings set for me by a group.

What is to be understood by unambiguous alignment of meaning? Let us observe the life of a child—or your own life before you reached the age where doubts arise. This will let you see that for you orientation then consisted of somehow knowing what everything meant. In other words, for an intact, unambiguous social community the world is interpreted in a set way, and when the individual begins to act, he acts in the direction of an interweaving of meanings that he does not create for himself, but of which he is informed, which is set for him by the group. If he encounters something new, the novelty is related to this context of meanings, which somehow ultimately has a goal. The new is fitted in, made understandable, appropriated from the standpoint of this end. Primitive societies have such a unambiguous alignment of meanings. Love, death, magic, etc. are laid down. Anyone who grows up in this society goes along with the accentuations of meaning, identifies with the society by viewing objects in the manner laid down by the society. He identifies himself not only by his way of life and his acts of compliance (*Mitvollzug*) but also by seeing an object from the perspective prescribed by the group. The bonding is so intense that, if one ends up with another group, one does not belong to it. The alignment of meanings one has brought along continues to operate within. It is through this identification with alignments of meaning that one is truly socialized. A social crisis always manifests itself somehow in the spiritual sphere since the alignments of meaning stand in a correlation to the social currents, tendencies, and oppositions present in the group. These are unambiguous in a primitive group, which is unambiguous in its orientation to meanings. It is necessary to go further. There is a tendency for the conqueror to take away from the oppressed—from their slaves, for example—the consciousness needed to orient themselves to the world from their own standpoint. Once integrated, the oppressed look at things from the standpoint of the conqueror. Spiritual tension arises when the underclass ceases to carry this into effect, when it fails to enlist in the sphere of consciousness. Distantiation is possible only when the unambiguous alignment of meanings ceases to be performed without difficulties. The religious world must be destroyed in order to have, for example, an experimental attitude towards life. Structurally this means that one is no longer self-evidently inclined towards a set and only possible goal of meaning. It is impossible to have the self completely absorbed in the execution of acts that tend towards this end. Distantiation from the things of the parallel and environing worlds occurs through the loosening of a binding alignment of meanings. The objects of the world are no longer fixed.

I have described the process of distantiation—what it comprises, the manner of its enacting, its structure. Now I ask myself, how does one or another human being experience the world in which he is encompassed. What constitutes the manner of experiencing? Through this analysis we seek to represent what is given, what is entailed. I am trying to represent the social preconditions for the emergence of such a human type. How would one depict distantiation? How would one characterize the posture (*Verhaltungsweise*) that has not yet enacted distantiation?

For this distinctive attitude (*Einstellung*) we in the phenomenological school have recently created a conceptual apparatus. Is it now possible to bring into view how one or another human being stands in the world, and is it possible to find words for this inner relationship? Drawing on expressions that have arisen in these settings, I shall endeavor to show what is so hard to show. Seen from within, what is experience for the man who has not yet given up his relationship to an orienting meaning (*Sinnziel*) and what is experience for the other? At issue is the relationship of being addressed (*Ansprechungsverhältnis*). The man who can live in only one alignment of meanings and who has not yet taken distance conducts himself towards things in a relationship of being addressed. We do not find a word for this anywhere. Language tends towards reification. The thou-relationship is a distinct kind of attitude and way of enacting life (*Lebensvollzug*). You relate to your fellow humans, if you have not yet distanced yourself, in a relationship of being addressed. The tree that addresses you is a tree experienced differently from the one you sell or the one which the physicist uses as the object of a quantitative investigation. This relationship of being addressed, the undistanced relationship, is the paradigm of a life that has not yet been distantiated. It is dissolved when one breaks off the relationship of being addressed, when one destroys it within oneself, and when one, so to speak, shifts the object into an it-position. Something that spoke to one, that was a purpose in one's own space of action and life, is put at a distance and shifted into the it-position. This expression is still not quite the characterization of the disengagement (*Loslösens*), because the phenomena in question are originally present as elements in relations between man and man. You can become an it when I speak about you. That is not the case with things. It would require a tremendous effort to characterize this it-position for things. This is so difficult for us because we have not yet characterized this sort of life-sphere in words. This kind of posture, which can be actualized only by being enacted, has not been thematized as yet. Language is just beginning to create new concepts for these relations, now that they become a matter of reflection. At this point, where one finds oneself at the margin of the linguistic situation, it is possible to see how language operates. Things that have a name today were all once in a state of inexpressibility (*Nichtaufzeigbarkeit*); and at that point adequate expressions were coined, just as today. And just as I constantly run the risk of applying to the world a coinage that is just breaking through, earlier men did the same.

While in earlier times one lived in a single alignment of meaning and had a relationship to the world of being addressed, the collapse of this situation gives rise to the fact that most things turn into something variable, without inherent meaning. They move into the it-position. While in earlier times that which addressed me could not possibly be variable, and the whole world thus, in this aboriginal situation, took the part of the agent and I myself as one that reacted, all this disappears with the disintegration of the unambiguous allocation of meanings characteristic of a given situation in the history of spirit. The things that address me proceed as follows: this is what I am; I cannot be different. Such a man experiences the world as world. The variability of being subject to being aligned in a different set simply does not exist. In a word, it is clear that the precondition for sociology is to be found at just this point, viz., that the variability of things is made possible by the fact that the frame of meaning (*Sinnzusammenhang*) that makes *a* world into *the* world is broken to pieces.

How did this happen historically? The second phase of the analysis localizes in history that which was stored and preserved (*aufgehoben*) in an act and from which one has constructively extracted the presuppositions. Where does it happen, in our frame of reference, that an unambiguous world interpretation, a contexture of meanings, is torn apart? We know that in the Middle Ages there was a relatively unambiguous stabilization of a world picture replete with the meanings of things. One knew the meaning of death, God, etc., how one had to address God, etc. For the essential things there was an unambiguous orientation. Conflicts about validity and the notion that the world could be different first arise in the Reformation, when it becomes possible to enter into a polemical relationship about these phenomena, when a new interpretation is attempted where there had been unambiguous interpretations. Different ways of seeing things take shape. The polemical attitudes push one another towards destruction; it is a matter of life or death. And then, suddenly, relatively quickly, the idea of tolerance emerges. That this phenomenon of tolerance could emerge has to do with the fact that it was suddenly possible for two types of world interpretation to subsist side by side, with the result that they rendered phenomena somewhat neutral, and that they possibly already created distance from them. The origins of religious and moral psychology can be found in the same age, in conjunction with the toleration movement. What is decisive is that the very phenomena to which one was formerly oriented existentially are now, suddenly, in the act of toleration, put at a distance. They are transmuted into reflexively comprehensible and causally explicable phenomena. This can happen only when spiritual contents are distanced to the point where their emergence, causality, etc. become themes. Tolerance is the first stage in the distantiation of phenomena. The state of being addressed by religion and morality is replaced by an altogether different attitude towards these objects, by a distantiation, through which a change in function comes into being. The following must be added: anyone who comes from a bounded world-view will be horrified by the situation of distantiation from the last things, treating them as variable. They will find it an act alien to life, exterminating everything. A strenuous effort is required to discover that this is not necessarily the case, that a new existential act is actually embedded in the distantiation from life, that it is constantly guided by a new unmediated act that aims at something which could well address us, that this distantiation is not only a putting to death but also a giving birth to something new. What is being put to death is already alienated from us. They are things we cannot perform without ourselves becoming separated from the act of performing (*Vollzugsakt*).

Lecture 3
The Distantiation from Life and Its Origins:
Social Differentiation and the "Sociological Human Type"

What we worked out in the last lecture in methical analysis, we must now present in ruthlessly condensed form, so that we have the whole line of argument before us. The topic is the analysis of the sociological human type, the analysis of the attitude out of which sociology first arises. The following claim has been made: This sociological human type, like the attitude belonging to it, is distinctly new; it poses an almost philosophy-of-history question in the history of human consciousness.

Here are our results. We begin with a concrete figure. We took Saint-Simon as our point of departure and we discovered there the phenomenon of the experimental life, which encounters all the objects in the world, as well as itself, in an posture of experimentation. The designation "experimental life" was taken from a character sketch. We asked when this peculiar attitude towards life first emerged. This attitude could only emerge when the religious one had vanished. For the religious person, experimenting with life is impossible. The experimental bearing presupposes the disappearance of the other. That is the substantive presupposition of a modern style of life. Viewed structurally, what does the disappearance of the religious attitude signify? Does not man at this next stage stand in an entirely different relationship to the world? We have identified the distantiation from life as the specific structural element. Man brought into being within himself what we have called distantiation.

Then we asked ourselves how this distantiation came about? Of what does it consist? It came into being by virtue of the fact that a group's unambiguous alignment of meaning was shattered. As long as a group is homogeneous, all things have the same meaning for every individual in the group, they are directed towards a common meaningful objective. Cognition (*Erkennen*) means to comprehend society, death, life, and all possible events from within this unified world view, to locate them within it. There is an unambiguous alignment of meaning, which is now shattered.

A further question: what is responsible for this? Why is there no unambiguous alignment of meanings today? Why is man poised among various possibilities for aligning meanings? We have pointed out that the grounds rest in the social differentiation of groups. The phenomenon of the substructure or base (*Unterbauphänomen*). Phenomenologically, a new attitude materializes. The unity of meaning disappears. We can trace the grounds for this further in the life of the group. The group differentiates itself. The social differentiation of the group is the most immediate cause of the differentiation of the group's alignment of meanings. As a matter of fact, every social differentiation attacks meaning. Is it then only possible to be oriented to meaning in an unambiguous way within a simple group, or are there diverse forms of social differentiation? Which of these forms brings about the destruction of a unified orientation to meaning? We want to amplify the point. Only the differentiations which create diverse circles

(*Lebenskreise*) whose orientation is antinomic by necessity. Social differentiation creates a variety of circles. A splitting in the alignment of meanings is likely only if the circles are antinomic by necessity. A further important point must be added. The possibility of the members of the group opposing one another in thought arises when the antinomic elements are subject to being driven so far by other factors that the antinomy rises to consciousness. It may also happen that oppositions exist but that they lack the intensity to produce a consciousness of the incompatibilities in the individual groups. There are factors in economic and social life, as we see, that necessarily lead to an antinomy of groups. The differentiation of classes builds on this. Yet one can think of a division of labor that would lead to a social differentiation without being antinomic.

A social differentiation can emerge without breaching the unified alignment of meanings or bringing about a splitting. In a word, we now want to establish that it is only certain kinds of social differentiations that may lead to the point where the alignment of meanings is smashed and a diversity of world views is present within a single life space. In this connection, you have already seen the place and importance of the analysis of the base (*Unterbau*). It is impossible, however, to analyze only the base, while passively accepting the spiritual domain as undifferentiated and fully isolated. That is the way to a completely primitive sociology. Marxist sociology begins with the base in its understanding of these phenomena.

One line of thinking describes very accurately what has happened in the history of the spiritual domain but tells us nothing about the reasons for those happenings. Conversely, the other side attempts to analyze the economic process as precisely as possible within its structure. If applied to the spiritual domain, the latter approach leaves it undifferentiated. It is my program to bring the spiritual history and the economic analysis together and to carry them out (*vollziehen*) with the distantiation required. If I dwelled relatively long on showing how such a thing as distantiation plays out in the spiritual domain, if I reconstructed the experiential context in which these processes originally arose and worked themselves out, I did so in order to see the superstructure (*Überbau*) in a more concrete way. That is decisive. The primary task of sociology is defined by the fact that we are alienated by certain experiential contents that confront us as if they could not be different—viz., this man is like this and the other is different.

The state of mind (*Geisteshaltung*) that took things as they presented themselves was once adequate. If one takes things as they present themselves, as if they were isolated phenomena, and fails to reconstruct the context in which these objects lived, what one has comprehended is not yet history. Beginning with the original experiential context in which such a thing could arise, I am trying to reconstruct the phenomenon of the experimental that is present in the sociological attitude. I recall the example of geology. It is the task of sociology to take the phenomena that first present themselves as isolated and to view them in their experiential context, of which the bearer is a social group. That is very difficult.

As we proceed, I will show the elements of such a procedure. I will show how one attempts to recognize in something apprehended the necessary inner premises that led to the rise of such a psychic attitude (*Seelenhaltung*) by representing it as history. When we enact (*vollziehen*) these steps in our experimental life, we are in effect re-enacting the fate of our ancestors, and we must carry it further by enacting the results of an attitude of generations, of which we may represent the final phase. If we had been born in a simple, aboriginal grouping, we would not have the attitude of "experimentalism." It is only because the situation of crisis is at one with us that we live grounded in this attitude. That is why it is a problem for us.

After this summary of the problem complex, we want to move on. We have seen what must have happened, viewing it from the outside. Now we ask how this splitting of the alignments of meaning looks from the inside. How is it experienced by the person who lives in this act, who has lost the unambiguous alignment of meanings of the group and who sees the world as from this stage of development. While I can describe the history of a stone—how it falls—from the outside, individuality is always present in human history. All study of human history is distinguished by its comprehension of this element of individuality. That brings us to the second phase of our inquiry: How does the falling man view this fall? What is distinctive about acts of experience at this stage? Things that have meaning for a group stand in a relationship of direct address as long as the unambiguous alignment of meanings remains. They speak to us. They are not present as objects of reflection—resembling in this a person whom I love or hate, who addresses me and is oriented to me. I am in a relationship of acting back. I answer. Such answering, such being addressed, comprises the most primeval way of relating to the world. It is impossible to conceive of it as different. One does not trouble oneself with thoughts; one simply adapts; one relates to it as to the sun that shines on one. It is the aboriginal situation. The world is simply there as world. It could not be otherwise.

What happens then? As soon as the antinomic situation is present and penetrates the spiritual domain, two worlds confront one another. Everything appears in a dual light. That is how it was at the waning of the middle ages, when everything could be explained through God, and through natural science as well. That is how it remains today, since every world view aspires to a gapless interpretation of things. In every case, a group's allocation of meaning is marked by the refusal to exclude any aspect of life from its explanations. Now there are suddenly two interpretations. That is the second stage of such a situation. At the beginning of this stage, the sides stand in a polemical relationship. The other is to be destroyed, to be put to death. Relations are polemical, with polemical depictions of the world. It is the era of the most furious attacks and the greatest intensity. The coexistence of the world depictions eventually leads to the result that the newer world depiction gains the upper hand. If the two positions are equally balanced, in terms of power as well, a reciprocal neutralization of the contrasting possibilities comes into being. That is the ideology of toleration. It arose after the religious wars. Everyone is right. It is not worth killing one another over these matters. That is why there are no more religious wars. There were other problems for the sake of which people killed one another. In a sense, the idea of toleration neutralized all these problems. At the same time, it comprised an inner act of experience, an act of wanting-to-be-rid-of-things.

How does the world look at the moment when one wants to be rid of it? How do objects appear? We have already anticipated the answer: they are devoid of meaning and variable. Secondly, they move to the it-position. Something that formerly addressed us moves to the it-position. It is not the position appropriate to material objects (*Gegenstandsposition*). The contradiction between subject and object is also valid for primitive man. But the it-position is something different. These are relations that have not been subject to scientific examination before but which phenomenology is beginning to see clearly. At this point, the possibility of experimenting comes forward. Moral philosophy, psychology and the like appear, as well as the beginnings of sociology, etc. Things that had not been subject to knowledge move into a sphere of distinctive knowability. First, however, comes the act of moving things to the it-position. That raises the question whether this moving things to the it-position, this wanting-to-be-rid-of-things is a dead act or an enactment of life (*Lebensvollzug*). That is decisive. That is the morality of sociology. Earlier we said that nothing to do with human beings can be treated like other natural objects. Our act of distantiation has simply emerged out of the situation of our lives. Intrinsically, a sort of obligation arises when one is confronted with something by one's life. We are reflexive in our vital activity because of the imperative context and not out of arbitrariness. Where does the act of reflection begin? In the attempt to identify oneself with an allocation of meaning. The process repeats itself in the fate of every individual who is subject to this course of events. The peasant does not experience it. For those who are affected by this history of consciousness, the situation entails an obligation, this distantiation is an inevitable process. The question is only what such a person does with it. Anyone who has taken up this situation sees things in a diversity of lights. He cannot act upon what is present to him with aboriginal naivety. He is subject to the experience that he is constantly becoming separated from the act of performing (*Vollzugsakt*). An uneasiness springs from this repeated separation (*Herausfallen*). He must reflect on it. It is an act of life that drives us to reflexivity. I must reflect on the situation that I must make present to myself. Things display a previously unnoticed reflexivity. This is nothing dead, but a searching reflexivity that originates in a necessity of life and expands from these origins to become, in the search, the most vital act of which we are today capable. That is because the reflective act is guided by a desire to take possession of the world. At first it is a differentiation, a separation from the act of performing. One looks things over. One begins to raise questions, for example, about the meanings of marriage or love. At the moment of thought, something becomes different. It is an estrangement from life. At the same time, however, one is searching in these thoughts for an act that one could put into effect (*vollziehen*), by virtue of being able to identify oneself anew with an allocation of meaning.

I want to characterize this process further. How does it look? The distantiation becomes both broader and deeper. There are no contents with regard to which a doubt could not arise, where reflectivity could not come into play. Religion, state, society, morals—all are subjected to the attitude of distance from life. This broadening is uncanny. The deepening consists in the fact that distantiation affects not only the objects of the external world and social forms, but increasingly also the sphere of the self. One gradually begins to speak of the ego as of a third person. The point is not that one speaks of the ego as of an object; one could do that earlier. This it-relationship is something different. One gets into position to speak of life as of an it. The apparatus of thinking and living moves into the distance. Psychological ways of examining our feelings manifest themselves. The process goes further and thought itself is put at a distance. Sociology of knowledge comes into being. One does not even identify oneself with the thinking one has used to become acquainted with oneself. One puts it at a distance, one moves it away from oneself. It is an activity of describing. We put the world at a distance, as well as the apparatus of experience and the apparatus of thinking. One is separated from the act of performing, and one can no longer identify oneself with an earlier allocation of meaning. An altogether peculiar relationship comes into being. Its highest intensification is when even this experiencing ego is suddenly put as a distance, viewed as an it, and separated from us. The problem of romantic irony is nothing but to bring what has happened here into view. It is a consciousness of self that is always only a spectator of itself, that views itself from the outside. This ironic possession of self is the endpoint of this act. One's relationship to self is as disjointed as to all forms: an ego that is spectator to itself (*sich selbst zuschaut*). To put it differently, one experiences oneself as something that could well be different. One is only a possibility of oneself.[23] This feeling of life arises with the process whereby an unambiguous interpretation of the world—that was more or less present in an unambiguous grouping—disappears. What is the next development? The point of departure has been shown. One experiences oneself as something that could also be different. That is decisive. That means that one incorporates the variability of the self-relationship into the experience. Searching gives way to experiencing. One experiences friendship, for example, by including the possibility of a different design of friendship in every act of friendship. We are talking about those who have a friend as well as specific ideals of friendship, and who, when they cannot achieve their ideals, no longer blame the friend but rather try to find out whether the ideals could not be conceived differently. The person whose reflexivity fulfills a need of life is the authentic model here. Those who merely play at reflexivity do not embody it. There are accordingly two types of sociology possible. One type simply plays with the fact that today one can today think about everything thus or so.

Do not think about problems that do not become acute! If certain problems do not become acute in your life, do not believe that you would not be a cultivated person without these problems. When this problematic reaches you, however, you must know what it means and what possibilities the situation opens up. Perhaps one person can then even help another. The person who carries this through incorporates variability into experience, albeit not always and not in a single leap. In one place or another, as we live longer, as the process of modernity advances, a problem emerges as an embarrassment in life, as a genuine crisis. Today one could say that there is hardly anything we could name that is not dragged into this problem complex. That is one of the reasons why today sociology is applicable in every domain. That is the situation. It did not begin today. It has been in existence for almost one-and-a-half centuries. It constitutes itself, it is repressed, and then it rises again. What have been the types of pathways entered by the human soul? If we take this problem complex as our point of departure, we will be able to reinterpret this, to understand the history of spirit in its most important phases anew.

First phase: Begin with the first pathway. Distantiation from life can emerge first of all from the standpoint of a utopia. I am expanding here upon some ideas in my book.[24] By utopia I do not mean an unreal portrayal of the future but a giving to the world a meaning which is viewed as a possibility for its future. This allocation of meanings attempts to take possession of all problem complexes: it becomes a world view. The present world is confronted by another allocation of meanings, as a utopian one. The impression arises that the world is variable, in contrast to the view of primitive man. This utopia which intends to achieve something in the world and strives for actualization finds the strength to cast itself free. But this is only one of the possible forms of distantiation, and it has its own corresponding sociology.

Lecture 4
Three Phases of Intellectual Reaction to the Crisis of Life: Utopianism, Romanticism and Existentialism

In the last lecture I reviewed the theme of characterizing sociological man. The topic was an analysis of the constellation out of which sociology in essence arises. Our task was a sociological examination of cultural formations. In this sense we are already in the midst of an analysis that represents a transition to substantive sociology.

Now that we have discussed the attitudes comprising the life-distancing posture in general, we shall today contrast these to the other attitudes possible. We must present the whole constellation of which such distantiation is only one possibility, and we must characterize the other attitudes with which it has to struggle and which are constantly in a polemical relationship to one another. We are actually undertaking an analysis of the underlying constellation, and this requires discussion of the political and philosophical foundations of the present age.

I said that the first type of attitude where distantiation from life can occur is the one where man uses a utopia as the point of departure for putting the contemporary world, environment, and inner world at a distance. His wishful dreams and his negative experiences consolidate themselves into a utopia, a counter-image, and this awakens in him the strength and capability to take distance in his consciousness from all the things that present themselves to him as final. The first root of sociological knowledge is the utopian relationship, the possibility of utopia. This forming of utopia already begins with the bourgeoisie. This class distances itself from the world, standing towards the world not as the conservative does but in a critical attitude. This amounts to the experience that things could be other than they are. The proletarian revolution takes over this possibility of things being different. Revolutionary sociology arises under the auspices of this point of view. It is marked by the fact that one is able to put everything in the present at a distance, to move it into the it-position. What speaks to the conservative is a given that is not even possible for the others. While the conservative melts completely into this world, without capability for reflection, the world is already subject to doubt for bourgeois criticism: it is shifted into the position of something questionable.

All sociology of the revolutionary kind—bourgeois, socialist or communist—is distinguished by the fact that it does not effect distantiation for the sake of searching for the correct solution for individual acts. Such sociology is in a condition of absoluteteness. What things should be—and how—is something already in hand One possesses a utopian counter-image. The opponents criticize the utopian counter-image. (The conservatives, in the case of the liberals.) The utopian counter-image is criticized as abstract. It has a definite form. One knows what one wants. The cost however is that one has not yet experimented with it. The reality is that the questionableness of the counter-image has not as yet been able to reveal itself. Revolutionary sociology has certainty and does not as yet experiment with the utopia itself. This cannot move to the it-position. As soon as utopia appears, a substantial transformation occurs, a new type of man comes into being. This absence of distance from the utopia provides the strength to take distance from everything in the present. The type of man who belongs to this stage has a unique structure. It is distinguished by the fact that he anchors his consciousness of self and self-confidence in a utopia. This is why these movements are so prone to the apodictic, why these persons—unwilling to expose themselves to an uncertainty they cannot bear—are inclined to anchor their egos' centers in a collectivity. From this place, there flows an incredible certainty of always knowing what one is about.

This attitude has something positive to it, but it also has its limitations. The positive consists in the fact that the self is not subject to being destroyed by the possibility of being put in doubt and called into question. In a word, activity is not crippled by doubt. The greatest concern is to preserve one's resolution. The danger consists in the circumstance that when a new and concrete case arises, where one would have to experiment with life, this abstract, tightly held, and prejudged certainty (*Richtigkeit*) makes it impossible to call the project radically into question. Here too, however, we must draw further distinctions. At the first stage, the abstract form is static and incapable of being brought to life. As long as a man is not yet sociologically engaged with the present, he passively belongs to it. As long as one remains wholly on the outside, there is nothing more to be done. If one is certain about the abstract goal, one will attempt, by means of utopian intensity, to fuse the group into a new whole. This posture comes under criticism when one confronts concrete problems, when one is called upon to move beyond rejection, to bring something about on one's own. At that moment the utopia is put to the test, and it can no longer maintain its earlier abstractness. Actuality can only assert itself through a thousand small acts of trial and error. That is when you can see whether a revolutionary group turns evolutionary or whether, so to speak, it suddenly has everything in its charge. At these stages, the group is faced by actualization. Then it must, in fact, incorporate the experimental relationship within its utopian posture. When one enters upon actualization, it becomes necessary to permit oneself and one's counter-images to be subjected to criticism.

It is the same in ordinary life.[25] The experimental posture imposes itself as a requirement as soon as a group ceases to stand abstractly on the outside. The world could not come into being if there were nothing but this abstract posture. What would happen if the abstract utopia encountered no resistance? Within every group there develops an inner differentiation, a splitting, and this serves as an evolutionary brake and regulator in relation to the absolute utopia. These things are decisive as formula for all group formations. The groups differentiate themselves in diverse ways, but this self-differentiation over against the utopian posture arises from the tendencies towards actualization within a social group. It would emerge even if—as every utopian revolutionary wishes—the remaining parties did not exist.

The differentiation of the psychic posture (*Seelenhaltung*) depends, in this case too, on the differentiation of the group.

How does the second phase look? We have a sociology. We can not only imagine a sociology but also possess it in fact, something that draws from the utopian core the strength to distance itself from everything present in actuality. This distantiation does not relativize its own utopia, but rather relates to it in direct address (*Ansprechungsverhältnis*). With the attempt to put the utopia into effect, it moves into a position where its imperative becomes actual (*des verwirklichten Müssens*). The hour of full experimentation strikes.

We have now arrived at the second form possible for a sociology and contemporary world view: when one is not anchored in utopia, but is rather swept along by utopia (like the German intelligentsia at the time of the French Revolution). The utopia sweeps the intelligentsia along. Then it collapses, followed by an immediate experience of disillusionment. In the meantime, however, one has learned to take distance from the world. Now comes the next wave: the strengths of disillusionment. With the strong means built up by the reaction in the interim, one uproots, distantiates the revolutionary utopia itself. But since the attempt is to interpret every world view and every element, we find every object in the consciousness of the intelligentsia cast in a double light, totally vacillating. We have the possibility of the revolutionary on the one side and the counter-revolutionary on the other. A conservative and a reactionary world view emerge. At this moment a profound process takes place. The possibility that the world has become completely unstable arouses fear, and the danger in the situation is also seen, viz., that all things are likely to distance themselves by virtue of the double attitude. The inner movement of the soul is then as follows: the attempt is made to reclaim the distanced contents—those which have shifted to the it-position—for a spontaneous performance of acts (*direkter Aktvollzug*). It is the aim to regain the contents of the past, traditions, and old allocations of meanings, and to achieve this through a directly effected act. They are to be reconquered. This is the situation in which Romanticism arises. Romanticism is the attempt to bring the distanced and differentiated contents back into the spontaneous performance of acts. The contents are to be possessed in as unmediated a way as they were possessed by men who were not yet differentiated. There is longing for the earlier primitive condition. All the past is made sacred. Everything is so desolate and vacillating now. What existed then was truth. Neoprimitivism, which has its origins at this point, emerges as a problem.

What is it that emerges out of this situation? Counter-movements too bring something into being in history. Not only out of revolution, but also out of counter-movements. In the attempt to enter completely into the earlier and lost execution of action, a new posture arises, the so-called empathetic understanding (*einfühlende Verstehen*), which arises historically precisely at this moment, in this situation of the collective soul. This is because the result of a future incorporation of spontaneous performances of action is nothing but empathetic understanding. One had spoken earlier of remote peoples in earlier times, but only as dressed in one's own costume, the soul's costume at the time of speaking. That is no understanding, but an expansion. Genuine empathetic understanding, the skill possessed by modern research in our sense, arises at this point, in this situation, where the intellectual subject became relatively free, where he lost himself and attempted to find himself, while lapsing ever again.

One can thoroughly understand another existence only when one has in some way and at some time become uncertain oneself. It is important to see these things. I am here reconstructing the original experiential context in which these things must have emerged, the things we believe existed, without our knowing, however, why they were there. We see history as individual phases. What we must do in sociology is to reconstruct the original context of humanity's personal knowledge and experience (*Erfahrungs—und Erlebniszusammenhang*).

The second great experiment of Romanticism in this situation of differentiation in life possessed its own movement of thought. It supposes itself to be something rooted but it is in fact an exercise of understanding. And in the activity of understanding (*Verstehen*) one is not rooted. It transforms the new situation and makes it into something that drives forward. The solidarity of our humanity which somehow arose in this life-space went on to affect other ones. Understanding develops in close alliance with the Restoration. As a practical matter, the problem complex of the capacity for understanding soon ceased to be a contested issue in all camps, but something grounded in the situation of the soul, accessible to us all. Even the utopian revolutionary is infected and takes on some of this posture towards life, even if, in the final analysis, he retains his absolute postulate.

Let us move ahead.

What is problematic about the Romantic solution is its attempt to substitute the activity of understanding for the act of direct address. One is no longer addressed by God when one understands religion. If one seeks religion one is no longer addressed by God, but rather possesses religion at the level of reflection. All of this shows the distinctive cunning of fate. Those who sought to become authentic and unreflective instead perform reflexivity in all their acts. At the stage of Romanticism, to have grasped something means to have possessed it reflectively. The past, which was at first naively absorbed, is ever more given the character of an object to be scientifically investigated. Opening up the realm of history is the greatest achievement of Romanticism.

Now we come to a final and most interesting experiment, dominant in contemporary philosophy, that originates in the situation just examined. It was necessary to get out of that situation, and so new individuals rise up who gain distance from Romanticism. A new problem complex emerges out of the collapse of Romanticism. Individuals who were Romantics abandon it because they discover that it was not in fact a life, and they dispute everything that had been newly gained from the Romantic posture. They estrange themselves from myth and religion. Yet one wants to hold on to something. That something was important in religion, the experience of being immediately addressed by God. God could be put aside. The point was the immediacy of life. The immediate and unmediated element in the intuition (*Anschauungsmoment*) of the world, the direct enactment of the existential act, leads to existentialist philosophy. What marks this philosophy is a tendency towards putting all things at a distance by means of an advanced consciousness of the distanced consciousness. In this attitude, one still does not understand the extent to which reflexivity is destiny. One simply has taken a hold on alienation from a world that has become reflexive. One has a yearning for the pure and direct act, an act that is truly addressed (*wirklich intendiert*) to oneself. One constructs a farsighted theory of existence, expounding its makeup and the makeup of authenticity, and arguing that everything depends on this actualization. This is not to be seen as relational. Rather there is something in man, a moment of being directly poised on the verge of a decision, of being attuned (*Eingestellt-Sein*) to something. There is a situation where man ceases to be reflective. Think of Kierkegaard's possibility of foundering (*Scheitern-Koennen*) before God. But there is no universal shipwreck before God, but a salvation by the act, by being directly addressed.

This position arises as a third stage, given the necessity of a position counter to the process of distantiation. It coincides in fact with the end of Romanticism (together with the appearance of the new revolutionary), as a result of this attitude (in Kierkegaard), and it continues to the present. Repeatedly it emphasizes and describes the location of the authentic reality (*wirkliche Wirklichkeit*) in man, that which cannot be rendered reflective. The existentialist act emerged, so to speak, out of the same basic posture (*Grundhaltung*) as Romanticism. While Romanticism, however, believed that it could negate the rise of reflexivity and sought to recapture the meaningful contents of the world, the existentialist position insightfully abandons these contents, although it yearningly conjures back (*zurückersehnt*) the act. Its fate is exactly the same. By speaking about existence, one destroys it. Existence is in fact something that has its being only in the performing of an act. It should be said that building a philosophy about it has positive results.

One re-cognizes (*erkennt wieder*) something that lay so deeply anchored and obstructed in man that it could not become self-reflective.
The truth is that this man is also a reflexive type. He simply wants to
avoid acknowledging the fact. By speaking of this other, he wants to
distance himself from it. It should be clear that I take this philosophy
with utmost seriousness.

It is not a Romanticism in the sense that one reverts once again to
the past. Instead, it arose with absolute necessity out of the life-crisis
of the present. And now to the alternative way to a solution. It is
naturally only after one has decided on a way that one can see the
negativity that afflicts this other life as well. The contradiction is that
one can will everything except the spontaneous performance of an act.
There are moreover very different currents within the existentialist
tendency. For one thing there is the danger, arising from these contextures of life, that this separation of everything from oneself and this
abstraction of the existential act from all concrete contents bring one
to a situation where the world becomes a matter of indifference (*einen
nichts mehr angeht*). One loses actual interest in the things of the
world. A graver endangerment of the existential act cannot be imagined. The world continues to matter in reflection. Now we are faced
with the possibility of a situation in which the act of existence will
cease to have contents, a situation in which it will become unable to
assert itself within time. But man's experience that becoming independent is a possibility takes place in time, if only in determinate moments.

The second paradox to be shown in this conception is that one fails
once more to recognize the self. By its denial of reflexivity this process actually perfects reflexivity. The most decisive thing, as seen
from a sociological standpoint, is to be sought in the fact that man is
alone here, that the culmination of liberal bourgeois isolation enters
into philosophy at this point. The ultimate decision is that man is
alone. He can see society as nothing but a total isolation, which he
cannot conquer. The meaning of living together, which is constantly a
topic for us, and notably its loss, cannot be understood from the truth
of this standpoint but rather from the fact that this human type is
decidedly a product of the pre-socialist period and that the construction of society as a plurality of isolated individuals is here absorbed
into the thou-experience. It is no longer grasped in the actual and
original form, as we are newly capturing it. We suddenly discover that

one person means infinitely more to another than he can imagine. Because this position does not see itself, it also fails to see that it arose in a distinctive context of experience (*Erfahrungszusammenhang*). How a man comprehends the ultimate loneliness depends on the constellation of life. When I explain the philosophy of isolation by the collective state of affairs I am trying to show that the other standpoint is far more comprehensive, since man discovers that he arrives at the experience of isolation only through collective experience.

Lecture 5
The Phenomenon of Reprimitivization as a Consequence of Distantiation from Life: Evasion or Solution?

I want briefly to fix our location, what is engaging us and why these things engage us. We have asserted that sociology is a knowledge of man. We know since Dilthey that knowledge of man in any form is self-knowledge and in this shape subject to quite different norms and structures than the knowledge of estranged nature. This is why, in order to see the structure of sociology or any science that deals with man, it is necessary, first of all, not only to look from the side of the object but also to observe the emergence of man, specifically in connection with the emergence of the man who is engaged in knowing in this instance. That is why, in order to comprehend this science, we first posed the question of what sociological man looks like, and why we made the effort, afterwards, to analyze the sociological attitude. The first step was to carry out the analysis in the case of the concrete example of Saint-Simon. From this analysis we took away a phenomenon that is manifest in his case and that we then made the basis of an analysis of the sociological attitude itself. As we probed more deeply into the attribute of being "experimental," we arrived at a broader characterization, viz., at the description of the phenomenon of distantiation from life. This phenomenon was central, as a specifically modern type of posture out which the sociological view emerges. We then probed further. We did not expend energy on the attempt to explicate (*aufzuweisen*) this psychic attitude (*seelische Einstellung*) as a psychological phenomenon (*psychologisches Phänomen*), but asked instead, how does this new attitude come into the world in conjunction with the social process?[26] We must always use the soul (*Seele*) as our starting point. Because everything that happens takes place in the psychic process. It is not possible to comprehend society except in the soul of humankind. It does not exist anyplace else. In this sense one could call everything "Psychology" since even the knowledge of physics transpires in the soul. But the physical is something objective, even if the experience of it takes place in the flow (*Ablauf*) of the soul. When some objectivity is also present, the knowledge is not psychology. When I grasp the reflection of the social process in the soul, this comprehension is not psychology. When you practice sociology, you will always have to invoke the processes of the soul through which society constitutes itself. You would be nothing but a psychologist only if you did not look beyond the constitution of the soul and failed to ask yourself what changes were taking place in the social organism to impose these changes upon the soul.

It is a psychological finding when I assert that modern man performs (*vollzieht*) this act of distantiation from life. If I then go on to ask about the reasons for the emergence of this distantiation, however, I have brought group phenomena into the inquiry and I have offered an explanation for these phenomena.

Distance from life means that modern man becomes separated from the performing of acts. The preordained group enactments are not performed, and, as he becomes reflexive, modern man discovers society. We have explained this phenomenon by the splitting within group entities in the modern epoch, an event that makes the segments of the group antagonistic to one another. In a word, the psychic phenomena that are our starting point when we comprehend modern man are set in relationship to what manifests itself in the social (*soziales*) life of the social body (*Gesellschaftskörper*).

To return to our topic and to recall the concrete example we used for the further development of the theme, we ask, what is this distantiation from life that I have been talking about? The original naive situation is as follows: a human being lives in a group, in the family, etc. Authority reigns here. As long as one is at one (*in Deckung*) with the group, the individual will perform without problems all the psychic acts that express themselves in obedience. Even if he does not do this, he will concede the principle of authority. He will feel guilty. He will not discover that this family is governed by the principle of authority. He will not see this social structure because his enactments occur in parallel to it. "I believe in authority as my parents do. I find myself at one with the acts they perform." As long as a group continues in such an aproblematical condition, sociological knowledge cannot arise. There is no distantiation from life. One does not recognize that the group is held together by authority, that the parent-child relationship is regulated in a certain form and oriented to specific norms. One has rules but does not recognize concrete problems of social experience (*des Sozialen*). Only when the individual becomes separated from the collective performing of acts, is it discovered that specific constraints are at issue, constraints that could be different than they are. At this instant, man takes distance from these constraints. An illustration is provided by a boy coming from the community of a rural family to the metropolis, where the old patriarchal principle has been dissolved. Today you can see that the parental relationship is transforming itself into a collegial relationship, that has yet to be shaped. Parents want to be comrades of their children, and teachers, of their students. This does not altogether work out since they are after all not comrades, but they do share a common direction.

If a boy, accordingly, comes into the city and experiences the possibility of enactments or valuations[27] different from aproblematical authority, he is no longer able to perform the old actions altogether aproblematically if he returns to his original home. This is his reaction, and the relationship that makes possible the education by catechism (*Frage-Antwort-Erziehung*) becomes problematical. The problem of authority becomes a reflexive problem. The valuations and constraints by which an aproblematical, naive group lives become an object instead of being altogether absorbed in the performing. Out of the breakdown of the old constraints, arises this modern type of man able to treat authority or the teacher-student relationship—i.e., a great many phenomena of life—as problems, and thereby, in this sense, to take distance from them.

I have once again brought the distantiation from life before us, in the instance of a simple phenomenon, as distantiation must inevitably appear in a situation of social discontinuity (*Umbruch*),[28] that is wherever the old forms of social life no longer suffice, when it has become impossible simply to carry through with the performing of an act (*Aktvollzug...vollziehen*). One becomes separated, and, in so doing, searches for the new form, which can be achieved only by turning what had been immediately one's own into a matter of reflection. That is the basic situation of modern man, who is compelled to redesign the old forms of life, but who possesses them only in a general way (*der*

Richtung nach). An example is the situation of the teacher, notably the comradely relationship between teachers and students, as well as between parents and children. This means that we do not really want to have a comradely relationship, which is, after all, the form appropriate to members of the same age cohort who are friends. Comradeship is experienced in this case as a negative form to set against authority. We experiment with this new form in every performing of it. The new life will not emerge through the emergence of a process by which new tablets of the law and new forms of the family are proclaimed, leaving us all in peace. The new seeks to form and to spread itself at a thousand intersections of life. The new life is born in a thousand obligations attending everyday enactments. As one relationship is unriddled, new problematic relationships rise up. The situation is further complicated at every transmission to a neighbor, and the like. Life and forms of life (*Lebensformen*) emerge in the guise (*Gestalt*) of this actual experimentation. A person who lives in the country and who has not as yet experienced the structural transformations of industrialism has no problems and should not be expected to have any. Where these things have in fact become problematic, it is impossible to go further without taking distance from phenomena that were formerly present in the unmediated performing of acts. You can see the sociological origin of the situation in which man increasingly distances himself and thus plunges into a new crisis.

We have described the sense in which this distantiation is at first unbearable. Life in such a situation, where it can always be called into question, triggers an extraordinary unease. So long as a community (*Gemeinschaft*) functions without being problematized, one knows what one is about. But in the contemporary situation, where more than one alternative is possible, even the fundamentals which could provide a standard of measurement have become problematical. That is a very radical unease, this insecurity of modern existence, which looks to sociology for orientation. Sociology serves by taking the distantiation from life, which first manifests itself in scattered and accidental guise, and treating it as a systemic problem, as the modern form of the search for the renewal of life. You cannot be savvy (*kapieren*) about the rise of sociology if you do not already place the rise of new things in the total context. Otherwise you have nothing before you but a hysterical person.

The initial result is an attempt to live on naively. Next comes the phenomenon of reprimitivization, which necessarily belongs, as an experiment, to the modern situation. As long as one has not understood the meaning of the turn to reflexivity by putting it in the context of totality, as long as one cannot come to terms with oneself, and as long as one lacks the ability to see the total context—and to see, from this standpoint, the only alternative possible—one keeps trying to turn oneself back (*zurückzuschrauben*).[29] "I will pretend that these problems do not exist." This formation, a person who artificially becomes primitive after he has already become reflexive, is the problem of the moment. Fascism, taken in its decision about the world as a whole (*ganze Weltentscheidung*), is nothing but reversion to complete primitivity and impressionist impulsiveness by types of men—among the leaders—who have already experienced the reflexive situation and who then say: "One cannot live like this any longer. We want to found dictatorship and order." That is how it is among the leaders. The process can be described quite clearly. Take Mussolini. He was himself a socialist, someone who had accepted Marxism—the most complicated form of thought and, as social orientation, the most sophisticated way of looking at things (*die feinste Betrachtungsweise*)—someone who knows a great deal about the class struggle, and someone who has heard the lectures of the sceptic, Pareto, who has taken disillusionment as far as it can be taken. When someone like that simply dismisses all these problems, he is acting out what we have seen in Romanticism. The problems are artificially simplified. This move is historically congruent (*fällt zusammen*) with the petit-bourgeois strata, rooted in the soil, who do not understand the situation, but who understand enough to know that the old order is not working. The fear of death is never as great as the fear of social breakdown (*Nichtfunktionieren*). "Until now, we have known the meaning of death; but if society dissolves itself, we do not even know what death is— and that is terrible." That is why it is understandable that these primitive strata should suddenly become explosive and incalculable. "I need nothing but elan and enthusiasm." This type of public and this type of leadership come to the same conclusion, although at completely different levels, and they both arrive at a theory of impulsive action.

A bad decision, but, as Carl Schmitt says, still more valuable than no decision at all. This situation of deprimitivization and artificial reprimitivization confronts us, and, as sociologists, we must understand it. The question arises, is this an ultimate solution (*letzte Lösung*)?

Can this be more than a matter of a few years? Is it possible for a consciousness that has already seen the total context suddenly to forget everything it has seen and learned from experience, and to become primordially simple? This is the problem of sociology. In primitive and simple political situations, it manifests itself as fascism. In a related form, it also emerges, however, in the most sophisticated philosophical ramification. The recourse in existentialist philosophy to the original existential act and the refusal-to-be-reflexive is a parallel on a much higher plane. One discovers that a thing is altogether reflexive and discovers simultaneously that there was once such a thing as the direct performing of an act, and one is enthusiastic for such an act, albeit without it having any concrete content. That is nothing but an extension of reflexivity. This way out, becoming suddenly enthusiastic about the primeval condition, is nothing but a repression of reflexivity, banning it to a sphere never entered by the normally reflexive person.

What is to be done? I believe that we cannot escape the fate of separation from the performing of acts and becoming reflexive as a result. That is our destiny (*uns aufgegeben*). The question is what we do with it, how we put it to use (*verwerten*). There are two definite types of possibilities. The one consists of playing with the possibility of questioning everything in turn, of putting life in question even where it has not yet become reflexive, of inventing (*spinnen*) problems. Such an abuse of reflexivity is indeed one of the possibilities.

I totally deny, however, that sociology poses this danger.[30] The alternative to the first possibility is to perform the distantiation from life whenever life poses the problem and compels distantiation, but to do this with searching intention for the new and real intensity. That is what I consider the fruitful new existential act. In it, we live just as naively as the primitive in his naive performing of acts. To unriddle the situation, the reflexive man probes just as nakedly and directly into his ultimate situation as the naive man. In a word, when sociology— with all its calling into question, its relativization, its distantiation— becomes the social organ (*Organ*) of a humanity that is forming a new world in itself, there comes into being—leaving aside the philosophical question of existence—the immediacy of a direct attitude to life. Sociology becomes the direct organon for a reformation of life. One is not trying to rush toward an overhasty answer. What one wants, rather, is really to vitalize the new in every situation in which this problem arises. This is quite an essential feature of our situation.

It is the point where the solution has not yet been found, but where in anticipation, the prime objection to distantiation from life is forestalled (*vorwegzunehmen*). Nietzsche was the greatest trailblazer of the sociological attitude to life (*Lebenshaltung*), just as I consider Marx to be the greatest sociologist. Ahead of his time (*vorauseilend*), Nietzsche clearly saw what was essential to the sociological attitude to life, and, in addition, he experienced in himself the step forward from the older human type. He said, among other things, that whatever is illuminated ceases to matter to us. What did the god have in mind when he counseled us to know ourselves? Was this perhaps intended to say that we should cease to matter to ourselves? A great question is thereby posed. Is life not put to death by the distantiation from life, the objectification of norms, the problematizing of so many things? There is a way of putting things in question that is distinguished by the fact that the questioning comes to an end. The greatest danger in becoming reflexive and distanced is that, while knowing oneself, one no longer matters to oneself. You are all perfectly aware that it is possible to drive sociological and psychoanalytical self-examination so far that mattering to oneself is destroyed. This is a danger specifically for the political attitude embedded in sociology. Sociology can become the instrument (*Organ*) for killing the political instinct.[31] I emphasize this negative possibility of sociology, and every active politician that rejects sociology for this reason is right to reject it. But I emphasize at the same time that this is just one of sociology's possibilities, the negative one. Nietzsche is right that the god who commanded "know thyself" may have wanted us to cease mattering to ourselves. That is possible. Man always has an escape route in an absolute distantiation from everything. The simplest way of turning something into a matter of indifference is to objectify it through this kind of knowledge. Reflection does indeed often have such an origin. Under such conditions objectification remains something positive because life must often neutralize itself if it wants to stay alive. But there is a different distantiation, which Nietzsche, in my opinion, did not yet see. He drove doubt to its highest point and then performed the first fascist act. The will to power is, after all, a first harbinger of fascism.

I want to close this prologue with a sentence taken from Freud: "Every psychic differentiation represents a new complication of psychic functioning, increases its instability (*Labilität*) and can become the starting point for a breakdown."[32] The sociological situation can lead to breakdown. Every intellectual person is right to be afraid of his situation because it can lead to breakdown. That is the greatest risk in the intellectual situation. This instability dominates the atmosphere (*Grundatmosphäre*) in the contemporary world of the intelligentsia. The same applies in a different form below, in the supposedly naive strata. Every new differentiation heightens instability, and every new organism must find its way anew, so as to be able to master the new sublimation and differentiation. I am of the opinion that ultimate mastery can never be achieved by a retrogression. We can only go on to the end , there to become original (*ursprünglich*) again, to have the world once again directly before us, in the searching act of reflection, and so to attempt to unriddle it.

I wanted to let you feel the danger that warns us from this pathway. This fear is well founded. We put ourselves at risk when we carry this through (*vollziehen*). The question arises, however, whether reprimitivization can be a way out. That it is an escape route, we know perfectly well. For now, I will at leave it up to you whether it is also a solution.

Lecture 6
Forms of Reprimitivization I: Deliberate Reversal of the Intellect in Fascism

First some supplemental points to the last lecture. For the problem of reprimitivization is so decisive and at the moment so much the fateful question for the intelligentsia as a social unit that one cannot simply break off, having raised the question, without completing the analysis. I believe, accordingly, that I must once more confront us with the problem. We can explicate this question in the context of the problem we have raised about the social situation in which this variant of the sociology represented here has its origin. We are in the middle of a representative sociological analysis of a given situation.

I summarize. Reprimitivization as a phenomenon suddenly became understandable for us from the panic situation that emerges with the general rise of distantiation from life. We have observed how man is affected by the fact that norms, values, and forms of life are no longer simply put before us under conditions of late capitalism, where different world aspirations complicate the interpretation of the world. Man can only help himself if he carries out the distantiation whereby he problematizes all the acts which the naive man carries out in agreement with his group. We have come to understand that subjecting the most self-evident forms of life to distantiation and problematization is itself a self-evident phenomenon, that it is not something to be condemned, but rather something that must happen of necessity in the difficult life-situation in which we find ourselves.

The next problem is posed by the question, how does the person look, the one who ever more often carries out this distantiation, when that person is examined in light of the fact, first, that life offers ever more opportunities to carry out distantiation, and, second, that almost everything is suspect as well as problematical to the stratum that has been entangled in the most recent predicament of life. What happens to the stratum that cannot but make it a rule (*zum Habitus machen*) to take distance? You can see that this is how a socio-economically constrained situation gives rise to the most refined (*sublime*) inner complications, complications that one must trace ever further and understand in their inner connectedness. At the beginning of a socio-economic transformation, it is possible to follow how the most refined impulses are connected to the situation of their origins (*Ursprungssituation*). If we recognize that a new human type has emerged, one that can deal with life only by taking distance from most phenomena because he can no longer accept preordained solutions, we will see that this type will be afflicted by a new illness, an illness that has never existed before but that is now a necessity. The illness is not a defect one can lose by improved habits; it is inherent in the situation. All one can do is to give thought to ways of shaping and bearing it. It is in connection with this problem that the phenomenon of reprimitivization emerges. Once we have gotten to know the person who is forced to take distance, we will realize that there will inevitably be a stage where a longing arises to be free of all these things, to be again as simple as before. The problem poses itself as follows: a further radicalization of disillusion, skepticism, seeing from all sides without achieving conviction. A solution through the rise of fascism emerges here with a certain inner necessity. This "must" is not normative in the sense that fascism *ought to* exist, but rather a reference to the imperative character of fascism's emergence among certain strata when they find themselves in certain positions. Sociology can explain the event by this situation, showing it to be the most available thing to try in order to become simple again. It is interesting that something we grasp at the level of a sociological problem complex, follows exactly the same course at the level of a psychic problem complex (*Seelenproblematik*).

It is evident that, after an analysis of Marxism, fascist sociology initially appears quite primitive and simplified. In place of the quite concrete view of class struggles, built up from the economic structural grid to encompass the things of the spirit (*das Geistige*), an ideology steps forward that has a very simple view of the process. It is a matter of a constant rise and fall, in the course of which elites replace one another from time to time. There is something to that. How and when and why these elites replace one another, however, and how they are built into the overall structure of the social body, all this is hidden from view (*verdeckt*). The theory is so simple that one has only what one needs for a fascistic type of action. This move to fascism occurs among certain strata of the intelligentsia. There too—as, for example, in the deeply skeptical type represented by Pareto—the vital spirit (*vitale Élan*) suddenly breaks through, the idea that one has no business with all that, and that one must consequently free oneself from the situation and become aboriginally simple (*ureinfach*). This segment of the intelligentsia is a specific one, whose idol (*Abgott*) is intuition. In Carl Schmitt we have an outstanding representative of this theory in Germany. He is the most sublime thinker we have today in the historical study of spiritual formations (*Geistesgeschichte*). It is a rare pleasure to read his phenomenological analyses, as when he discusses parliamentarism. The ability to see things in their multiple meanings is clearly on view. His teachings nevertheless culminate in a solution with just one slogan: Decision. This means that we can no longer get along with parliamentarism in the present state of things. Where the solution might come from is not as important as that it arrives. It could even be communist. This solution could however be no less ascribed to fascism. Of itself, communism is embedded in a structural theory that necessarily reserves decision to itself, while in Schmitt the decisive step, the decision, is added on, derived from an altogether different context. This spiritual structure (*Geistesstruktur*), present in Carl Schmitt in the most sublime form, is the basic structure of fascism in the domain of the soul (*im Seelischen*).

I tried in the last lecture to show that there is a specific point in common between the inner condition of the intelligentsia that becomes decisionist and the masses that stand behind it. For these masses who are estranged from their place of origin—petty bureaucrats, those recently arrived from the countryside, and the rest—are in the same position as the intellectuals, who have experienced everything through spiritual analysis. Driven by the combative assertion (*Kampfdrang*) that one cannot live without decisions, such a man also wants explosive action. The push to decisions, high and low, is a point of coincidence. If you follow the fate of the intelligentsia in the context of social groupings, you will always notice that motivations are different in the intelligentsia and in the mass, but that it is always possible to find the point where they can converge. We will have a chance in our tutorials (*Übungen*) to see that the Romantic intelligentsia at the beginning of the nineteenth century stood in a specific relationship to the reactionary orders (*ständische Reaktion*). A retreat to antiquated medievalism was present in both, but it was meant differently by the one and the other.[33] We have come to understand that reprimitivization appears as a necessary solution, first, for strata that are unsettled by the present situation but not in sight of the new solution, and, second—more generally—in response to the strain of seeing too much. But this leads to the following problems.

I want to lay out a whole range of problems with great care. In keeping with sociological method, this will expand our problem, but it is nevertheless part of our task.

The first question arising is whether someone who has engaged in analysis up to this point, someone who has become seeing and knowing—whether such a man can suddenly become primitive again? Is it possible to live like that? Can these tensions be borne, or will they not, rather repeatedly break through the actual, vital life? Is it possible in the long term to live with a consciousness more simple than the one possessed earlier, and yet to remain in command of the situation? Is there any chance that a man, who has in principle reached a position to see through himself and who has already intellectually taken distance, could begin again at a lower level, to live and act there? A thousand observations that you register in your own lives speak for the possibility. A consciousness that knows something but then attempts to become simpler somehow acquires a hysterical structure. There is no doubt that there is a persistent spontaneous return of the genuinely vested knowledge that has grown in us as a result of our experiencing a certain stage of life. And if one keeps shouting "I am simple," one falls into a state of nervous tension, a condition that clearly demarcates a certain type of modern intellectual. Such an effort to outshout oneself is one of the most characteristic phenomena of our time.

That is also the great argument that ultimately speaks against this situation. I do not believe that it is possible, in the long term, to overcome an inner condition that is demanded of us simply by disconnecting (*abhebt*) from it. The scaling back does not actually succeed. That is not to say, however, that it may not in fact be performed, that individual persons and entire nations cannot attempt this regression, or that this type of man does not reappear. But rather that such a man must always break down, either in himself or in the next generation, which has to deal with even more complex situations.

As a sociologist, I am not in favor of simple solutions. For this reason, I must now go on to tell you what speaks against the unambiguous position I have just taken before you. It is the radical disturbance created by the relative truth in fascism. I will tell you in advance that, for me, fascism can never be this final solution (*Endlösung*). But if I am a sociologist, I must allow the other alternatives to come as close to me as possible. In a dialectical movement, I want to show how far the relative truth of the alternate possibility extends.

I want to share with you the meaning of dialectical thinking, something that can never be done except by underlining it in the course of its immediate performing (*Vollzug*). Dialectical thinking is not when one schematically sets thesis, antithesis, and synthesis against one another, but rather when one allows the mutually destructive enactments of living reality to assert themselves (*zur Geltung kommen*) within oneself, and then strides forward to a solution. I convey the thesis with everything that speaks for something (*Sache*), drawing on an inner experiential process. Now I am trying to show a countermovement, that which tells against that thing, and then finally, drawing on the historical powers living in us, to identify whatever comes into being (*zustande*) in ourselves. I want to formulate the alternatives as antithetical and then to find a relative equilibrium for our time.

In school we learned a frozen dialectic that no longer retains the vital impulse of the dialectic. We shall see how vital dialectical thinking arose out of the situation of the nineteenth century. One suddenly had the feeling that it was no longer possible to formulate the truth in simple theses, but that one had to participate in the living movement that spoke in favor first of one and then in favor of the other countertruth, and only from that standpoint to go searching for a solution. Note that it was Adam Müller[34] who actually discovered this thinking for political life and that Hegel simply offers a systematization and more radical thinking through of the form of thought already present in the political sphere.

At present, I am at carrying through a kind of dialectical exposition of the elements of life under examination. With the thesis, we have indicated the things that speak in favor of the fact that an achieved stage of consciousness turns itself back. I want to put before you everything that is relatively favorable to reprimitivization. That move is the antithesis. One might say, perhaps with a certain unsettling degree of justice, that life may be creating a vital self-correction with these explosions, this flight, this grasping for the past. Perhaps our ability to see has become broader and more comprehensive than we can stand, and our intellect has a wider reach than our practical volition. What may speak for reprimitivization, then, is the possibility that this backward turning (*zurückschrauben*) has its justification when it comes to vitality and not in the intellectual sphere. The thesis affirms that it is impossible to reverse the development of the intellect. We are human beings, however, and perhaps we have acquired a head that has become too complicated for our lives, not to speak of command over our readiness for action. If that is so, the fascist movements may represent an attempt at correction, a backward turning, which may unexpectedly permit us to restore an equilibrium. We are talking about certain phenomena of vitality that are observable in other spheres. The sudden eruption of sports, a phenomenon of the rediscovery of bodily strengths and simplification of the situation, is perhaps a vitalist correction (*Vitalkorrektur*) of the overextended mental activity we must carry out. Several phenomena exist, all associated with hyper culture (*Überkultur*).

We want to continue pursuing what is relatively valid and unsettling in this counter argument, turning now to a particular instance I read about in Freud.

During the World War, he wrote a treatise on the theory of the experience of death in war and peace.[35] It went like this. First he made the following profound observation. It is part of the makeup of man that he cannot really imagine his own death. Although every man says, "I will die," he is convinced in his unconscious of his immortality. You can observe this in yourself. You do not in fact live as if you were going to die.

Dostoevski's *Idiot* provides an example. The idiot's greatest experience is that he was condemned to death and then pardoned. And he tells what he experienced in the ten minutes that were supposedly his last. He says that he experienced something of utmost grandeur, namely nothing at all. The past collapsed into a single entity, and he said to himself that if he could live longer, he would want to live always with this intensity. And he was pardoned and lived on as before.

We do not live, in fact, as if we were carried along by the intensity of death. We do not really live under the sign of death. We do not have a vital belief in it. In contrast, we possess a thoroughgoing and objective conception of the death of the other. The other dies, without a doubt. He is lost; he is abandoned. Only the death of the other is credible. But the situation is not so simple. According to Freud, this simple duality is the duality of primitive man, the duality of primitive experience. A collision between the two experiences of death, one's own and that of the other, takes place, according to Freud, as soon as a family member dies. We stand, it appears, in an ambivalent relationship to any family member. Most immediately, we are in a relationship of identification. He becomes, somehow, part of ourselves. In our love of ourselves, we love much in him. For the first time, we perform the unique act of recognizing that the other is also an ego. Our return from this is a flash of terror in the face of our own possible death. If he can die, I see the eventuality of my own death in a completely new form. On the other hand, however, our stand towards our family member is ambivalent. We hate his otherness. At some time and place, we discover his otherness and hate him, essentially, only for this. The psychoanalytic layman does not admit this observation. A cultivated person does not permit himself to acknowledge such an experience. We must repress this because the dominant morality does not allow us to carry through with such a thought. Such repressions often bring about neurotic conditions. Freud teaches that it is precisely the cultivated person who cannot make his peace with this hatred, and that conditions consequently arise in the psyche (*Seele*) that disturb the equilibrium. It is part of this problem that we all possess a dual experience of death—first, that of the other person and, second, the absence of knowledge of our own. From this he infers the primitive and simple aboriginal experience (*Urerlebnis*) that the individual who comes out of an unbroken assurance of life (*Lebenssicherung*) goes to war in certainty (*Bewußtsein*) that nothing can happen to him. There is an experience of the death of others, then, and a non-experience of one's own, and culture seeks to overcome this duality by attempting to generate an empathy (*Mitempfinden*) whereby I comprehend the death of the other as my own. We call it humanization when the experience that I undergo in the case of family members is ever more widely extended, so that I am ever more under the threat that I too may die.

Freud asks next about what happened in the World War. During that time we suddenly dispensed with the latest cultivated manner of experiencing death. We fell back into the original—perhaps barbaric—primitive form of the experience. It is the other who should die. The enemy is the other. We ourselves are, however, immortal. We could tolerate the predicament only insofar as we restored this original primitivism in ourselves. It is a regression in the enactment of culture, turning from modern, cultivated experience to the primitive way of experiencing. What does Freud think about this? He writes: "Is it not for us to confess that in our civilized attitude towards death we are once more living psychologically beyond our means, and must reform?"[36] It is possible to live psychologically beyond one's own means. It is possible, according to Freud, to go further psychically than is permitted by the circumstances. This experience of death which arises in a cultivated person by means of empathy, arises in civilized, urbane situations. From this form we receive too delicate a soul, something not yet permitted, according to Freud. Why? If we are still at a stage primitive enough to engage in war, we cannot live with such an apparatus. It is our duty, according to Freud, to turn ourselves back in order to endure life, to bring experience to the level of the actual conditions. "To endure life remains, when all is said, the first duty of all living beings," says Freud.

The process of reprimitivization is in accord with the principle that there are also psychic attitudes today that cannot as yet endure life.

You see the dangerous power of the antithesis. A thinker who fails to think so as to permit the possibility of the contrary thought to come so close as to threaten him with annihilation is no thinker. Thinking is perhaps a mission. I have tried to show this power to you, although I can think of no more atrocious thought.

I would like to offer a sociological interpretation of the Freudian truth. It is not a question of one human mental state that races ahead and another that remains behind, but rather of a human stratum that races ahead and the present state of an established social situation. It is not a tension within the individual, but rather, it is offspring of a modern society who gain, as products of the highest cultivation of urbanity (*Verbürgerung*), a psychic life, an apparatus of thought and a structure that is in contradiction not to life as such but to the life forms belonging to the other strata. It is clear that the primitive peasant hardly has this brokenness. He goes to war at peace with himself, and he enacts the old, original experience of death.

There are, in sum, social tensions between the experiential world of the self-distanced, cultivated intelligentsia and the real social core (*realer Sozialbefund*), and these tensions are the medium for the society's existence. The sociological inquiry becomes ever more distantiated under such circumstances, and the ever more decisive question becomes, what is to be done?

Lecture 7
Forms of Reprimitivization II: The Standstill in Orthodox Marxist Thought

We are digressing to address ourselves to the problem of regression and reprimitivization. We have presented dialectically—i.e., through the living movement of the spiritual processes—how this problem emerges as a problem of life, a crisis of life, and as a problem to be mastered by thought. First of all, we established the thesis that the reprimitivization and regression represented by fascism in politics and, psychically, by the irrationalist tendencies that associate themselves with fascism, must, in the final analysis, be quite impossible. We posited that as presupposition. Something in us balks at the thought that—after consciousness has seen through itself, after it has attained to a high level where it is capable in principle of understanding all transactions from their contexts, and comprehending its own ego once more in its self-distantiation—that such a consciousness should suddenly act as if it did not know these things, as if it were fresh and youthful in itself and could plunge into life with its original naivety. We said that a certain kind of bracketing was in play here, since we are confronted with the phenomenon of an advanced consciousness reversing itself to a more primitive stage. This gives rise to special kinds of hysteria, especially in the intellectual stratum. If one were working on fascism and counter-revolution, it would be essential to investigate the social location of this intelligentsia with great care. I have had a chance to look more closely at this situation in Hungary, where the intelligentsia is quite generally affected by this psychic manifestation and exhibits the whole range of such hysteria, and where a certain form of hysteria suddenly appears as an illness whose etiology has not yet been investigated.[37] I do not know how things are in Italy.

I do not want to deny what must be admitted right away: first, that these things too can be made fruitful and, second, that there is a big difference between Italian and Hungarian fascism, in that the former has known how to carry away (*mitzureißen*) productive strata. It is part of the unfolding of the contrary argument when I have to acknowledge that every past culture, in truth, had to fashion the positive out of the negative and to bring cultural creation into being on the basis of negative tensions. With these remarks I have already arrived at the antithesis, and I am compelled at least to understand the relative necessity of this causal emergence, thereby going to its comprehensible aspect. As antithesis, then, there arose the question if this regression may not be a process necessary in the development of society, as Freud, for example has shown that the outbreak of war flung us back, in our experience of death, to the stage of primal man. Freud affirmed, in the name of vitality, this being-flung-back, this regression, notwithstanding his regrets as a man of culture. As long as a situation is incapable of overcoming war, a man who wants to live cannot but turn himself back to the primitive experience where only the other dies.

I have presented this idea so as to give it its full weight. One other thing to be noted in Freud's analysis is that he always speaks of man as such, as if man were situated in an inner contradiction in which his intellect races ahead and his instinctual structure remains behind, as if this discrepancy occurs in the isolated individual, while we know that the discrepancy is in fact divided among strata and that we can fix these sociologically. The Freudian view is correct, but it must be reformulated as follows. There is a stratum that is far in advance of the instinctual structure, viz., the group of intellectuals. The existence of such a cleavage is social destiny. This is not a class stratification because it has an altogether different character. The duality must be acknowledged. This type of man is formed in a certain way by the shape of life, his way of loving, his experience of sexuality. He is sublimated to such an extent that he can live only in a civilized milieu. On the other hand, the strata who remain rooted in the soil—using the expression in a value-free way—stand closer to the original way of abreacting the difficulties of life. For them, at the beginning, the war is not a psychic catastrophe. Only later, as the war continues, can they turn to revolt. At first, however, it does not go against their instinctual system. This discrepancy between the different possibilities entails[38] that society does not have a homogeneous structure, that these two strata collide and are thrown upon one another—in sum, that while initially seeming to live isolated from one another, these strata now abruptly become an acute problem for one another. The incursion of an earlier and less mature social condition upon a rapidly advancing one is actually the problem. We experience the same discrepancy in ourselves.

Above all, we have seen from a sociological point of view the duality of the urban civilized strata, on the one side, and populations rooted in the soil, on the other. This duality is also present in individuals, namely [in the coexistence of] the forward moving instinctual sphere, sublimation and intellectual sphere with the primitive instincts. This tension may indeed be replicated in the individual and its antinomy may structure individual lives, but only if the individual is in a position where he must prove himself in both spheres, if he is not socially enclosed—never seeing other social strata, or experiencing, for example, only the aristocrat and never the peasant. An example of this last might be a count's daughter who does not clash with this completely sublimated world through any of the enactments of her life. In the case of her father, however, who must also rule, we find that he will experience the duality of structure in thought and soul. In the sociability of his own circle, the cultivated aristocracy at the highest level of cultivation (*Kultivation*), he is completely at one with himself. He can live for his self-cultivation. On the other side of his existence, however, he is in a situation of warfare, and there he must be brutal. Thus he possesses an apparatus of sublimation and also, if you will, a primitive or reprimitivized sphere of his existence. In such a case, it may well come to a mighty collision in the individual subject, but this is not a subjective tension but rather a mirroring of the fact that the life of this man develops two sides of his existence and that the individual is thus a reflection of his social structure. The tension of his social sphere appears as a tension in his own life.

Now the justification for these various excursuses. The point of what we are doing is a search for a new method through which we can shatter the fabrications of the schools. From the previous century, we have inherited the illusion that knowledge is a closed and teachable system, and that everything known comprises contents of instruction. This misconception derives from the institution of examinations. It is the hallmark of examinability. In sociology, I have no reason to reenact (*vollziehen*) this procedure. I will show you that living thought is a process of constant self-expansion, where it is possible to introduce by pedagogical means a precept that incorporates self-discipline and methodical self-observation. That is the direct enactment of thought. Sociological man does not think according to a scholastically systematic method; he feels his way through the intermeshing weave of the actual situation. Because we destroy this capacity in school, we create individuals who can no longer think authentically in their lives. That is why I want the original movement of thought to assert itself. My self-interruptions are intentional. I want to show how one can reach out ever further, beginning from a single problem.

The fact is that the individual incorporates the social situation in himself, that our count and his daughter live in the family under completely different conditions of life and that they are bound to exhibit completely different structures because they are required to abreact and assert themselves in different circles of life. It is similar with the countess, his wife, who once enjoyed the integral life of a noble daughter but then acquired certain partially concrete cares of the household, as well as a husband subject to the duality. These tensions derived from a social situation are absent in a working class family. From these tensions, arising out of the social situation, emerge internal family tensions.

I have experienced, in a concrete case, how feelings of unhappiness arose in the wife out of the circumstance that her husband did not display the same sublimation, the same stage of refinement as she.[39] The tensions generated by life originate as tensions in the family and generate certain differences which, if they cannot be abreacted, turn into neuroses. A situation social in origins thus reproduces itself.

I have attempted to show how social tensions reproduce themselves in a marriage, how farm laborers influence even the marital tensions of the aristocratic family, how tensions can be communicated to the life of the household and family because of the mirroring of social tensions in the tensions of the individual. Now I close this excursus.

What is now the state of the problem which threatens us, the necessity of regression? I want to say the following: There are two forms of reprimitivization. I have thus far only mentioned the crassest form, a form I must absolutely oppose. I have not yet mentioned the really problematical one. You must not forget that there is not only the form of becoming more primitive that results from a backward turn, but also one in which one permits an achieved high level to grow rigid (*erstarren*), a form in which one immobilizes a stage of thinking in order to safeguard the security that is threatened by distantiation from life. By rigidifying one of the highest forms of thinking, one resolves the original sociological situation of doubt, the capacity of seeing things from many points of view.

The form under discussion now is orthodox Marxism. We want to grapple with (*sich auseinandersetzen mit*) this alternative, to specify it sociologically, and to ask what it means. We must both appreciate and express the fact that the emergence of an orthodoxy is inevitable in certain situations. The question of when orthodoxies arise would be an interesting dissertation topic. When are they socially necessary, and when do they dissolve? Since these questions have not yet been researched, I can only pass on some speculations. It is clear that an orthodoxy must arise within every social location where the occupants must remain unreconciled with the social body at large.

Every reactionary social stratum, especially of the older generation, once it is cast down from its position of dominance and comprises a membership without prospects for individual redevelopment, is compelled to consolidate its old collective self-determinations, together with its partisans, and to do this in an intolerant form. While the new generation, which may have the opportunity of reorienting itself, will at some point attempt to ease the boundary lines and to erect justificatory ideologies of collaboration. That is where orthodoxies are dissolved. Every stratum that cannot assert itself except by opposition will be forced to certify this opposition by positing its thesis as absolute.

One must then ask how it is with large organizations? We know that the Catholic Church has a rich store of dogmas. In this connection, it would be necessary to investigate what the Church's store of dogma means when examined from a social-functional point of view. One must be careful here. It may be that the [Catholic] Center Party (*Zentrum*) has certain dogmas that are left untouched but that are in practice nevertheless very elastic.[40] Just as in Catholicism. These dogmas are maintained by reinterpretation, since large bodies are necessarily elastic. A sect can remain rigid, unqualified for decisions (*undezisionshaft*), while a group or a church in a variety of situations—like the Catholic Church—changes itself according to the political situation and acquires an extraordinary flexibility. Social Democracy too, which is extending itself in the direction of flexibility, is so much under threat that it is losing its contours, its basic forms.

If someone wants to correct something, to make it different, it is impossible nowadays for him simply to stand there and proclaim that he wants things changed. He must know the sources of error and illuminate them sociologically.

This brings us to the root of the matter, if we are talking about orthodoxy in Marxism. For the social strata that do not arrive at the point of collaboration or that cannot do so, only orthodoxy is at hand, and it may well represent the proper form for them. Now the question arises for the strata in this situation, whether such orthodoxy is self-evidently a regression. If I were a miner and very badly off, I would certainly be an orthodox revolutionary. We can see clearly that this way of thinking arises from this specific situation.

That leads us to ask how the attitude of affiliated intellectuals is formed. One of the keenest challenges[41] is whether the intelligentsia can in fact affiliate itself. The intelligentsia has undergone something like sublimation, self-distantiation. It has passed through this stage. And this intelligentsia undergoes it persistently—ever since it defected from its original group, when the intellectual abandoned the earliest unambiguous possibility of seeing the world and entered upon a level of consciousness with multiple possibilities. For the essence of modern cultivation (*Bildung*) is that it embraces, in principle, many alternate ways of seeing. Becoming truly cultivated means experiencing all possible ways of seeing and thinking. There is present a tendency to see multi-dimensionally, but at the same time, a great uncertainty. Simultaneously, the intellectual identifies himself with a position that is not altogether his own, but that is in some measure consonant with the dissatisfaction of the intelligentsia with the world as it is. This dissatisfaction accords with the dissatisfaction of the proletariat. This is at once the source of identification and a dualism in the intellectual's stand towards life. He is under a compulsion, especially if he affiliates himself with the most extreme group. He finds himself in a situation where he is constantly binding his consciousness to the sanctioned decision that he receives and experiences with the others. This causes the following tension. He understands that this dogmatizing, this nail-ing fast of certain things, is very fruitful from the standpoint of action. Collective action is possible only when the direction of action is un-equivocally laid down. He also understands that this orthodoxy is prescribed on the basis of a situation that is not actually a complete fit with his own. It means the presupposition of axiomatic propositions. A new experience can only be taken in by fitting something into this axiomatic structure. Insofar as this latter is particularistic, certain things can simply not be successfully mastered.

It is part of the original nature of thinking that, on the appearance of new facts incapable of being fitted in, one widens the compass of thinking. Progress in the physical sciences is like that. First came the facts, then a hypothetical system as context. Certain facts are mastered in this way. Then new facts of a certain kind arrive. They cannot be classified, we say. I revise my premisses and find a new hypothesis that does justice to the new facts. Every orthodoxy that lays down a framework is advantageous to a point, as long as it is limited to the facts constituting its formative experiences (*Urerfahrung*). When new constitutive facts appear, however, things become difficult.

I want to say something at this point about the sociology of closed systems. Every orthodox thinker has the advantage of having a closed system and he sees in this a guarantee of truth. He possesses this system by virtue of the fact that he regards the things he cannot master as peripheral. He does not care to see them. From my own standpoint, then, I must regard orthodoxy as a regression, and I am compelled to say, in the interest of truth, that an open system is the truly social system. It is possible that the world is ultimately a closed system that we do not know. One must obviously keep the boundaries of the system open, however, if one aspires to totality. This question of open or closed systems is also sociologically differentiated. One of the most important insights of the sociology of knowledge is the power of the thought that even such philosophically conceptualized questions can be discussed from a variety of standpoints. Fascism is a regression that does not want to grasp the world as unity, in order to let its hysterical assaults be justified. The denial of system belongs to this type of regression. On the opposite side stands a fundamentally different type of relative regression. It possesses precisely the contrasting attribute of upholding the absolutely closed system—and it fixes this at the stage of social development that is most advantageous for an absolute general attack. If the intellectual wants to think for himself, however, and if he dispenses with all collective wishes, he most prefers to think in terms of an open system, constantly putting it in question. I do not think in an intuitively erratic way, but see things coherently. I seek a totality of society in a structural interconnectedness. But I have not predicated a single possibility, but rather coherence that aspires to totality but that holds itself open to facts that cannot be comprehended from this point of view.

This raises the second important problem, whether a defensive maneuver anchored in an orthodoxy is good even for a party. There is a great contradiction. On the one side there is the demand for a decision. The intellectuals' posture that inclines to participation in all possibilities requires a decision. On the other side, there is the observation that Marxism is fruitful only if it represents a way of seeing, the highest form of social insight. Is a way of thinking still capable of such insight if it suspends its movement at a certain stage simply because it wants security for action and if it thereby runs the danger of becoming so rigid that it cannot apprehend any emerging novelties not susceptible to being automatically fitted in? When such things emerge, one cannot and will not take part in any expansion of thinking, out of concern for decisions, so that a regression gradually renders the once elevated stage of thinking rigid and is in danger of jeopardizing the elasticity of thinking formerly inclined towards optimal vision. As a result, this position is itself caught in an antinomy. On the one hand one wants things to be closed and has no use for the uncertainties of the intellectual, but on the other side one has need of self-expansion. Out of this ambivalence in the situation is bred a struggle within the party itself.

Lecture 8
The Ideal of Dynamic Thought:
Orthodox Thinking as a Type

We have analyzed what we assume to be two fundamentally different forms of regression. The first type was fascism, a psychic attitude toward the reflective and the experiential, where men deal with their circumstances not by proceeding within the situation in which they find themselves but rather by enacting a reprimitivization, attempting to shape life as from a different stage of life. There is also a different kind of regression, which stops the natural process of expanding the vision, of self-overtaking, by scholasticizing a given system of world view or science. It rigidifies this system and, in the guise of orthodoxy, renders it static. While the structure of thinking originally tends towards unceasing self-expansion, orthodoxy signifies the acceptance of a given stage as absolute, and the treatment of things that become newly visible only insofar as they can fitted into this design. The circumstances under which orthodoxies in general arise is a sociological problem.

To begin with, I want to develop a phenomenological account of such thinking. The most important point was already indicated during the last lecture. The distinction between open and closed systems can be the criterion of orthodoxy. The sense of superiority enjoyed through the possession of a closed system is often a sign that this security, this closure of world view, is considered more important than calling things into question. But there are also much more primitive varieties. The most refined form is one where systematization conceals self-arrest. I want to add that the inclination toward rigidity does not happen through political impulses alone. Schools are an example in academic life. What does this mean? That one fixes a certain basis of thought in place and fundamentally rejects anything new that cannot be fitted into its system. That is also a kind of closed system. In political life, however, the phenomenon is much more important because here the objective is not just a small sphere of life but a world view intended to cut deep. It must be emphasized that the greatest danger in any such arrest lies in the fact that it interrupts the original function of thinking—to begin anew, to apprehend freshly, to process novelty, and to expand itself—and that defensive maneuvers become increasingly dominant. I cannot deny that every act of thought, even in its original form[42] contains a defensive maneuver. In the very formulation of a concept, I already exclude something. Even if I were to attempt to remain absolutely open and always ready to break through boundaries, I would close myself off at the moment that I demarcated something. It is a question of balance, however. Whether defensive maneuvering so dominates thinking that it becomes nothing but incessant defensive maneuvering, or whether there is a balance.

The primitive form of defensive maneuver takes the form, first of all, of finding something to be nothing but a novelty in thought. When persons who dwell within the well-marked confines of an academic school are confronted by a new fact they will attempt to devalue it.

Such devaluation and trivialization is the most primitive and simplistic type of defensive maneuver. The second step is somewhat more refined, looks a little better, but amounts to exactly the same thing. They ask, is sociology a science at all? In this case, they have a fixed conception of science that they refuse to relax, and on this basis they reject what is newly emerging. It is a more refined act of thought to play the premises of a concrete doctrinal structure off against an innovation. As noted, this carries out the primitive defense in a more refined manner. Instead of rendering things more flexible by backing up, loosening the premises and broadening the concept of science in order to be able to comprehend the new mode of knowing, they cling to the premises that obstruct the infusion of the new fact. It is an essential act of thought. In living thought the principle of locomotion consists in easing back when things no longer work out, rather than further rigidifying the underlying problems that impede the approach of the new.

A second form of intellectual defensiveness is when one, instead of undertaking an easing back in principle, pushes the logical foundations into the foreground. Something already anticipated in the last lecture belongs under this heading: the phenomenon of the closed system. It is not out of the question that this is the ultimate goal of humankind. Perhaps it is in fact the case that the entire reality of things is a closed interdependence of events—perhaps the whole economy is a closed system, although system and structure are not the same It could be that everything that happens does so within a total interweaving, a fastening together (*Verklammerung*), something we could observe until now only in its small intermediate links. The whole is integrated by an unequivocal structural tendency (*Strukturlinie*). Even if all this were the case, if the world had such a structure, I would still be of the opinion that one could make use of the system only if one sought after knowledge from specific points of departure and constantly pursued an ever more expansive system. It is unlikely that the expansion of a single point of departure could arrive at a structure capable of comprehending totality as a whole. It may be—the matter is as yet unsettled—that the fascist deed coincides with reality, that reality is in fact spasmodic (*sprunghaft*), hysterical. It is however equally possible that reality has a structure in which several structural tendencies are implicitly present and likely to intersect at a given moment, that every thinker is positioned in the medium of one of these wavelengths, that an image of the world abstracts itself from this location and is perhaps recognized at a later stage as a single wavelength which only appeared to represent a closed system, some kind of closed structural image—but that the world itself is much more multi-layered than the particular wavelengths we register.

When we sketch a material happening, we get a silhouette. We have a cross-section of reality. We thus have a closed picture of reality, but if things shift, you get a new silhouette of reality. Systems are various silhouettes that capture a cross-section of a three-dimensional reality. One's own system may be nothing but a silhouette. The empty assertion that everything has particularity is meaningless. If one can say that particularity is present here and there, one must reckon with the fact that this particularity has already become visible. If I am ready to see that something is a silhouette at the same time as it comprehends reality, it is impossible to do anything but see it as a silhouette of a reality. I believe that I have done nothing but use the methods of Marxism to make evident the particularities that have come into view. By this means I still cannot arrive at a closed system. I cannot transcend the particular meanings of the various silhouettes by exhibiting them. I must locate the point from which I grasp them.

I want to emphasize that my examination does not consist merely of the observation that all things are particular. That is no trick. Rather, the question is always, why and how and from which standpoint is something particular. Playing one silhouette off against the other increasingly reconstructs the complete picture. That does not mean, however, that every silhouette, every aspect is as good as the other. It also does not mean that I want to integrate the particular claims by taking their average, and that I imagine that I can thereby arrive at truth.

There you have the defensive maneuver: simplifying the views of the opponent until it is possible to make such assertions. The criticism of my work consists mostly of typical defensive moves. This problem is the great problem of the day.

We have reached an unsettling stage. All thinking has stopped. It has converted itself from searching the world to defensive maneuvering, where everyone has his assigned line of march and nothing else is taking place.

A typical misleading question is, what is this novelty? Is it psychology, sociology, or what? Labels are demanded. If these are in order, then everything is all right, and it is no longer necessary to give the matter further thought.

The first thing I heard about this lecture series was: "But this is psychology." I myself believe that I am making sociological analyses.[43] But that is not important. Have I said anything essential or not? It makes sense methodologically to delineate the boundaries between psychology and sociology. That is quite a different question, however. It makes sense to render the system of science more flexible. But to limit oneself to labels when confronted with concrete questions is merely a defensive maneuver.

A second defensive maneuver is to ask not "is it true?" but "is it dangerous?" All such critiques say: very interesting but terribly dangerous, dangerous for all the parties. First the academic world, then Communism and, in part, Socialism, then the Catholic Church. All alike, without distinction, strike an identical pose. We can use this analysis. It is a good discovery. But we ourselves are of course not ideological; we are absolute. We occupy the absolute position. We go along with this book; we must let ourselves be enriched by it. We also adopt the method, but only for the enemy. Our own position is absolute. That is repeated by all the parties, even though this whole undertaking has aimed at nothing but to show that everyone comprehends everything from some point of view and that we now find ourselves in a situation where thought systems that have been marching separately have become transparent in their experiential biases and could even be analyzed anew.

That is very important, because it became necessary to recognize something pointed out to me by a collaborator. There is much truth to it. It is possible to devise a world historical construction showing how we can reach socialism. A measure of probability speaks for it, but also for its opposite. It turns out that this terrible history of humanity has provided only a few rays of light, lasting only a few hours, when it has been possible to think freely. There has been no knowledge (*Erkennen*) in the thinking of the East, bound by magic. Until in a happy hour something like free thought arose in Greece. Perhaps we had something similar during the Enlightenment. This ray of light, this small intermission, is coming to a close. Our present moment is defined by the fact that no new world has been able to consolidate itself after the dissolution of scholasticism and, consequently, intellectuals have been able to shift about. Now, however, we are arriving at the next stage, where great power centers embodying mass concentrations confront one another—and where these will also absorb the intelligentsia. Then we shall get—at the level of a high stage of development, of machines, of peak accomplishments of technology—exactly the same thing as scholasticism. We cannot say whether this will arrive at a unified scholasticism. However, it is clear that we have reached a stage where this intermission, this short time of enlightenment and relatively free research, is endangered, and where it will be incorporated in the intellectual apparatuses of the various large organizations. And every thinker is completely absorbed by his organization. This construction is a hypothesis, but there is something right about it. It is possible to recognize the trends. In this case, however, it is incredibly important that we keep pressing ever anew the search for what I call the constant breaking-through (*ständiges Durchbrechen*), moving beyond static biases and discrete points of view. Skepticism too is a peculiar business. Do you think that a person is skeptical because he is a bad fellow? Do you think that the great skeptics of the past were skeptics because they were badly brought up, something that academics and the like feel to be the case? Skepticism is a necessary function in a certain life situation. Skepticism emerges at the moment where the opportunity arises to call one view into question by means of another, an opportunity due to the fact that a new world power has arrived and provides an opportunity to frustrate and cast doubt upon the other.

There is a certain design in thought (*Denkintention*) that endeavors to think without stop and that finds help for this will (*Denkwollen*) in the many situations in which one can illuminate one actual possibility from the standpoint of another. Absolute standpoints are not given to any human. He lives in a historical situation. There are perspectives from which it is possible to effect a loosening. As a practical matter, this can happen only by means of this choosing between one and the other. One may well ask what will come of this. While I am thinking, this does not concern me. I have to carry through the mission that is revealed to a human soul, to a human spirit at a given hour. I can understand it when the major political parties raise the question of danger, and I recognize its legitimacy. I cannot and do not wish to forbid the raising of this question. I value it because I have a politicized consciousness and know that politics cannot be banished from the world. It is however necessary to realize that this can only be the first question, because if you pose nothing but the question, "who is harmed?" to yourself, you lose the capacity for insight into the new and newly visible. If, as a result of this question, the Catholic Church, for example, abandons a new insight because it is damaging, it declines a spiritual mastering of this fact, it remains backward and harms itself because there is a further insight able to go beyond the first.

I want to include several other categories of criticism for analysis because they also contain defensive rejections. I am deliberately considering these objections because my lecture is not intended simply to transfer some information but rather to confront the issues that concern me at the moment. It is possible, for example, to say dismissively that mine is some sort of bourgeois thought, since the ideal of free thought—this disguised concept of individual personality, according to which it is the self-emancipating person who always discovers the new truth—these are typically bourgeois matters. I am doing nothing, it is said, but inadvertently demonstrating the legitimacy of the category "bourgeois." Yet my research aimed to show that there is in fact such a thing as conservative thought, that it is determined by social class authorities (*Instanzen*), and that it penetrates into the categories of thinking. In this case one cannot say that it is legitimate to operate with the category of "bourgeois." It is impossible moreover to discard all the things created by the middle class (*das Bürgertum*) in the Nineteenth Century because it is bourgeois. It is an ambiguous situation. Are we ready to scrap all industry because it is bourgeois? That is quite impossible. It cannot simply be the case that anything that springs from this source is nothing, that anything that seeks to salvage values from this time can be dismissed with a gesture of rejection and presented as nothing. The actual situation is that, as a socialist, one undertakes a selection among the bourgeois elements one wants to retain and those one leaves behind. The question is "Can we use this?" "Don't we want to salvage this?" Or is it really possible to dismiss it all with the judgment "bourgeois?" A strange situation.

I have done nothing but to show that this concept of "bourgeois" has long been outdated. I have attempted to show, by means of an analysis of social locations, that this historical concept originates in conservative points of view and that through reliance on it one is led to move in illusions. As well, I have exposed the concept of personality as partly aristocratic. In a word, I have exposed the defensiveness of these gentlemen who prefer to know nothing at all about the social problem constellation. As soon as I reach this point, I have almost entered what Freud called the situation of retroactive obedience. In this condition, there is a slackening of all the impulses that might allow the correctness of a particular insight from elsewhere to spring into view. It is a situation without ambiguities. It is the polar exaggeration of the counter-position. It is a very influential opposition that exaggerates matters so far as to make it appear as if the proletariat would not know what to do with this relatively free thinking, these values of personality that should after all be preserved. If one attacks even these impulses towards openness, if one takes this type of liberating skepticism as bourgeois, one is using the latter concept merely in a defensive mode. The point is not that the sociologist destroys legitimate concepts but that he dismantles the layer that is nothing but the will to defensiveness.

I would like to go further and to show concretely the desperate situation that has confronted us in a discussion here, where Marx's majestic doctrine that a bourgeois thinks in bourgeois fashion is grotesquely inflated to yield the interpretation that a bourgeois utters only idiocies in .everything he says. That is driving the matter to absurd heights. It is maintained that a bourgeois professor is incapable of seeing that the Russian Revolution take place in the domain of world revolution. Is a professor of the present epoch similarly incapable of understanding the counter-argument as soon as he attains to the stage of Marxism?[44]

Matters are no longer so simple with regard to the bourgeois and proletarian realms, although a polarizing tendency remains and certain strata are unambiguously bound. I simply wanted to show how necessary it is to struggle against such interpretations within one's own party when they lead to a paralysis expressed in its most extreme form by utterances like those I have reported. If such things are often repeated, the attitude will triumph in the group.

There is another Marxist theory that is also dangerous, viz., the theory of the best chance for uncovering reality, the chance supposedly possessed by the proletariat, as if it had in its hands the self-revelation of the world spirit, to speak with Hegel.

I believe that proletarian thinking in its Marxist form does indeed have on its side the greatest wealth of capabilities for understanding at the present historical stage. But if this system of thought is immobilized at a certain stage of its development, the situation is reversed. Then the bourgeois stratum can extract from Marxism everything for expanding its own outlook and repeatedly enrich itself from its opponents, while he who is unwilling to move beyond the orthodox rigidities of thought simply wastes his opportunities.

Lecture 9
Immobile and Dynamic Thinking—Orthodoxy and the Intellectuals

We have tried to analyze the symptoms of defensive maneuvers in thought, the typical symptoms present in many intellectual tendencies but especially in every kind of orthodoxy. I have also explained why I am doing this. Every human being speaks, lives, and operates within a concrete life, and I have no reason, even at the lectern, to pretend that we are trying to locate an absolute truth in absolute space. Instead, our task is to carry out (*vollziehen*) the sociological concretization of our own situation. In the beginning, in this introduction, it may be the task, in order to build a basis for mutual understanding, for me to point out the barriers to entry which might increase actual misunderstandings by a thousandfold and which may be removed by taking the obstacles as theme. I naturally do not pretend that I am necessarily in the right. It is my task to give utterance to what everyone senses, and we can discuss afterwards whether I am right and how these difficulties may be overcome. I have shown how political circumstances produce and compel the growth of orthodoxies in certain situations, and I have yet to discuss the relative inevitability of such things.

First I had the task of showing you an ideal image of a dynamic kind of research, carried forward by the intellectual instincts (*denkerischen Instinkten*), and to provide you with the characteristics of such committed thought. I have collected a few of its most visible marks, together with the counter arguments to it, and I have thus far systematized and presented the following marks of the orthodox mode of thinking—or, let us say, of all modes of thinking that characterize the defensive maneuvers of the opposition.

I repeat. As we have often experienced, the most primitive form of defensive maneuver consists of asking "What is that? I want the labels." I have shown how this comes most frequently from colleagues in the discipline who are unready to accept the new science, who reject the whole problem situation, and seek to impede it by the petty tactic of demanding the label. We have already established this as the most elementary way of rejecting a newly emerging matter. An elaboration of this maneuver consists in saying, as one starts to think, that it follows from the concept of science that this thing is impossible. But that shows simply that the concept of science was grounded in past achievements, and thus that the defects of inadequacy in the apparatus invoked for assistance become ever more apparent. What is decisive for the sociology of knowledge is that the deeper one goes, the more radical and dangerous is the rejection. Trivialization can be met by counter-trivialization. But if the other has principles, the hidden defensive maneuver is not so easily seen. The sociology of knowledge must then bring those principles into question by means of a loosening move. This is an essential function of the sociologist of knowledge. For all values and problems raised, he must inquire into the concreteness of the world view, into the secret will governing the thought apparatus—in order no longer to leave these things hidden, but to identify himself with them. This is a conscious reception, a conscious self-identification. The thinker consciously identifies himself with his thought apparatus, but not in an unconscious way. The sociology of knowledge prepares the way for a new phase of thought, because it teaches how to carry through the loosening movement of thought and, in a situation in which discussion is no longer possible, makes such discussion nevertheless possible to a degree.

There are two forms of defensive maneuver. "That is dangerous," says every party. One does not say, "that is true" or "that is untrue," but "that is a danger to this or that." I have conceded that such a statement of the problem is valid from a political standpoint. But to think this way too long means failure at the emergence of important new discoveries. That is the greatest danger. I admit that it is hardly possible today to express a thought that is not somehow politically relevant, a danger to someone. Whether there is any action that is ethically indifferent was already a question in classical antiquity. In this ethical world view, everything is ethically relevant. In a political world, everything is politically relevant. Everything is to be included and, from world views to ethics, everything has a dangerous side. If there were nothing present but this criterion, any productive movement in thinking would come to a halt. If we want to see clearly what is of use and what of harm, then I deny that one must be confined to this point of view. The tactic of opening up the intellectual apparatus avoids the great danger of all dogmatism, which allows a system to become fixed at a certain stage.

The third danger of the stricture to be opposed is its operation with overly narrow and rigid categories.

I have tried to show how much cognitive value there is in the confrontation between bourgeois and proletarian thinking in Marxism. But how dangerous it is if one applies this slogan without thought and ultimately rejects everything to be found in the bourgeois world, never asking whether certain things do not abstract themselves from what is bourgeois and whether they cannot consequently be taken along. This is the danger of an overly restrictive categorical apparatus. In Marxism, certain stabilization tendencies are manifesting themselves through the party apparatus, but these should be combated from the opposite pole within the party.[45]

There are dangerous dogmas that—although they may once have had productive meanings which we can articulate more precisely today—can under certain circumstances become a danger to thinking and knowing. The example to be cited here is the notion of the proletariat as bearer of the world spirit. In itself, something valid is happening when one acts in the consciousness of having been chosen. This arises out of the chiliastic spark of this thought, but it implies simultaneously a certain determinism in outlook. An example of such a combination is the notion that world history is working for us, that we are the vanguard in step with what has been determined to happen. Total opposition and determination by a group fully excluded from the regulation of things in the world gain a flaming beacon in the feeling of wanting to break the world apart in the name of the world spirit and in the belief that the world spirit is working for them.

The odd thing is that this intellectual configuration allows no room for freedom, for the fact that man chooses a situation for himself. When a bourgeois observes this, he is frightened by the fact that this is a determinism and that the basic theme of bourgeois thought has no place in it. That one finds oneself in step with the world means that the thing works by itself. It is interesting that the bourgeois should take such a stand, since if he did want to identify himself with this [orthodoxy], he would do it out of his situation of choice. Although the proletarian is not placed in a situation of choice, the absence of freedom is no restraint for him because he is in step with his situation, with which he has identified himself. As proletarian strata commingle with strata for which the situation of choice would be available, the gap in the system that has been present for the bourgeois also opens for them. At the moment when the situation of choice emerges, a place opens within the life of the individual where he must decide and move from freedom to necessity. Considered abstractly, the problem of man having to come of necessity to a decision at some point exists for the determinist as well, if he is not to become a Revisionist. This situation is also not surrendered in original Marxism. It is our task to move it to the center of attention. I just wanted to develop this line of reasoning in order to show that this chiliastic feeling of having been chosen contains a very subtle set of problems, which may be simply expressed by saying that determinism has the feeling of finding itself in step with the world, but that the more concrete this situation becomes, the harder it is to sustain determinism as a world view.

And the notion that the best chance for understanding the truth lies in the doctrine of being a priori in step with the world belongs to the mechanisms of repression. The danger arises of being unable to master newly appearing insights and developments that must always emerge in life. The situation of imagining that we have the key to the universe in our hand may well turn into an intellectual complacency that one should oppose in one's own party. That is why I have transmuted the doctrine of being chosen into a doctrine of the best chance. A chance has to be seized; it can be lost. There is no doubt that the proletariat has the best chance for understanding the social structure. It is necessary to arm oneself against the loss of that chance. It is essential somehow to receive with candor everything that comes up. One may well ask about the political consequences of a thing, but one may not execute a defensive maneuver before the thing has even been taken in.

One might say that the most important hallmark of the bias inherent in any thought and present as the essential characteristic of orthodoxy is intellectual defensiveness, a maneuver that answers every proposal with "we absolutely will not do this." One of my collaborators recently said that one can fight against this quite easily if one watches the opponent. I do not find mistakes in myself. These I do not see. If I want to control myself, just as with Freud's experience of death, then the reflected rays from others gain the power to reveal that I could be like that myself. It is important that these problems be specified. Discussions can proceed quite differently if one can distinguish these defensive maneuvers in the discussion itself. Today's discussion consists of everyone simply absconding from his own small boxing-ring, leaving the other just standing there. If there is any one task set for us, it is to create, so far as possible, a platform for a possible exchange of views, a platform for a material discussion (*Realdiskussion*).[46]

In contrast to thought impaired by defensiveness, the thinking that I want to call non-orthodox is distinguished by the following: like reality, it is in motion, and not only by taking in new contents but also by broadening its basis in thought. Consider the example of the natural sciences. There, if one has models of thought and sets of axioms with which one cannot comprehend new facts, one discards the old basic system without qualms to accommodate the new data. Where the individual is not politically bound, he faces nothing but obstacles that can be overcome by the fruitfulness of his experiments. In political life, however, things are not given merely as fact to be registered, but as tied up with a volition that is in fact also attached elsewhere and that must be liberated when one sees that this attitude is impeding orientation to the world. Thought that is truly free participates in this movement by returning to fundamentals. The second technique, more difficult to enact (*vollziehen*), is where one sees that one's intellectual points of departure (*Denkansatz*) all originate in a point that is particular. At the moment when volitions meet, when localities and regions—not to speak of classes and status groups—that had separately formed certain views for themselves converge in a common stream, the opportunity presents itself of seeing that each locality, each status group, each class lived in only a corner of the world, that each was particularly oriented towards a distinctive axiomatic set, and that none of them was absolute. The basic structural logic of every human being is to see his particularity as absolute. The new insight may mark the first stage of a cosmopolitan situation. Certain ways of thinking take form in certain stages of life, and this moment may present the stage at which it is possible to confront diverse developments.

What I have been attempting to carry into effect (*vollziehen*) is to use this situation in order to move in the direction of such a possibility. I do not know what will come of this. But the opportunity is presented by the convergence of these biases (*Tendenzen*). Uninhibited thinking that does not blockade itself is obliged to revise its attitudes at such a moment. It should not be thought that being tied to interests invariably makes one blind. Under certain circumstances they may make for clear sightedness, especially for another's character. Envy and love, like other bonds affecting one's being (*seinsmäßige Bindungen*), can make a person clear-sighted. One must ascertain how the particular views can be fitted to the enlarged plan of the comprehensive framework. I cannot deny that one must search gropingly in this direction, that one starts by becoming more uncertain. But that is inseparable from the situation. Yet man would rather know it all than think.

Now I want to direct your attention to the highly important positive valuation of orthodoxy, which nevertheless has its limits, and from these latter I can show you, after pointing out the dangers inherent in orthodoxy, what comprises its relative justification.

The political doctrine of theory and practice has a splendid insight, namely, that no image of the world that fails to eventuate in a specific type of political practice can be fruitful.[47] A decision about the world (*Weltentscheidung*) which offers direction but, because it remains contemplative, inhibits decision (*Entscheidung*) is politically useless, according to this doctrine. Here too, I want to allow my opponent to encroach upon me as far as possible: that is my duty. Now I want to admit right away that the most difficult point about my kind of thinking is that, at least at first, it suspends decision. That is inevitably implicated in this position. As soon as I establish the point [about the particularity of standpoints], I will continue to do what I have been doing, regardless of my standpoint, but I will put off any sort of decision. The project cannot be carried out except under the sign of a suspension of the final act in deliberation, the will to action. I admit that it is necessary to have a consonance between theory and practice in a world view, which must be directed towards the deed. My solution, rather than being unswervingly self-enclosed, is ambivalent. It is a theory that has a theoretical man in front and a practical man within. These things do not coincide; they seek for one another and want to meet; but they are not designed to match one another, as in every theory that is genuinely political. It is, however, an illusion to think that, as a factual matter, political practice is so unbroken even in Marxism, as events follow their actual course. How could one succeed in bringing about a self-enclosed theory without ambivalence? The real situation will constantly disrupt it. Only in its ideal type, is a system always self-enclosed. You can observe this in yourself, whenever you attempt to classify (*zurechnen*) people. Classification is always difficult. It is always possible to classify a person ambivalently. It is always a question of making a choice. Life in its enactment (*Vollzug*) is also ambivalent. I will shortly show the character of its ambivalence. Orthodoxy is evidently suffering a crisis of ambivalence at the present time—or why would they listen to what I say and why would it unsettle them? Only because it is recognized that the proletarian situation must possess two qualities: first, unambiguous guidelines for action and decision, guidelines that may not be disturbed; and second, it is necessary to be at the height of right consciousness, and this cannot be as readily guaranteed as the militancy of the political will. Even within the party two tendencies oppose one another. On the one side, a group maintaining that the firm contours of the theory, the decisiveness of the willed course not be rendered uncertain by a wide expansion of outlook, by calling into question things that one should not reflect on, lest the decision be lost in the process. On the other side, a group in the party urging that to operate in discussions with nothing but slogans causes the disappearance of the cognitive value present in the theoretical elements. The ambivalence experienced by the individual in himself functions in the party in the guise of distinct groups.

You will grant that there are in fact two groups constantly struggling with one another in the party. We shall depict them schematically. First, the intelligentsia that seeks to expand beyond the framework of orthodoxy in order to guarantee an enlarged view and thus to avoid the loss of realistic consciousness, and second, the other group that is prepared to sacrifice realistic consciousness but not the unwavering aim and lack of ambiguity in the purposes of political decision (*Entscheidung*). Ambivalence is actually split up in this way. You can see it in large organizations but also in smaller spheres of life. Sociology has the task of shedding light on man's reasons for loving or hating, and on the ways in which the experience of the individual functionalizes itself in large groups.

What we have identified (*aufgezeigt*) as ambivalence in the individual is a vital ambivalence in humankind. I would like to say that it is not possible to answer yes or no to the question whether one should decide in favor of decision or expansion, i.e., self-expansion. One cannot in fact proceed other than dialectically. It depends, first, on the phase we are in, and, second, on the group with which we identify ourselves.

First, a some points about the phase. In a situation of the deed, a moment of decision, in my view, one can do nothing but to carry through (*vollziehen*) orthodoxy's step, to fix the sphere in place, and to carry through in actual fact an unambiguous step on behalf of life. Life requires the ambivalence of both the posture of searching and, at the moment of attack, the stage of decision as well. The party requires this too.

I would like to say that orthodoxy always becomes the decisive spiritual element at the moment when the necessity for action is unconditionally given. Its function is always to guarantee a decision. It must be in charge at such a moment, its supremacy is temporarily the truth. But even in the party of orthodoxy a self-relaxation must take place (*sich vollziehen*), the formal rigidity must be suspended, whenever there is a breathing-space, where things are not at the stage for striking out. In these phases, the elements whose functioning I find in the intelligentsia must be taken up. The intelligentsia are not a god and they do not hold the truth in their hands, but the point is that within the parties, no matter where they stand, they usually have the mission of fulfilling this task of the hour, which is expansion, loosening, seeking. From the recognition of this ambivalence, the position which I represent, the absolutizing of searching and loosening, comes to know its own limits. At this point I concede a relative justification to the necessity for a type of orthodoxy. I recognize my own limitations. It is possible to admit that certain things could not be sought, that certain things could not be carried through (*vollzogen*) without being reprimitivized. The turning back (*zurückschrauben*) to fascism from this level of unconstrained thinking is possible only on an interpretation that this solution is perhaps a part of life. With this, however, one gives up the autonomous movement (*Eigenbewegung*) of one's own life. The problem whether this solution may not belong to life, to the structural logic of society, emerges impressively in Nietzsche. This is the move in the direction of truth in fascism. He starts out by finding the fascist solution, but then he recognizes the possibility of a second solution, viz., that, without self-abandonment or the surrender of one's dignity as thinker, one can make this second kind of regression—the orthodox stabilization of volitional decision—visible to certain groups, with all of its self-limitation and self-enclosure.[48]

Lecture 10
The Role of the Intellectuals in the Present Situation:
The Attitude, Subject Matter and Method of Sociology
(a Reopening)

We have been occupied with the question of how we should present and solve the problem of the situation of our own souls (*Seelenlage*), the situation in which we find ourselves specifically as the stratum of intellectuals . You will recall that the question of regression arose, that we posed the question about the possibility of reprimitivization becoming necessary, that we conceded much to our opponent and took his arguments extensively into account, and that we finally had to ask ourselves: what is our view of the solution he offers us, how should we judge it? Our own answer was that the solution could only be dialectical. One cannot say unequivocally that we must simply renounce our own character, which has become refined and which has taken upon itself all the burdens of knowledge. In certain situations, however, we must renounce it. The dialectic consisted of the fact that one does not pretend to have an unequivocal solution for all situations but rather offers solutions that are differentiated according to situation. It is impossible in any other way. Anyone who respects counter-arguments must also delineate their field of play within the solution. Since I have attempted to show the meaning of dialectical thinking, I want to make it manifest in this case too. It means that one does not simply lay out a unilinear course of things, but poses as well the antithesis presented by counter-arguments. By this means one cannot arrive at a solution as simple as that of someone who has only considered one solution. The answer will be particular, one that contains itself within itself. Our answer to our substantive question, then, was that there are specific situations in political struggle where the intelligentsia must necessarily renounce their distantiation from life, their exaggerated reflexivity. The intelligentsia must, however, use all situations in which there is, so to speak, breathing room, where the opportunity to reconsider things arises, in order to make the case for self-expansion. The intelligentsia have experienced that it is possible to reflect on things and to see total situations where others see only particular ones. In the situations that comprise the breathing spaces, they must permit their capabilities for seeing through themselves and getting behind things to come into their own. During these moments, they have the task of easing rigidity, the task of representing in the various parties the possibility of self-expansion. I have remarked on the extent to which warring parties are dependent upon—and large organizations destined for—development in the direction of rigidity. The larger a newspaper becomes, the more capital is invested in it, the more the readership is firmly grounded in its political tendency, the more complicated it is for the newspaper to change directions. The readership becomes accustomed to a certain spiritual attitude. And if someone in the leadership were to determine that the attitude was wrong, he would have to redirect the entire organization, the investors, and the readers. It is a large problem from the standpoint of the ossification of the press that the reorientation of life is much more difficult to carry out (*vollziehen*) in the case of great organizations. The same is true of parties. They are much harder to redirect than sects or individuals. But life has a structure that presses towards redirection. It presents new situations to which one must attune oneself, which one must newly evaluate. And if through concrete forces of socialization one is compelled to remain ever more rigid, to think only along one line, this redirection will not be performable (*vollziehbar*). For that reason, large organizations like the Catholic Church must somehow allow individuals to operate freely and to experiment on their periphery.

Let us recall the significance of Jesuitism. You see that an extravagant fellow goes off to rethink everything and to act on his own, and that the Church, as soon as this starts to prove itself, removes the man from the periphery into the center and capitalizes on his achievements for itself. That is done wisely, for a large organization cannot in fact give shape to a spiritual redirection from the tendencies internal to the organization. It must bring about a productive symbiosis among peripheral figures, an independent intelligentsia, in order to retain the capacity for change. Every party will have to find the elasticity to enable it to establish the right balance between a well functioning organization and the experimental field at the periphery. This fact gives the outsider a new function.

Until now we felt that we were superfluous people. The future, it seemed, would feature great organizations, with their fixed opinions, mobilized against one another, while the independently thinking intelligentsia stand by, essentially powerless. Now there is at least a promise, looking from the point of view of further social development. The great platforms of opinions and parties will confront one another. We are living in such a period. If you look carefully at what was added to our analysis today, however, you will see that there remains a certain chance for this outsider intelligentsia. There are two types. One is the total outsider who belongs to no party. The other joins a party but neither sits at the organizational center nor functionally represents the organizational will. He is always humored a little, but also always needed. He is most highly productive and important. When a tactic in the spiritual realm (*Taktik des Geistigen*) is at issue, it must be duly assessed and taken into account. This spiritual mode of destabilization and experimentation is a decided necessity even when viewed from the standpoint of the great social party organisms.

If we take Marxism as example, we find that there too a certain truth is posited together with the specific party organization, a distinctive doctrine that originally arose in the head of a free-floating intelligentsia (*freischwebender Intelligenz*) and that was subsequently standardized beyond the stage of being an outlook. It contains incredibly fruitful elements but can only be fruitful if one steadily experiments over and over again. When this doctrine turns into a rigid dogma, one that fails to process new problems, this kind of thinking turns into a defensive maneuver. This condition can only be avoided through a steady stream of insights from individuals who have a chance of experimenting. The party can hardly afford to introduce a new dogma, since it would have to instill such a novelty in the masses, who have been instructed in the old truths only with great effort. The risk that if I think something new it must also be instilled does not exist for the individual. Hence he has the possibility of loosening things up. Things that have traditional importance for the organization do not constrain him. This relative—not absolute—freedom provides the individual with the opportunity of seeing something here or there that the other fails or does not wish to see, although he could see it too. If this outsider stratum is working right, it must also be given a chance of gaining acceptance for itself and its truth. At the periphery of every organization there must be a level of new discoveries, a possibility for discussion, where experimentation goes on. That is the point of the insight I have been offering you. Provided with this chance, we must understand that we cannot renounce our native ability to call things into question. Those whose task it is to represent party discipline and the established world view will reproach us for this, they will note the negativism in our conduct (*Verhaltensweise*), and judge us to be unreliable customers. In the interest of the productivity and fruitfulness of the party, however, one must not renounce this capability, which comes from being an intellectual, the ability to see things not only from one side but from many.

That is our answer to the question whether the intellectual should join in with the party. For he knows that alone he is nothing in a world where only collective forces can create reality. But he must not identify himself totally. He must know that his function consists in constantly seeking and expounding the right perspective.

I want to address briefly one more objection raised against me. "If you propose to us that we accept regressions when necessary—because it is also regression if one occasionally renounces the work of loosening things up—then you are teaching a truth that we would be unhappy to accept, namely, that all social life necessitates lying. One might say that fascists can do this with justification, since they confess that one must renounce one's own ultimate truth in conflict situations, since such questioning would stir up uncertainty. They confess that all socialization requires the lie." The question just formulated arises, in my view, of necessity. And I have earlier pointed out that the basic concept of the necessary evil was already promoted by Nietzsche, who promoted, with its help and in sophisticated form, the social significance of the lie.

I would like to set before you a passage from *Beyond Good and Evil.* "The falseness of a judgment is for us not necessarily an objection to a judgment; in this respect our new language may sound strangest. The question is to what extent it is life-promoting, . . . preserving, and . . . cultivating. And we are fundamentally inclined to claim that renouncing false judgments . . . would mean renouncing life. . . . To recognize untruth as a condition of life—that certainly means resisting *the emphatic feeling for truth* in a dangerous way; and a philosophy that risks this would by that token place itself beyond good and evil." (Quotation not literally correct [km]. Cp. Nietzsche 1966: 11–12).[49]

Listening to this quotation, it must be clear to you that in its deep structure (*Urstruktur*) it is a form of solution that we call fascist. Nietzsche's greatness lies in the fact that he anticipated a crisis of the soul at a time when few could see it, that he anticipated something that confronts us as problem, so to speak, in everyday life, that he anticipated all this in his isolation. The shock is just as great today as then. But today, because of the dynamics of the dispute, we are further along in alternatives to this solution. He was right when he observed empirically that the truth people possess does not fall from the skies but is driven by vital impulses, that this truth does not exist in a free-floating realm, but is connected with human beings, their desires and instincts for life, that these differ according to their different situations, and that life can only understand truth from the lives of men. To this point, I subscribe fully to his thesis. The sociology of knowledge has no objective other than to transform this intuitive insight into methodical research, by means of which one first makes claims from case to case and then empirically shows (*faktisch aufweist*) how it is that (*wieso*) a given life-solution belongs (*gehört*) to a given life-situation (*Lebenslage*).

Where Nietzsche is wrong, however, and where we cannot follow him, is in that we add something and believe that the facts he describes ought not always to remain as they are, that we use the insight, on the one hand, to understand how we are bound down in detail (*Detailgebundenheit*) but, on the other, also utilize it for self-expansion. In this process forces are liberated that stream from particular boundedness towards totality. Furthermore, we do not take the position that we should simply go along and affirm that thinking is nothing but vitality and that we are accordingly prepared to turn ourselves back. We say, to the contrary, that when we penetrate to the fact that life possesses structures of vitality in certain areas and when we penetrate to the necessity of stopping short from time to time, we enact (*vollziehen*) this as a cognition, and we regard it as a seeing ever more clearly and not as a degradation. That is the great difference. One can enact a reprimitivization by saying, I want to avoid seeing things that one can already see. That is a retrograde movement. We are unable to do this. What we can do is to see even more clearly and to say, instead, that at this and that particular moment, in the sense of a rationally comprehensible tactic, we want to put a temporary stop to the uncertainty harbored by sociology. That is seeing even more clearly than is at first made possible to us. The point is that one includes in one's understanding the idea of life, that one takes cognizance as well of the existence of vital instincts, and that one recognizes that other men and strata exist, that we do not live isolated in space, and that we are influenced and shaped by this circumstance. That is no reprimitivization but rather a recognition of the temporal forces at hand, which we recognize in their actuality and figure in our accountings. The insight into the irrationality of social forces does not lead us to irrationalism, but rather leads us to say that man must think through anything he is able to think, he must take cognizance of the life existing in the actuality of his times and orient himself to it—especially when the society is in shock.

There is a difference between deliberately making myself dumber, on the one hand, and, on the other, becoming aware of a certain situation and adapting myself to it. That is what is decisive about sociology for the intelligentsia. It has discovered that other people also exist. The question is whether it embodies a primal experience, whether one has had a true encounter with this fact.

In these acts of thought, one discovers that it is a benefit to one's own thinking to know that certain enactments of thought (*Gedankenvollzüge*) cannot be followed through (*vollzogen*), because there are strata in social space that do not react adequately where they are. If I were to keep doing what I would do as an individual, my thought would be in danger of being isolated. One discovers in the course of becoming reflexive in this way that there are things that contain another world, that my experience cannot fulfill itself because there are, in the final analysis, members in the society who could not keep up with this, that the existence of other strata enters into my private life. That my own experience is interwoven with other lives is the most authentic discovery of sociology. That is how it is with language. My words are not my contribution; each one is already given. The fate of the language community contains the fate of the community of thought. We discover ever more layers, in contrast to the intelligentsia of last century, which always considered itself as something elevated and now discovers that it cannot save itself until it has saved the society as a whole. That is effected (*vollzieht sich*) not only not only by the political deed, but also by one's own reorientation (*Umstellung*), so that one is able to think through situations, including one's own, in a sociological manner, that one poses the sociological problem of the intellectual by oneself, that one sees that we are in quite a unique position of running ahead of vital life, a position that I must always encompass in the position of the whole. You will have understood that the individual is always thrown back upon the state of the soul in society. To think sociologically is to act out (*vollziehen*) at the level of thought what one already possesses in fact, it is to connect one's position to that of the others. With this, I close this section. Its purpose was to specify the place of sociology in the contemporary crisis of life. The concrete occasion was our encounter with sociological man.

Our starting point was the appearance of the *"vie expérimentale"* which was traced further to the distantiation from life, to the crisis of the person who takes distance from life, and to all the questions that emerge at that point and are associated with it.

Now we want to return to the problem we posed at first. We have said what sociology is. We have tried to give a very vivid picture of the intelligentsia that has become sociological. We have specified the intelligentsia and the sociological human type. We have said that a science is not determined by its appropriate attitude alone, even if it can only be truly understand in this medium. It is a new departure when, in the introduction to a science, one first portrays the man for whom it became timely (*aktuell*). But we must also satisfy our other requirements, and sketch not only the attitude but also the object and method of the science.

Starting out from the sociological attitude alone, we arrive at the broadest possible concept of sociology. Such a broad concept of sociology does exist. But the research character of sociology is not specified by the fact of the sociological man. That only answers the question why life everywhere poses sociological questions. How is it possible that a single discipline is able to turn almost everything into a subject of its research. Sociological man is actually a situation in the philosophy of history, whose problems are posited together with the present. But there are varied forms of concretization. Psychoanalysis, for example, arose out of the same distantiation. There is a certain commonality in the type and manner of apprehension. Psychoanalysis as well as sociological examination of spiritual phenomena presuppose a certain kind of distantiation from life. Up to a point, the psychoanalyst does the same thing as the sociologist, inasmuch as he considers certain contents that are simply accepted as given by the naive person and takes renewed distance from them, reaches behind them, extracts that which is fatefully constraining, and identifies the factors in which it originated. Both arise out of the same situation, namely that men have lost their unequivocal orientation. While the psychoanalyst wants to explain everything by reference to the individual soul, the sociologist wants to draw explanations from the life of society. In a few years, we may see more clearly the stretches across which the sociologist can and must apply psychoanalysis and, obversely, where the sociologist must help the psychoanalyst, since the latter lacks the tradition to see social functioning as well as the functioning of the inner apparatus of the soul.

We have hit upon the following divisions: sociology as attitude, as method, and as subject-matter. We have described the attitude. It consists in a certain distantiation from life, which I have depicted. Is there now a sociology as method? It will exist as a distinct specialized science. We use sociology to designate three phenomena which we must keep apart. What is generally called sociological is first a characteristic outlook on life which is effected by man without science: the distinctive sociological distantiation from life. The second is a specific method which almost all human sciences aspire to actualize—the sociological method is applied everywhere and it is winning through. We want to pose as problem the commonality of the method which the distinct disciplines collectively install. I want to show first that this is unequivocally a specifiable sociological method and finally that there is a area which sociology must develop for itself as specialized discipline.

I will describe in different stages. I say that we are the only ones with a method. In the human sciences [in general] we have not brought it beyond knowing the style of thought needed for examining a spiritual formation. Take literary history. One gets the impression that the author simply narrated whatever came to mind. There is no guideline to explain why this or that becomes the theme. Does sociology provide an unambiguous guideline? Sociological method consists in seeing spiritual contents in a certain way. It experiences the contents quite differently from the man of everyday, insofar as his attitude is not sociological. While man in a pre—sociological attitude experiences contents immanently, sociological man constantly transcends this immanent attitude and sets it in brackets.

I shall give an example. When it is written "thou shalt not steal," that is some kind of norm, and the [ordinary] human sciences address this norm directly. They accept it in the same form as the one who posited it; they enact (*vollzieht*) the validity it implied. The validity is not challenged. It can only be violated. As a practical matter, however, validity is recognized. When sociology has such a norm as problem, [in contrast], it brackets the validity of this object. The norm becomes a fact.

Supplement
Sociological Method

The following continuation of Mannheim's tenth class derives from the lecture outline in the archives of Kurt H. Wolff. There is no indication whether the text is complete.

A science is not determined by its attitude alone. Up to this point we have established only a very broad concept of sociology. But the method has not yet been specified. The sociological method arises out of the same crisis as the psychoanalytical one. Both presuppose distance. Both "reach behind" and "extricate." Man loses the unambiguous setting of norms. Both sciences will certainty unite at some time: individual and society. Both will someday be slogans for each other.

Only sociology has a method. There is a guideline for sociological method. Sociological method examines contents in a quite specific manner: while man in the pre-sociological epoch experiences contents immanently, sociology brackets immanence and looks at contents transcendentally.

For example, not "Thou shalt not steal," but "It is asserted that you should not steal." And then, "When was that asserted?" Science produces new methods. Sociology puts contents at a distance. The validations enacted by the man engaged in life are reflected as facts by the sociologist.

1) Sociology transcends (looks outside) the immanence (that which remains inside). Under which circumstances and in which society is fish eaten with a fork.
2) Sociology dynamicizes cultural formations. It is a human tendency to let the flow of things become rigid. E.g., one speaks of a third person as "he is" instead of "he becomes." Antiquity and scholasticism operated with the categories of being and becoming.
   It is important that man does not label himself. "Thou shalt not steal!"— Jurisprudence already ordains that the rich must be punished more than the poor. The pathos of sociology is the variability of man. "How would things be if this were thus or so?" Historiography has already executed this step.
3) Particularization. Every man is inclined towards taking himself and the world situation as absolute. (E.g., during the Renaissance, the story of the passion was portrayed in Renaissance clothing .)

Can we master the global tensions or must we suffer shipwreck upon our own history? Our time.

The possibility of change arises from the situation of becoming. That is the origin of the question, what could you be, and what could you do in order to become different!?

Mere negation is only the establishment of our mobility. A form of thought may be destroyed only when there is a need.

What does sociology do with the experiential contexture (*Erfahrungszusammenhang*)? Particularization consists not only in the discovery of a situation rather than the situation, but also in the fact that the entire life of individuals and individual groups is particular. As if mankind were a large man. DILTHEY. And sociology removes us from loneliness. Cp. Speech! Reconstruction of the original contexture of life.

Where does man learn and experience (*erfährt und erlebt*) something? Contexture of experience is the social process.

The idea of functionalization. For, how does sociology connect spiritual happenings to society? Category of function. Contrary: internal life history. (Binswanger, *Internal Life-history and Life-function.*)[50]

It is important at every stage to think of oneself as object and in categories of objects. Aristotle objectifies everything. St. Augustine: Experience of self (*Selbsterfahrung*). Heidegger: The history of functions has a different history than the internal life history. Classics of functional observation. Aristotle and the four categories. Similar to sociology. Here are the economic equations, and dependent on them the spiritual equations. Not an it-position but an account rendered for the life that has passed. Since Augustine. The religious meaning of the conversion is clear, but "Life-history" also begins here. (Misch, *History of Biography*).[51] Moreover, the individual discovered. Religion was only the shell from which the new man came into being. Today the two tendencies fight one another. Both are important. Sociology has to occupy itself with the tension between these two possibilities.

Two ways of viewing (*Anschauungsarten*) being: life-historical and functionalist thinking.

Contradiction between internal life history and life function. What is internal life history?

Internal life history: when one examines one's life with a view to important points which, differently determined (*räsoniert*), would have shaped life differently. In short, from a constructive center. Any factor on which life depends.

Things lacking in meaning gain their meaning from this decision. Everything depends on the personality. Not until this point of view is it possible to narrate something life-historically. (Cp. Conversion which lends meaning to the past). As long as the conversion experience is not experienced, every narration is objective/epic, as in the fairy tale, "The Carpet of Life." In sum, no internal life-history. Internal life-history only when all happenings are viewed from some experience of the center of personality.

In this way, the unique sequence gains individual relevance. The impression that there is only one uniqueness arises at the hour of birth of the experience of personality. (Something different from the consciousness that everything is different. In that case, the individual is a combination of general characteristics.) In this case, however, uniqueness through meaningful events. If this is erased, all that remains is the combination of general characteristics. Everything general is seen in this same way. Only from the subjective: "Every individual has his typical fate." Subjective motivation.

The point of view grounded in the theory of function. Dominates in sociology. E.g., why do men work? (Life-historical pre-sociological answer: because they must, from ambition, out of interest in power, etc.) But a functional view says: the worker works from pressure or tradition, the academic and employee, from ambition, the leading industrialist works from a search for recognition or power-drive, etc.

The decisive thing: the motivations are traced to the social process. Inner happenings are secondary, they are caused by the social. There is something true in both views.

Odd that the foundational truths of Christianity are here fulfilled: sociology shows that the other lives in everyone, that all men are brothers.

2

Heidelberg Letters:
Soul and Culture in Germany

Born in 1893, Karl Mannheim enjoyed a precocious career as a young intellectual in Budapest. Admitted as a favored protege to the circle of Georg Lukács, the foremost cultural innovator in pre-war generation, and gladly seen as well in the circles of the social reformers grouped around Oscar Jászi, Mannheim could count on a hearing from other non-Communist emigrés after the victory of the counterrevolution in 1919. In 1921/22, he published two literary letters in Hungarian in Tüz, an emigré journal published in the formerly Hungarian city of Bratislava, assigned to Czechoslovakia by the peace settlement. From the text, it would appear that Mannheim planned on a longer series. There is no evidence about his decision to stop after the two installments translated below, but it seems likely that it followed logically from his resolution to seek habilitation as a sociologist under Alfred Weber and Emil Lederer, a choice of a career as a German academic.

These letters are still written at a distance. Mannheim writes as one of the scattered "shards" of the Hungarian emigration, sharing with his fellows some lessons that may be learned from the German experience, as well as a some insights into German culture gained by virtue of his outsider's status. Four aspects of these documents deserve special notice, the notion of Germany as a model of decentralized culture, the vision of Heidelberg as polarized between the spirits of Max Weber and Stefan George, the ironic attitude towards the German tradition of humanistic cultivation, and Mannheim's continued identification with a neo—Romantic ideal of charismatic reconstitution of uni-

79

fied meaning, notably by way of a rather non—committal dedication to the recovery of religious belief when its moment strikes. These themes reflect the problems that will occupy Mannheim during his remaining years in Germany. He will depend on pluralism and openness; he will opt for Weber but never abandon the hope of reconciling the disillusioned followers of George; he will propose an alternative to humanism as the core of cultivation; and he will attempt to emulate the Hungarian poet, Endre Ady, whom he praises in these writings as being able to make creative use of the impossibility of resolving the tension betwen politics and a God who must remain invisible to a "nonbelieving believer."

In style and manner, these writings are unlike the others collected in this book. They were written in Hungarian, but the present translation must regrettably depend on a German translation, controlled by use of an earlier loose translation directly into English from Hungarian. The German version is turgid in stretches, notably where it reaches for its most "literary" effects, but it is impossible to say whether Mannheim displayed greater skill in his own language. For present purposes, the important thing to notice is Mannheim's orientation to a kind of thinking and writing that is remote from strictly academic norms. He was never to be content to write only to "the profession."

Our addition to the original unrevealing title highlights the two concepts, "soul" and "culture," with which Mannheim was closely identified during his years in the literary circle around Lukács. His Hungarian readers would have recognized the extent to which he was reviewing and reconsidering the arguments that were central to his 1917 Hungarian publication, named "Soul and Culure." Above all, the letters are a reflection on education, his own and that which is to come.

I

We Hungarians live dispersed, one here and one there, and every point in the world is further from another than before, yet our curiosity is more avid than ever. Since I first arrived in alien lands, I have felt like an advance scout, like an observer sent ahead to watch a small group of people, to find out if something is finally happening somewhere, if there are also human beings among the unfamilar houses. I peer into every open window, guess at the gestures of the gesticulating speakers and at the unspoken words of the restrained silent ones. When people come together, I am there; when they learn, I learn with them; and I would also wish to live with them, to settle down–but I cannot find my place.

The Hungarian jug is broken and its hundred shards have been hurled in a hundred directions.[52] These precious few persons, the circle of those who mostly knew of each another, are scattered, and when two or three come together by some chance, they eagerly ask after one another. I want to know not only the fate of each one but also everything that he has seen with Hungarian eyes in the most varied corners of the world; and I am surely not mistaken when I suppose that it is the same with others, and that they are interested in what a shard cast away in Germany has to tell them.

I must confess from the outset, above all, that the world under discussion here does not reflect the total cultural life of present-day Germany. From these lines, it will be possible to glean a characterization of nothing but the small, thin layer comprising progressive intellectuals in Germany today. It has always been the case and it remains the case today that those of us who write somehow belong to them; and as we write, we are also sampling, although unknowingly, the points of view, the prejudices of our own caste. And when we write what is ostensibly the history of the spirit, we are only reporting the adventures of a few trailblazers and we act as if we and these few select persons were the axis of the world.

Modern times commenced with a highly symbolic deed. With a Copernican gesture, man discovered that he is not the center of the universe; he acknowledged that the universe does not in fact revolve around the one who sees it, and that the crown of creation is not necessarily man. Despite man's recognition that he is not the center of the universe, *writing man* has continued to live in a Ptolemaic world; and only through the reform gradually advancing in most recent times will writing man perhaps grasp that within our terrestrial order neither the scholar nor the journalist is the center of the public life of social movements. Development does not take its orientation from his questions and viewpoints. To view matters only through the eyes of the cultivated is to look at them from a remarkably narrow angle of vision. As it has been the fate of women until now that (with one or two exceptions) it has always been men who have described their lives and most hidden feelings, so, in other spheres, thanks to a paradoxical determination of things, we can see the characters and fates of non-writing, non-cultured men only through the lenses of the cultivated. It follows from the nature of things that Tristan loves and Don Juan "loves around," and that neither of them writes an essay or drama; and we see their figures only through the contemplative categories of a poet or writer, while the real problem is how the figure of Tristan or Don Juan would look if they had described themselves. The ultimate paradox in writing is that it aspires to be objective and realistic and to reproduce the complete blueprint of things, but that it is always only in a position to put one of their perspectives on paper.

There is only one help for this, which is to become conscious of this fact and to acknowledge it freely, to include a transformation table, the angle of observation, by means of some form of notation, so that the reader can add or subtract, expand or contract – in keeping with the key provided by his own soul and interest.

That is exactly why I preface everything with a single point. At this time–and perhaps it will some day be different – I am interested above all in the lives of those to whom I belong. We, the multitude spread all over the world, are the only international rootless scatterings without ground under our feet, we who write and read books and who are one-sidedly interested, in writing and reading, in the spirit alone. Who should actually be included in the caste can only be decided from case to case, because the matter is not simple, as if one could consider the external indicators of writing or reading as the key to the actual difference.

Just as not everyone who performs on stage is an actor and not every scribbling bureaucrat is a statesman, so only those who put themselves in the service of the spirit to such an extent that it is truly located at the center of their lives, and that its presence can be felt in every expression of their lives can be assigned to this caste. This can also not be solely decided by the criterion of whether a person participates in cultivation [Bildung] in the deeper sense of the word or whether he himself shapes and creates something verifiable and new by means of written and printed letters, but only whether the entire form of his life gains its ultimate meaning from these qualities and activities. Cultivation, true humanism, forms men into a new kind of stratum, cutting across the economic and other sociological classifications. Cultivation also shapes the most spontaneous forms of life and transports man into an isolated world incomprehensible to others. While the cultures of China and India created an externally visible caste for these people, our isolation is sometimes hidden from view, since the stratum does not possess such an unambiguous mark of recognition.

When I think about the general and mistaken beliefs that are a consequence of *not having such a mark*, it always amazes me how much closer I am to those who participate in this cultivated humanism and how much closer they are to me than they or I are to those who share their nationality but are an altogether different kind of people. I respect their efforts (and time may eventually grant meaning to their strivings), but I simultaneously scorn the lies of those who, under national or racial catchphrases or the slogan of class struggle, want to fulfill the romantic dream that they are at one with the race or class that they programmatically represent.

There is something beautiful in the attempt to close the gap, but one must nevertheless both see and admit the distance remaining, and one must also know that we possess an almost hopeless longing, for the sake of which we struggle and with which we lull ourselves to sleep. We want to find a home, a world, because we sense that we will find no place in this world. Ady[53] says someplace (towards the end of *Portus Hercules Monoecii* among the *Confessions and Studies*)–it is a pity that I do not have it with me and cannot cite it verbatim– that there is a really difficult problem in securing the possibility of life for these few who press ahead. It may be possible to assist everyone else, and even the economic problem may sometime be solved, but it would be self-deception to think that this would bring us even a jot closer to solving this difficult task of bridging for all time the distances among the souls of men. Perhaps there will be more who will, as a result of the elimination of external obstacles, attain to a life of the soul and spirit–and this elimination of obstacles must not be omitted–but we will simply increase in number as a result, and the problem of finding a home for the spirit somewhere on earth will become more difficult, even statistically.

As I wander about and observe things, I ask myself how those anointed or victimized by the spirit live in Germany after war and revolution. What occupies them, what moves them, what lulls them to sleep, what is happening in them and to them, where is this narrow world moving? When I speak of the present-day German, I am think-ing, with a deliberate narrowing of meaning, only of this thin layer; and, with all my reservations and condemnations, my love turns nevertheless towards them. Because I believe, despite everything–and perhaps this is only my partiality—that something is being readied and formed in them that can become important in time. Perhaps when I understand them and their causes well enough and am aware of the limits of such knowledge, it may be that I will be able to assess the radiating power and influence of this purposely restricted circle, by means of which it is able to work upon large entities, extended worlds.

These letters are written from Heidelberg, a small university town in Germany, and yet they must not necessarily become "provincial letters." The reason why it may be possible to see the soul of the larger Germany from a small provincial town can carry us further. It has to do with the cultural decentralization of Germany. The bearer of the diverse spiritual movements is not one and the same cultural stratum of a single place, a great city. Rather, the new experiences, events and thoughts have their origins dispersed among the numerous small cities of the country. The whole originates from many traditional sources, from many roots in local soils. The provinces, the towns are thus not the last derivative, peripheral echoes of the life of a single cultural center, but the living sources themselves. This may be another reason for us to pay attention to the German situation, because the Hungarian cultural problem, if it was once identical with the question of centralization, is now at one with the question of decentralization. The emerging Hungarian culture could be annihilated so suddenly only because it was centralized. A single spiritual *stratum* of Budapest, so to speak, was the bearer of the movement, and by chasing it to the winds it was possible, as it were, to devastate spiritual life with a single blow. Today we can only follow a second path—like that of German culture —where the dispersed spiritual forces join together anew in the many small centers, involve themselves in the existing provincial cultural initiatives, and lay the basis for a future decentralized Hungarian culture.

That a decentralized culture produces an altogether different picture than one that is oriented to a capital city is shown by the German spiritual world. The many-branched origins lend German spiritual life not only a variety of colors but also a breadth that offers unusually many opportunities to anything new that presents itself. Every movement has its own local character, its paternal site, from which it takes its departure, and any traveler quickly discovers which of the many spiritual tendencies arose in a particular city. Every city has its own distinctive atmosphere (they are very proud of this word), that slowly takes shape, and if one pursues the question it is still possible here and there to uncover which attribute of its general spiritual disposition was given to the town by one or another earlier or still living outstanding person.

The culture of the town has the advantage that the traces of the residence there of one or another significant person are long preserved and that they enter not only with their contents but also with their form of life as a whole into the spiritual atmosphere upon which subsequent developments feed. The human being is more present in the culture of the town and not so impersonal as in the variety of the metropolis that neutralizes everything. It is not only the contents that undergo further development, accordingly, but rather that forms of life, attitudes, thought and vision are also inherited; and there is much in the air that is common property and comprises cultural treasure created in common. That every thought first finds its home in a small circle and spreads only *slowly—submission* to such a trial is only to the good of the contents that are thus disseminated.

Naturally, this decentralized spiritual life originating in the towns has its dangers as well as its advantages. The small city offers the genuinely active person, and especially those who dispose over political or some other form of prophetic ability, too little opportunity to express themselves.

This probably spelled the fate of one of the most important men of recent years, Max Weber, who had at his disposal everything that would have fitted him for political leadership: unbounded sociological and economic knowledge, a feeling for political realism, an animated temperament—and yet his influence on the course of things remained minimal. As a professor in Heidelberg, he could only play a guest role in politics, and, although many other things also conspired against him, it is because the current of vital political life could not carry him past the dead spots that he is known today only as a scholar. Max Weber is only one example of the blockage of energies that is only one of the great dangers of provincial culture. The other lies in the petit bourgeois quality that is imposed upon even the most outstanding persons by the strength of the lassitude of social life. One has to be here and to see how petit bourgeois the "torch bearers" and "reformers" are in their everyday lives, the extent to which it is merely ideas that they proclaim, and the narrow frames in which their lives play themselves out. There is also something touchingly naive in the way that the distinguished are allowed to press forward and rage in the matters that concern them most, but how they allow themselves to be constricted within very narrow bounds in their daily lives. It is not enough to read their writings, because there has hardly ever been anywhere and at any time a deeper abyss between the work and the man than here and now. With unprecedented courage, they write words that smash through everything and wield their pen even too lightly; but the man himself, the one who wrote this, is in every trait of his life peaceful and submissive, without a single gesture to emancipate the soul. The antagonism between petit bourgeois life and cosmopolitan thought becomes evident with unprecedented force here, because in the life of the town it is not so easy to sidestep a problem as in the metropolis, where the control over forms of life is slight and life shapes itself without resistance, as thought does.

All of this is today no longer quite the case, especially because in recent times Berlin is taking on on ever more significance, in spiritual matters too, and because it consolidates spiritual movements of the most varied origins, confronts them with each other, deprives them of their local color, and throws them together, in a mix, into the German smelter—finally to unify them, amid chaotic noise.

If I had the choice between, first, constantly traveling around, su-perficially seeing Berlin, Munich, Dresden, Cologne, as well as the other places, and writing cultural reportage about them on this basis, or, second, remaining somewhere in one place and observing life from that spot, I would choose the latter. I have in any case seen most of the cities, and I could, as a traveler and on the basis of only passing impressions, describe their contents, which could also be read off their books. But that does not interest me. What occupies me is how the people conduct themselves towards these contents, how they live with them, and how much is actualized of that which may only exist as a letter on a page. To this end, one must live among them, somehow in the same place. To be sure, one must also know what is happening outside the walls, but how the new ranges itself alongside the old, and how the ideal is reconciled with the reality become visible only in a cross-section of life in a place. And because the process of actualiza-tion in cultural life is strongly stereotyped, it is quite likely that the remaining places can also be better observed through the orientation to a fixed point. To avoid pushing the city on the Neckar one-sidedly into the center of the German sphere, I want to add a few words before I look at things from local standpoints, in this introductory letter, about the general spiritual attitude that characterizes present-day Germans, not only here but everywhere. From the standpoint of philosophy of history, the constellation is such that the many local deities, local movements, set forth on a campaign to conquer, if not the world, the whole of the country. What would have been, under different circumstances, a scholastic teaching tied to one place, one town, leaves its locality today and, because the people, in the attitudes of their souls, wait hungrily for belief and instruction, every movement finds adherents beyond its own narrow native domain. The general loss of direction, emblematic of our time, meets the multiplicity resulting from the German cultural decentralization and drives the individual into the confusing maelstrom of spiritual currents. Most German educated people today are covert sectarians, adherents of some isolated movement, see the world through the lenses some "ism," and attempt to orient themselves amid the confusion that surrounds them with the help of some not very sharply contoured principles. No more than elsewhere in the world, is there here the "one cause" in which everyone can believe and which they can endow with the saving grace of partial truth. But not even the individual believes fully, with the complete fanaticism of conviction, in that to which he has pledged himself. Everyone is somehow suspended above the cause he has accepted. Perhaps this is still the legacy of the Enlightenment of the Eighteenth Century, which left deeply cut tracks ineradicably in the human soul. Even if its contents and the obsolete Enlightenment doctrines are ever more repressed, and even if a longing for a new religion and a new belief now seizes men, the "attitude of soul" remains what it was. In his soul, the present-day German is in truth cast loose and without support. He is a seeker and reasoner in his understanding, however, and it is his deepest paradox that he reasons about things that are irrational and precede understanding and that he organizes things that arise out of organic development alone. After the Enlightenment, Romanticism opened the floodgates for the pre-intellectual, the presentiment, belief, and instinct. Man's understanding gained the insight that there are things prior to and alongside of understanding and that insight now wants to reach beyond itself by its own means.

That is why the Germans' reflections must be viewed as longings only and not as reforms. The fundamental form of their thinking is the program, and their life is taken up with sketchy notation of new possibilities, and there are in fact no contents with which one could fill these frames. And because it is the fatality of programs that they always seize upon something accidental, something moving on the periphery of life, and place it at the center, it is possible to build new world around them only artificially. One discovers rhythm, another, dance, a third, education, and others again, belief, God, the Negro, style, unity, and the theatrical scene. And whatever one of them accidently seizes upon becomes the center of the universe, the cornerstone of resurrection and the promised land of the life to come, whose sole apostle he is.

Everywhere there is the watch for prophets; the air is full of prophets, great and small. One swears by Steiner, the other by Spengler. There is Blüher, Kayserling–centers that reform whole cultures, there are the apostles of Wyneken and George.[54] There is an unprecedented readiness in men– a readiness of the spirit, but not of the soul–for some sort of salvation, there is a certain emptiness, a sense of want, that nothing succeeds in filling. It is for just this reason that the present-day German intellectual lacks distance. He sees no difference between small things and great because he is, in appearance, always moving among great ones.

They are all attractive as individuals because all of these movements contain some partial truth–the "Free German Youth Movement," the "*Wandervogel,*" "Georgeism," and the rest–and, when we free them from their pathetic husks and relocate them from the artificial center, we can assign them to their due natural place in the totality of life. That is why it is meaningful to occupy oneself with them–and in the view from Heidelberg, they can all be reached–because a future life is laboring in them, and all of these rudiments may at some time find their place in a larger unity. At present, however, it is only a laboring; and perhaps there is something sad and lovable about this enthusiasm without distance, because it has been the fate of each of us that we have brought more love and, above all, more longing to things than the present world could satisfy. We have become ripe for something, but there is no one to harvest the fruit, and our soul fears that it has ripened for nothing but a barren withering.

II

Heidelberg is the city of autumns and springs. In winter, man covers himself and waits or reminisces, seeks refuge in the library, or he contemplates, standing on the shore, the gloriously spanned old Neckar bridge with its stone arches. Romantic painters have memorialized the old castle, the moon and the rich foliage countless times, and anyone who spends twenty-four hours here as an Englishman finds it hard to separate Heidelberg from the romance that has so often penetrated its image. When a person lives here, however, and it begins to be self-evident that the moon shines, and when the giant cask that is displayed in the castle also ceases to rouse the imagination all too much, he discovers the many hard lines and the salutary precision that are buried more deeply in the architecture and surroundings, a treasure worth discovering. At the time of my earlier tourist trips, as we were leaving some attractive place, I often thought, as the guide wound up his spiel and while the monotonous rhythms of his memorized speech still rang in my ear, how bounteously this city, this place, must reveal itself to those who remain there, who do not see it in the momentary flash of a superficial adventure, but who pace it off with their lives–and never see anything else. As someone left behind at one such tourist site and as its admirer, I now walk about in the town and in the park and feel as if I were translating one of my old thought experiments into reality by being there. Man faithlessly abandons so many minutes, as he rushes from one thing to another, why should I not seize hold of this minute and say that this time I will use this opportunity to the utmost?

Heidelberg's beauty is that of an Italian setting transplanted to Germany. What Riegl says about the architecture of Salzburg also applies to the environs of Heidelberg. The Italian and German landscapes come together here. While the southern-Roman and northern-German do not meld together in gentle gradations in Salzburg, however, and an Italian architecture appears before us with harsh suddenness, purified in the German surroundings, matters in Heidelberg depend on the sunshine, whether the softly blending colors of the German woods catch our eye, or the atmosphere of the brilliant Italian blue skies, opening wide vistas upon a setting delineated in a precise system of lines. Just at the point where the Neckar, this small stream, prepares to leave the valley encompassed by the ruins of medieval castles and to hurry into the great plain, there, at the foot of the last hill, lies the town. The river still carries with it the aroma of the flowers and woods of the valley, but one has the impression that this is dammed up in the lagoon-like estuary and cannot stream into the plain, where the Americanized city of Mannheim rises, an alien planting. This Heidelberg possesses a certain seclusion, the protected status of a glass house, and I always think of the world as of something outside, something external, although the enclosing walls are nowhere to be seen. But this is in reality not a seclusion but only a protected status, because just as the city still lies in the valley but with half of it face turned towards the Rhine plain, so in, spiritual matters, life is rounded out by the unity of separation but not by closed-mindedness against the outside. The primary achievement of Heidelberg is that despite its tradition, while the tasks and problems of the generations steadily succeeded one another, it never sank into the sterile conservatism that always only turns, like a whirlpool, about itself. It is cosmopolitan despite its tradition, because they have been accustomed here for centuries to strangers, and, beyond the transient foreigners, the streets are thronged with students in hordes, renewed every summer and winter, who populate the many small, ever emptying rental rooms. This streaming in and out, this readiness for ever new faces, alters the attitude of those who remain. Everyone feels that what he does and says is impelled outward in human form and also strikes targets that lie elsewhere. Sometimes in the evenings, as I stroll past the walls of old houses, I have the feeling that the wind of medieval dead cities left behind the modern trade routes wafts over the houses–there appears a souvenir of Rothenburg and Bruges–but when I enter a room illuminated by yellow light and there are people sitting around the table, young folk, their eyes shining, and the talk is of new pains and new joys–then I know that we are alive, and the torpor bred by the sense of abandonment falls away from me.

One also ought to discuss how this world appears from the outside and what the background may be that sets off the movements of the life we shall be depicting, that which most immediately captures my eye. Heidelberg's spirtual life may be calibrated by two polar opposites. One pole consists of the sociologists and the other, the Georgians. The ideal-typical representative of the one is the already deceased Max Weber, and that of the other is the poet, Stefan George. On the one side, the university, and on the other, the unbounded extramural world of the literati. The one lies in continuity with the Protestant cultural tradition, the other orients itself by Catholicism. These contrasts do not hold up without remainder; they are merely rigid schemes whose aim it is to indicate the contrasting components of the manifold intersections of vibrant life. University life cannot be represented by the person of Max Weber alone, just as he was much more than the university; and it is similarly not possible to mark the Georgians simply with the stamp of tendencies towards Catholicism. And yet this confrontation is justified, because this is where these two world-views took form, as well as the more general contradictions—as with Catholicism and university and literary culture, which take on their local color from their contacts with these two poles. Because in this instance Catholicism and Protestantism signify neither a racial nor a religious difference, but rather the features of two kinds of past, whose traces manifest themselves in the spiritual attitude and the coherence of the teachings of the present-day tendencies, it is also impossible to make the remaining distinctions into positivistic measurements, as if one could divide individuals into two groups on the strength alone of their belonging or not belonging to a religion or the university. The division can depend only on their closeness to the one or the other, their affinities to one or the other attitude. Themes, questions, posture and manner of speaking, association and socializing are different in the two worlds. The Georgian, you can recognize on the street, and the sociologists, at the lectern. Terminology and words are in conflict even where the deviation in essence has not yet been articulated.

Georgianism arose by virtue of the fact that a poet drew several individuals to him with his works, but especially with his person and essence, and that this relationship, which originally extended only from man to man, merged into a united community.

There are numerous forms of human association. It may be a matter of external interests, external defense, an impersonal grouping around spiritual contents, and a mere mutual attraction without any spiritual contents–social contacts. This last, resting on nothing but colorless and contentless mutual association among persons, soon consumes itself. Where people live together without contents or a common will, despite the absence of belief, their mutual attraction eventually turns into mutual indiscretion. The substance of their lives together then consists of nothing but their regaling one another with petty problems, mostly about love affairs. And, because the attitude of people today is in any case excessively psychological and analytical, a common experience and common happening between two people is stymied in such cases at the very ouset by the fact that the very first seeds of a happening are analyzed. Constant mutual confessions and psychoanalytical reflections perform largely the same function in such relationships as gossip in a petit bourgeois environment, whose task and origin are, from this point of view, the same, viz., to replace belief. The second factor capable of building community is an ideal, a common religious, philosophical, political aspiration, that unifies inwardly and builds a front against the outside. If this is the only thing holding them together and nothing else has power, then this form too has limits set to it, to render it sterile. An ideal, a goal, would be too impersonal a principle of choice for men, suspended above them and in no way adequate. An ideal makes souls close only in a comradely way. It is not a sufficient criterion because it brings into the community people who do not belong to it with their souls, and it keeps away many who are only unable to accept its objective contents. At this point, there emerges a resemblance to a community united by interest. Although this is something different in essence, and more than the other, here too the emphasis shifts, due to the dynamics of things, from the aspect of inner unity to the aspect of external defense, exclusion.

Finally, there is a kind of human association that can be designated by a word at home in sociology, a "charismatic" community, in which most often the emanating power of a single individual's soul collects the others around him. Not objective, spiritual contents, remote from the soul primarily hold individuals together in such a community, but rather this other kind of attraction of soul that emanates from the soul of the leader to the others and may be called magical. In such communities, unified by the human soul, contents also slowly take form. But the coherence of these contents cannot be derived from a logical or traditional context. And because the supra-objective center of the soul slowly draws these contents to itself, the necessity of their coherence too can be understood only through this unity of soul. Timeless examples of such unity of soul are Jesus and his disciples, who grouped themselves first of all around this charismatic center, whereupon doctrines of varied origins first fused together into a "system." In such a common existence there are as yet no dogmatic ties, and the criterion of heresy is not the contradiction of some thesis, but a sin against the holy ghost of the unifying soul.

The existence of a charismatic person and the possibility of his effectiveness is not given to all times. The atmosphere of spirit and soul are not equally welcoming at all times, yet we recognize such a person even in the hardest of times, someone in whom dwells at least the kernel, however undeveloped, of such a substantial effect from soul to soul. Something of this attraction must be present in George, since the form of association of his adherents, its non—objectivity— the unity beyond objectivity among his followers—bear its marks. And just because such associations on a charismatic foundation are so rare and because I still somehow retain the belief that the new man can truly transform himself neither in the family nor in the school, nor in the life and politics of the external world, I consider it important that this kind of common life exists in our time. From the fact that things take on existence only as they are placed (*Hineingestelltsein*) in their times it follows that not every form of life or experiment in common life abstractly possible can actualize and develop itself in every temporal setting. Certain forms of life require certain substantive contents for their development; and when they are compelled to precipitate themselves among contents that are not appropriate to them, they atrophy—they suffocate on the way things are. Charismatic community is the most profound form of human life in common and it can therefore actualize itself only in the most profound contents. The contents appropriate to this form of life are those of belief, of religion. Because at the time when the George-Circle emerged (and to the present day), belief in its most profound form was not a possibility for this stratum of individuals, since it was not alive to the extent necessary to serve as an integrative, unifying experience (and because they were honest enough to intuit and feel this), they (spontaneously) chose the most profound contents then available, humanism, as the basis of their association. Georgianism emerged in the nineties of the last century, at the very time that naturalism began its triumphant march. George's development was nourished by sources quite different from those of naturalism, and he quickly ended up in opposition to it. His historic function may be seen in his having helped to divide the forces of naturalism in the interests of a wider development. In his youth, George experienced (just like Ady) the great change of sentiments in Paris. He too was first affected by Verlaine (and the Parnassians), and as was true of Ady with us, who was at first the assembly point of a generation given to aesthetics, Georgianism constituted itself at first as a loose collection around a literary aesthete. (Hofmannsthal still belonged to them at the time.) The experience of Nietzsche and the undertaking to feel their way into the national language also lets their developments be viewed as similar at the beginning of their paths. Only what came after separates them completely, and this rests in part on the differences between the Hungarian and German worlds. Ady soon entered alone upon the lonely *via crucis* of the "unbelieving believer;" the understructure of the struggles in his soul is composed of the two extremes of the terrestrial world, God and politics. He fled from one to the other, and, because for us the intermediate region of life called culture does not exist, with the help of which one can acclimatize oneself to earthly life, and because he would not rest content, his grandest poems arose from this. While Ady's extraordinary genius created his substance out of scarcity, it may have been the plenty of German life that gave rise to temptation in George, as well as the limits that impede the expression of the soul. George had aestheticism as his starting point and, although he left it behind, impelled by the dynamics of history, he never freed himself of it completely. Since in Germany one is located in the flow of a great tradition, it is possible, for a time, to forget the chaos yawning in the depths of life and the soul. There are partial tasks that the individual has inherited from earlier generations and in which he can inscribe his life with his fate. In our case, the actually living soul is confronted with the whole of life, everyone must do everything, and no one can linger over individual things. With us, it is only possible to live from soul to soul. People love one another only individually (to which the heightened importance of lovers' conflicts is to be ascribed). In Germany, the possibility for communities that are more than associations with practical objectives existed, communities that could waken the illusion of protectedness and the finding of a home.

So the George-Circle turned into a closed, spiritual-aristocratic community of persons who shut themselves off from all events in the outside world and envelop themselves in themselves. They struggle against the age, insofar as they condemn its derangement, but they do not aspire to intervene in the course of things, and the charismatic core that holds the members together develops nothing but humanistic contents. In Germany since the Renaissance, it is humanism that has provided the principle that has given form to brotherhoods and communities, as well as the articulations of the principle in the preoccupation with history, literature, and the past. Philology, which is in itself a dead and desiccated science, here gains entry into life and becomes the factor that renders it social. It is no accident that, after the humanists, the bearer of the rococo and then the cooperation among Goethe, Schiller and Humboldt, followed by Romanticism there emerged just such a cultivation, one that renewed the past and absorbed it from the standpoint of the new. Through this form of association, created in the course of centuries, streamed an energy that demanded charismatic persons, and the soul donned these contents, philological in the final analysis, as its mortal coil. The members of the circle were mainly writers and historians, and the most valuable among them was Gundolf, from whose vision of the German literary past one could sense that his points of view grew out of a unity and that his research was no aimless circling about its objects.

And yet there is a certain discrepancy between the nature of their solidarity of soul and its contents. Even if their aristocratic posture is not political or social, its principles nevertheless resemble ever more the ideology of a prosperous person living on an income. Its extraordinary abstractness is nourished by essentialist intuitions of the grand historical perspectives rather than by the concrete demands of everyday and of life. [Here are their arguments:] The crumbling German spiritual life must be saved through a new myth; it is necessary to recur to the great historical powers—those of the authentic German beginnings, those which have so often regenerated the north-Germanic and German shares of Hellenism, those which are being newly resurrected. It is necessary to struggle against the Protestant capitalist principle and, if the Catholic Church as positive confession is also too narrow for them by now, its worship remains a relevant, life-shaping factor. They reject socialism because it appeals to the masses, but the *Volk* appears as the actual substance. And to it clings a magic aura, the language. Everything brought by the Enlightenment, much of which was wretched, they condemn, and they would hurdle over the things that nevertheless remain the historical and contemporary presuppositions of their own spiritual existence.

Even more characteristic than all this is their battle against "the watchword of progress," and in this, interestingly, they are close to the standpoint of neo-Catholicism. It makes sense to look more closely at this position since in this they offer the counter-example to socialist doctrine, with its affinity for enlightenment. [They argue as follows:]

Modern man has accustomed himself to see the way of history as a straight line continuing to infinity, which is why his motto became a constant future-oriented progress. In Hegel's words, one could call this conception a "bad infinity" because it is something to which one can always add something else (as in a numbers series) and that never becomes complete. The symbol of experience for the Georgians is the circle, the constant return to the same points at a new level. For such a view, history is the ever new appearance of a limited number of possibilities of soul and culture, and its ideal is self-enclosure, inner plenitude, and not the constant reference beyond oneself. That it is possible to see history under the sign of such of such antagonistic symbols [as do the Georgians and their socialist opposites] rests mainly on the fact that those making the arguments focus their attention on different cultural manifestations. Someone who contemplates the course of technology, science or civilization will see the symbol of historical development in the straight way to infinity, but someone who looks, in contrast, to literature, art and religion takes away from this inner experience the realization that only deepening is possible here, and no advancement. In these spheres, the later manifestations of temporality are not at the same time the more perfect. The religious self-immersion of the soul's substance or its blossoming forth in the work (in its proper signification) do not run parallel to the development of civilization.

From their polemical position against the "watchword of progress" the Georgians also attack contemporary science, which is, in their view, only a factor of civilization and not the expression or emanation of the soul–nothing but aimless destructive analysis.

Viewed from the outside, all this could also amount to a nationalist and conservative ideology, but since they are politically passive and, as individuals, the bearers of a cultivation with very wide horizons, as well, it is not possible to measure their value by these necessarily fragmentary theses–and even these theses are different when we look at them from the closeness we have experienced for ourselves and not as hackneyed phrases of a tactical external confrontation. Many productive insights result from their opposition against their times, and their literary and general public criticism has exposed many evils in present-day German life. On the other hand, however, their fortune resembles that of reformers who castigate their age but deeply share its faults. Just as Moliere censured the preciosity of his times in his "précieuses ridicules" and never suspected how mannered he was himself, so do they, who want to put life itself in place of the many analyses and programs, create nothing but literature and programs.

As long as the charismatic core remains alive, it lends meaning even to contents that are not adequate to this essential nature, but as soon as it ceases to operate, the contents gathered out of humanistic studies—since they are not adequate bearers of the soul previously associated with them—fall apart, and they become simply theses among the many other German theses. Viewed from within, the Georgian community is a well-intentioned experiment by "intellectuals," who have become isolated in present-day society, to solve the problem posed by the homelessness of the soul. Their solution is that of shutting their eyes. In order to lull themselves to sleep with the feeling that they have found a grounding, they seclude themselves, wrap themselves in the contents of culture and—omitting the world from their objects—they alienate themselves. The lagoon of life sheltered by the hills of Heidelberg lets them convince themselves that they are actual, effective, and important, but it would only take a small storm–and they would become mere symbols of a time gone by.

3

Science and Youth

Mannheim was first introduced to Frankfurt not in person but in print, on November 30, 1922, in the pages of the higher education section of the influential liberal newspaper and Max Weber's favorite forum, the Frankfurter Zeitung, *His article was prefaced by these comments of the editor:*

> In recent years, science has been accused of being alienated from life, of increasingly losing its relationship to the present. There has been much debate over the possibility of regeneration of our academic institutions of cultivation. From these doubts and wishes has emerged what is really valuable in the "politics of higher education." The criticism by the youth has sometimes condemned the good along with the bad and in the exuberance of striving for innovation they have denied every tradition and its pedagogical value. It is a good thing to discuss the pros and cons of this problem with scientific calmness. The following essay, with the aid of some concrete examples, seeks to demonstrate the value and the deficiencies of academic institutions and their significance for the cultivation and preparation of the youth.

Mannheim was an acquaintance of Siegfried Kracauer, who joined the FZ in 1919 and soon became one of two leading editors of the cultural sections. It is only a surmise, however, that Kracauer opened the paper to Mannheim's contribution.[55]

For the student, entrance into university means adjustment to a spiritual reality that came into being without his help and that, indifferent to his psychic needs, lives its own autonomous life. Now a struggle of self-validation or failure begins for the individual, a struggle to translate the concerns he brought to university into new aspirations: "A farewell to adolescence in the anticipation of manhood." A tension between science and every new generation is inevitable, but the university is a pedagogical institution only insofar as it mediates between the autonomous realm of science and the young individual talents, ultimately resolving this tension in favor of creative work.

If we are truthful as we observe the development of individual students from this point of view, we must confess their defeat, a suppression of essential human and scientific instincts by the contemporary scientific machinery, operating on its own momentum. Let me offer some typical examples.

One of the students whose development I want to trace arrived in a small university town fresh from the political movement, full of enthusiasm, energy, and dedication. Discouraged by the superficiality of party journalism, he wanted to devote some years to study. In the beginning he experienced conflicts of conscience as to whether he could allow himself the time for such work. Others among his comrades were already sacrificing their youth and lives to the work of political organization. He came from the rushed metropolis to the life of a small town still bound by tradition, and he took offense at everything, he rebelled against the town's contemplative silence, and he raged like a wild man against the attitudes firmly established within an environment adapted to what was considered to be the one authentic academic tradition. After only one semester, a surprising change had taken place. He had become calm and thorough; he had learned a great deal; and he would almost certainly not have written any of his earlier articles. He hardly ever spoke any longer of a return to the political movement. It was not just that a certain political dogma now seemed wrong to him, since he could have, after all, adhered to another. His whole political engagement was gone. The fire was extinguished. More out of a need to settle unfinished business with his earlier self than from inner conviction, he says now and then that he may some day take up once more his abandoned plans and rejoin his old companions.

In his case, the life of science provided much that was beneficial: viz., theoretical depth, reflection, and clarity. But his instinct for life, that appeared to be as important for the greater whole as for himself, was broken, in part redirected into theoretical work. This conversion of a spiritual and psychic potency benefitted his scientific work. Unlike others, he did not pursue theoretical questions motivated by nothing more than scientific, quasi-philological interest. He was moved by problems grounded in actual life. By the time he received the answer to his questions, however, he had forgotten that which was best about him, his profound quest, the impulse that had driven him to ask his questions in the first place.

Another student came from one of the metaphysical-religious fellowships so common nowadays. When I first met him, he was an inward person, intensely charged with a fullness of heightened spirituality, and he lived with a perfectly philosophical attitude toward things. He surrendered himself to every detail of his life with his full capacity for experience. There was also something mendacious in him, something that smacked of self-satisfied pathos and often of exaggeration. The function of the lie at this stage of life, however, is quite familiar. It manifests dissatisfaction with one's inability to be in constant readiness. He was a student of philosophy. What happened after two semesters? His whole spiritual intensity was weakened; his internal torments were transformed into philosophical, historical problems; and, in the end, those questions, for whose sake he had turned to his books, were completely forgotten. In place of his unceasing pursuit of essences, there arose self-estrangement, perplexity, and a lack of vital interest in the philosophical questions that accidentally came his way.

A third student, whom I first met at the end of his studies, was an art historian. Whenever he spoke of paintings, there was such a frenzy of horizontal lines and vertical lines that I had to ask myself whether he had any sense for art at all. Then we discussed literature once, and I was astonished by his deep insights and manifest feeling of simple joy. I asked him: "Why don't you study literary history? You seem to have a better feel for it." His ironic answer did full justice to the situation: "I don't want to spoil this pleasure for myself as well."

What is common to and typical of all these cases is that a number of instincts and attitudes towards experience, which would be of great importance especially for the cultural sciences, were fatally subverted by "the turn to science." These students had managed to retain a comparatively strong measure of inwardness and intensity due to the fact that, before entering university, they had, by their adhesion to a living fellowship, acquired a pre-scientific access to the spiritual realities to which they then dedicated their scientific care. In their cases, the result was at least a conversion of all their vital energies into particular cultural energies. How many others are there, however, simply transplanted from one school desk to another and perhaps also endowed with less intense sensibility, who can now see things only from an attitude of dutifulness and through a prism of problems prescribed by the scientific enterprise?

Adding to these dangers, ones that arise largely from the nature of scientific thinking itself, is the presence of scientific "schools," such as the current dominance of a mainly historical attitude to things. Both factors, thinking in schools as well as historicism, are phenomena that arise in part from the immanent movement of scientific thinking itself. They are in part signs of a developed spiritual culture, but, for younger students, they represent simultaneously a threat to the clear-eyed statement of problems that they have won on their own. How many have already gotten to the point where, whenever they really want to think a thing through with science, they first simply throw the whole "scientific clutter" aside and only afterwards work in the "literature" to keep up the appearance of being scientific? The reduction of one's own problem agenda to the formulations ready at hand, the rethinking of thoughts along lines derived from school traditions, inhibits a candid view and promotes the inclination to orient oneself less by the things themselves than by readily available, imported thoughts about them. The dangers to thought in general posed by an all-inclusive scientific enterprise are akin to those we have noted with regard to the dangers of a scientific attitude to an attitude of man as a whole : a narrowing of the scope of vision, a transmutation of unmediated interests into technicalities of thought.

It is certainly easier to criticize this state of affairs and to entrench oneself in an oppositional position than it is to comprehend the actual situation in its inner necessity and to find the remedy within the situation as it actually presents itself. Some of the tensions between life and science simply come along with the structure of life and the essentially autonomous development of the scientific cultural process. It would be nonsense to demand that science accommodate itself to every generation and ultimately to every individual. Only the active collaboration of the new generation and its entrance into scientific work can make any difference and gradually effect a redirection. Vague programmatics are without use. Moreover, not all of the factors comprising "life" are as pristine, pure and intense as it may at first appear. The spiritual tendencies that may be present in unscientific, semi-scientific and pre-scientific forms as undercurrents in the movements of the spirit as a whole have their histories too, and they are often nothing but decayed specters of obsolete thought. Compared to these, strict scientific thinking represents an intensification by virtue of its concentration on a focal point. However, the vital undercurrents rise to the top—and rightly so—whenever the scientific tradition becomes rigid; and whenever the teaching institutions, as mediators between life and the dynamics of culture, are unable to effectuate a valid exchange of cultural and scientific energy.

One is impelled to ask whether the great impression that these extra-scientific sects are making on the youngest generation, specifically in scientific matters, is not connected with the fact that many university teachers, misappraising their own vocations, view themselves as nothing but purveyors of a scientific tradition and not simultaneously as the stewards of the freshly streaming flow of life. Out of a misunderstanding of the purely contemplative scientific attitude, which can properly be imputed only to the finished intellectual product, they forget that the intellectual process, the work of research itself, is not something that can be abstracted, something that exists for its own sake. It is, rather, nourished by extra-theoretical, extra—scientific interests and forces. Once these connections are severed, bare thought and observation will continue on their own for only a short stretch. In attempting to turn the young student directly into an ideal type of the purely theoretical-contemplative subject (the subjective correlate of the intellectual product, abstractly considered) one excludes all the capabilities that alone furnish a wider foundation for productive thought. If the scientific environment achieves the instant transformation of the young student into such a cognitive personality type, then we see a severing of the vital connections that led to science, and thus also to the motivating principle of true scientific thought. If some students escape, however, we should not be surprised if they use their repressed energies of life and culture to seek psychic-spiritual satisfaction in such pre-scientific speculations. More vague, indeed, but also more alive, simply because they comprehend the whole of the subject in thought and action.

Science in its present state of development, in sum, has become an autonomous force abstracted from the totality of life. And yet, while it advances in part by its own immanent principles, it is nevertheless intertwined in its development with the life process as a whole. One of the sluice gates through which life has access to this formation is the constantly renewed generation of fresh people, young scientists. These people stream towards the existing scientific enterprise from an always changing environment, one that produces not only new contents but also new attitudes to things; and they draw near while constantly working this environment through in an always novel, organic manner. Accordingly, the pedagogical task of the teacher is to re-channel, as far as possible, the full breadth of this life into the scientific stream. The teacher's task is not simply to represent the interest of the developing science but also to advance the interests of the developing scientists. The task of a teaching institution is not only the elaboration of unresolved problems, however necessary from a systemic standpoint, but also the steady conversion of the interests present in the students into corresponding questions for inquiry. The concrete ways and means of this pedagogical task can be discussed, however, only insofar as there is agreement on its necessity. If there is denial, however, there will be an inner split among the thinkers of the future. Its ultimate logical consequence can only be that what is thought by this new generation, science itself, will be rendered completely alien to those who have worked for it, dedicating their lives.

As life is inwardly structured, the realm from which ever new formations of culture emerge is most accessible to the god-inspired chaos of the youthful consciousness. Advancing in age, the creative person may be in fact only finding the form proper to something he had intuited in early youth and retained by a sort of recollection. The mere continuation of life (which we can call maturing) will by itself, up to a point, cause a certain weakening of that quasi-religious intensity in which every conviction is driven by inner excitement. Aging is not merely an advance in years or an quantitative accumulation of experiences, but a gradual shift that takes place, as it were, behind our backs, in our point of view towards the totality of new impressions that pour in on us. This process finds its most marked expression in the fact that we came to most things in our lives—occupation, marriage, and the like—for reasons quite different from those which lead us to cling to them. If we demand a sudden interruption of the inner development of youth, however, we are not only hastening the organic process that would move along without our intervention, but forcing it prematurely, and spurning the origins of spiritual life in individuals and communities.

If today one were to ask the best of our youth in their student years, however, how they came to their science, what inner reasons drove them to dedicate themselves to precisely the problems that now occupy them, they would have to say, "We have forgotten our reasons."

4

On the Incorporation of Research in the Journalistic Medium *(Zeitungswesen)* into University Science

In April, 1927, the Institute for the Journalistic Medium (Zeitungswesen)
was opened in Heidelberg in connection with Alfred Weber's Institute
for Social-and State Science. Mannheim was a lecturer in the Institute
and a number of his regular students attended his courses there (Demm
1999: 128–137; Blomert 1999: 38–48). In the Summer Semester, 1928,
Mannheim held a colloquium on the sociology of public opinion and
the press. The basic themes of his colloquium, the prospectus of which
has survived (GLA), are continued in the newspaper article below,
written in 1929 for a newspaper trade publication. The most striking
theme in the abbreviated prospectus is the distinction between the
knowledge conveyed by sciences and the practice-related communica-
tions specific to journalistic media. A related theme, familiar from
Mannheim's 1922 FZ article, is the necessity of bridging the gulf
between university science and everyday life. This continues to be an
important part of his pedagogical philosophy during his Frankfurt
period and after.

The incorporation of journalistic science into the curriculum of the
university advances the widely noted process of bringing science closer
to life. This process, endorsed by some and scorned by others, will
gradually prevail in the other disciplines as well. It is most evident in
the advance of sociology, whether as independent discipline or as
bourgeoning method of observation that bids fair to displace all other

types of observation in the specialized sciences. This development could lead to a leveling of general academic standards, but also instead to a regeneration of our academic knowledge.

Such a regeneration always requires a science that is practiced institutionally, since it is precisely to its institutional framework that science owes most of its advantages as well as most of the limits placed on its chances. The institutional framework guarantees, for example, the continuity of inquiry. At the same time, however this inclusion within a framework hampers reorientation, as well as the adjustments to new life situations that would otherwise emerge spontaneously.

It is not in our power to prevent or interrupt this process of bringing the sciences closer to life—even if we did oppose it in principle—but it is entirely up to us whether we promote this development in the direction of its deepest possibilities or simply allow it to take effect in its most superficial tendencies.

The example of sociology shows us clearly how it was possible to deepen a modern spiritual attitude, which unquestionably had something flat and trivial about it in its American manifestation. Max Weber's work provides the proof that one does not achieve a spiritual reorientation—a new discipline, sociology—that is made necessary by modern developments simply by copying foreign models, but rather by allowing the corresponding problems to emerge out of the context of one's own life and questions, and by achieving the new position towards life from one's own starting point.[56] Correspondingly, scientific attention to the newspaper may also lead to contributions to the problems of the human sciences (*Geisteswissenschaften*) beyond this narrower area, and this in a manner and direction that these sciences would never have come to see in their subject matter on their own. Such a reciprocal fertilization of journalistic and university science can only result, however, if the newspaper researcher gains the insight that his discipline has not yet achieved the rank of a science when it has merely addressed the practical problems of the craft, and conversely, if the human sciences increasingly bring into view that their special themes (history of literature, history of art, philosophy, and so on) are simply portions of a wider continuity, extracted from the contexture of life, and that they cannot understand the "higher" objectifications of life if they have not found their source in the "everyday togetherness" (*alltäglichen Miteinanders*) of men.

If a new life ideal appears in literature, if philosophy keeps finding the basic problematic of being human in new areas, this usually corresponds to a shift in the ideals of concretely existing men and a fundamental change in the ways in which man stands to his fellow-men and, most intimately connected with this, with himself.

Thus, if the student of the human sciences attempts to return to the point of origin where spiritual formations are still "spiritual *life*," he will reach the stratum of "everyday togetherness" whose direct expression is public opinion and the press.

It is, accordingly, the problem of the sociology of public opinion that forms the meeting point for the intersection of two lines of problem that have been developing separately.

In the last decades, the human sciences have increasingly appealed to the stratum of happening that one could call "spiritual life" in their explanations. As an expression of this tendency, a philosophy emerged that was actually called philosophy of life (*Lebensphilosophie*). And the study of the newspaper must increasingly recognize that if in its method it wants to understand the newspaper not simply on its own terms, but methodologically in terms of larger comprehensive totalities, it must refer back to the phenomenon of public opinion.

Philosophy of life and the sociology of public opinion, thus, both address one and the same object, the same sphere of being. While in the former case, the need to grasp the "spirit" from the standpoint of "life"—from the stage of becoming where nothing has as yet hardened—emerged only gradually out of the study of intellectual history (*Geistesgeschichte*), the situation is different for the sociologist of public opinion. For him, life in its ordinariness (*Alltäglichkeit*), where the new configures itself in constant integration and the old that proves itself must constantly reproduce itself, is the unmediated theme, the research area proper to his choice of subject.

In philosophy it was Dilthey in particular who directed the eyes of the human scientist toward the "pre-spiritual" sphere, toward structural research of the "context of life;" and lately it has been the most recent currents of the phenomenological school that move the same sphere into the foreground through discovery of the problematic of "ordinariness" from the philosophical side.

Thus the inner development of philosophy and the human sciences, on the one hand, meets the candid need for a deeper foundation of new disciplines that emerge from the practice of modern life, on the other; and it is only a matter of being clear-sighted enough to locate the point where the new need of practice has its point of conjunction with the question complex of the traditional sciences, itself in continual modification.

This point appears to us to lie increasingly in sociology, in a sociology that is, on the one hand, in a position to absorb the problem complex of philosophy arisen out of the new life situation, and to do so by way of mediation, and, on the other, sufficiently elastic, holding itself constantly ready to be impregnated by unmediated empirical reality.

From the perspective of the science of journalism, however, it is precisely at the topic of a sociology of public opinion where this attempt at integration can be undertaken. The analysis of the structure of public opinion is simultaneously a philosophical, historical, sociological and journalistic phenomenon. The investigation of its problems effectuates the reciprocal penetration of practice and university science that we called for just now in merely programmatic terms. If we seize this opportunity, we can derive a paradigm from this to the effect that engagement with the demands of the day does not necessarily bring with it a leveling of science, and that, on the other hand, being an empiricist does not necessarily mean abandoning the center of questioning. At the present moment, it is entirely up to us, by means of a timely comprehension of the new situation, to rejuvenate what is established with what is just arriving, and to ennoble the new with our inheritance.

5

The Intellectualism Dispute

Protocols of the Joint Meetings of the Seminars of Professor Alfred Weber and Dr. Karl Mannheim. Heidelberg, February 21 and 27, 1929

It is a measure of the spirit between Karl Mannheim and Alfred Weber and among their students that the two colleagues organized a joint seminar to discuss issues arising out of their public disagreement at the meetings of the German Sociologial Association the previous year.[57] *The point of departure was* History and Class-Consciousness *by Georg Lukács. The document clarifies Mannheim's complex relationship to the "Hegel-Marx" of Lukács, as well as the nuanced terms of disagreement between him and Weber.*

The first seminar opened with presentations by an Alfred Weber student and a Mannheim student. Friedrich Bran, a journalist from a publishing family, wrote his dissertation, "Herder and the German View of Culture [Kulturanschauung]," *under Weber. He shared the interest of his mentor and Curtius in German-French rapprochement. Hans Gerth was a student who was especially close to Mannheim, and acted as his de facto Assistent in both Heidelberg and Frankfurt. He followed Mannheim to Frankfurt, where he wrote his dissertation on late eighteenth-century liberal intellectuals in Germany, a project originating in Mannheim's "Liberalism" seminar but concluded under supervision of another professor, after Mannheim's ouster. He was a member of a socialist student group. A non-Jew, he moved to the United States during the Nazi period for political reasons, and he is best known for his collaborations with C. Wright Mills, including his work as the co-editor of* From Max Weber. *Gerth spoke for Karl Mannheim at the 1937 meetings of American sociologists, when* Ideology and Utopia *was subjected to sharp criticism, notably by Hans Speier, another former student of Mannheim.*[58]

Two participants of the second seminar, in addition to Weber and Mannheim, are recorded as intervening. In 1928 Alfred Sohn-Rethel resumed his studies in Heidelberg after a six-year stay in Italy. He wrote his dissertation under Emil Lederer on the theory of marginal utility. In 1933 he emigrated first to Switzerland and then to Britain, where he developed a Marxist theory of the origins of German fascism.[59] *Paul Eppstein, who had been an* Assistent *under the economist Sally Altmann, had earlier taken part in the discussion of Mannheim's presentation in Zurich. He taught economics and sociology at the Commercial College in Mannheim. He was later shot to death in the Nazi concentration camp Theresienstadt.*[60]

A scientific edition of the German text, collating the drafts available in various archival sites, has been provided by Eberhard Demm[61]

As an appendix, we include Karl Mannheim's letter to Alfred Weber on his 70th birthday, mailed from Budapest during Mannheim's exile in London. Weber, in turn, was a political outcast in Nazi Germany, more nearly in inner exile than in inner emigration. The letter is self-explanatory and self-evidently sincere, despite some mannered formulas.

Protocol
of the First Meeting of the Joint
Seminars of Prof. Weber
and Dr. Mannheim. February 21, 1929.

After introductory reports by Mr. Gerth and Mr. Bran, in which Mr. Gerth briefly presented Georg Lukács' conception (in *History and Class-Consciousness)* of the dialectical method in Marxism as well as of the phenomenon of "reification," and Mr. Bran offered several theses against this conception, *Professor Weber* formulated the most essential points of his agreement with Lukács and subsequently the questions most needing clarification.

He distinguished the Marxism expounded by Lukács in his book as "dialectical materialism" from the philosophical position of historical materialism as a positivistic method of viewing history, which must be judged empirically according to its fruitfulness for specific research tasks and not philosophically, like the other. Yet the central problems of the sociological point of view in general have been posed precisely by Lukács, and the discussion will therefore concentrate on them.

Prof. Weber emphasized his agreement with Lukács on the following points:

1. The attempt to elevate the total concept of history once again to our consciousness, and also that consciousness as a whole, together with all of its consequences and the entire development of consciousness, are included without exception.
2. The conception that the totality can be grasped only if one wants something from one's own present.
3. That Lukács demands and attempts a de-absolutizing of the rational and of intellectualism. Prof. Weber emphasizes that he has made it one of his prime tasks to assign intellectualism to its historical place, to uncover the no more than relative value of the rational comprehension of the historical world of objects, and to fix the limits of intellectualism.
4. That Lukács posits processes instead of fixities and generally demands for history a thinking in processes. Although Lukács mistakenly maintains that such thinking was first discovered by the proletariat.

Then *Prof. Weber* posed the following principal questions:

a. How is the concept of totality in history to be determined? Is it supposed to be valid universally, for history in its entirety, or only in part, i.e., only for the capitalist epoch of history?
b. Is the dialectic a comprehensive philosophical view, a universal thinking? Does it also apply to the cosmos, to knowledge of natural?
c. What about the manner of including the course of consciousness in the historical process? The historical process is dialectical—determined by social antinomies, to which consciousness is shown to be relative. But how far should this go? Is there any possibility at all for discussion between different points of view, or does social position simply take the place of all logical argument as

final arbiter? Then all that would be left would be to ask someone, where do you stand on the subject-object relation? for example, or where do you stand on religion?

d. Lukács claims that the subject-object relation is surmounted in
dialectical materialism. This surmounting is no doubt as important a question as it is difficult. According to Lukács, such surmounting has succeeded for the proletariat, for whom subject
and object coincide, as do consciousness and action in relation to
history. He, Prof. Weber, is also in search of a way to surmount
this dualism, but in his view this lies in creative intuition. The
question is, then, how does Marxism understand creative action?
Or, if Marxism does not deal with it, how is it to be included?
(The question about the surmounting of the subject—object relation was not further taken up by the subsequent discussion.)

e. This raises the very last question: is the completion of form
(*Gestaltetsein*) the ultimate value in itself, or is the dialectical
antinomy of the process the ultimate by which one should orient
oneself?

Dr. Mannheim then answers. He emphasizes first the agreement that
aligns him with the standpoints laid down by Prof. Weber in his first
points, in order to turn next to the questions posed by Prof. Weber.

1. Re: presupposing the concept of totality for history. The sociology of history must orient itself by totality. Every individual
historical fact that is comprehended by everyday consciousness
only in its isolation must be understood as somehow coherently
related to all other individual facts in a totality. What remains in
question is only the "how?" of this coherence in a totality.
2. He also sees all consciousness, without exception, included in
the total historical process.
3. He too says that one can know history only if one wants something from it. This is a factual point, not a normative one.
4. Re: the question of de-absolutizing rationality and intellectualism. Dr. Mannheim understood Prof. Weber to say that intellectualist thinking is the property of only one specific historical
epoch, not necessarily to be met with before or perhaps after.

Prof. Weber: He did not mean to say that. Intellectualist thinking, rather, has had a place and always has a place in history, but only as an instrument of existence (*Dasein*) and of concrete tasks in relation to existence. The intellectualistic is to be restricted to this function as mere instrument, however, because it has no part in the setting of ends. In this matter Prof. Weber declares himself a Bergsonian. The modern phase of history is intellectualistic because it makes the intellectual and the intellectually comprehensible into the highest arbiter. Opposed to this are the limits of mastery over existence. These are the limits of the intellect. In other epochs of history, the highest arbiters and the orientation poles of existence were determined meta-intellectually—as Plato's metaphysics, for example, is based on vision rather than on rational coherences of validity. To extract this meta-intellectual vision, however, he made use of intellectual instruments of thought.

Dr. Mannheim: I wanted to address this problem in connection with question (e) because it is ultimately connected with it. Then Dr. Mannheim explained his position on the question of "relativizing" intellectualism.

By "intellectualism" he means a theory of thinking that maintains that correct judgments can be discovered on the basis of something immanent in thought. The paradigmatic image underlying such a conception is that all possible truths and correct judgments that are thinkable are all present, valid simultaneously, as in a book, where one can look things up, now on page 200 and then again on page 400, without regard to the historical situation in being. He wants to posit a different conception of the rational in place of this intellectualistic one, one where that which can be thought at a given point in time is inwardly connected to the thinking historical subject's condition of being, and where the only thinkable thoughts and truths are those that coincide with the point one has reached in being. The paradigm of forward movement in contextures of thought is not comparable to a book but rather to a stocking, where, when the mesh is loosened, thread by thread is also loosened in a connected process. Nothing can be drawn in except the elements of the thinkable and knowable that have been (existentially) reached by the steadily expanding process of loosening. The threads of possible thought must always be reeled in from their having existentially become a problem. The connection does not run from thought to thought; it is, rather, always mediated by an actuality of being. (The last point of agreement with Lukács emphasized by Prof. Weber—thinking in processes—is not expressly mentioned by Dr. Mannheim.)

Dr. Mannheim next turns to the questions raised by Prof. Weber:

ad (a) Re: the question of the universal or partial validity of the dialectical totality conception of history. There are passages in Lukács where he maintains that the grasp of historical materialism weakens as one moves away from the capitalist epoch towards earlier times, and where he conversely also considers it likely that the validity of the materialist interpretation of history will cease beyond capitalism. For his part, Dr. Mannheim gives preference to the validity of the Marxist conception of history for the capitalist epoch, and he is prepared to concede economism a preferential heuristic value for pre-capitalist epochs as well, because we have gained, as a result of our mainly economically determined problem situation, a good eye for the significance of the economic in history as a whole. By this method, we make visible in the longitudinal section of history precisely the configurations that are practically most important for us today.

ad (b) Dr. Mannheim leaves open the question of the validity of dialectical thinking for the cosmos and the knowledge of nature, and he does not consider it very important.

Prof. Weber: He does, however, attach importance to this question and he deliberately placed it in the sequence of questions so as to draw attention to the question whether dialectical or proletarian thought does not—just like bourgeois thought, which oriented itself in a one-sided way to natural-scientific thinking alone—represent merely a partial point of view, a partial thinking (i.e., that it is not valid perhaps, first, for all of history, and, furthermore, for knowledge of nature.)

Dr. Mannheim: He confesses his adherence to the conception of Marxism which sees interconnections of thought as a chain which invariably originates in a contemporary necessity, in a spiritual, psychic, physical necessity. The problem of the validity of dialectical thinking for the knowledge of nature does not as yet constitute an essential problem—not yet for Marxism either—and it is better to await the historical ripening of a problem than to erect premature conclusions. This last was exemplified earlier when the thought of natural science was made into the paradigm for thinking as such and all theory of knowledge was oriented to it, and yet existentially connected (*seinsverbunden*), living thought emerged alongside. There will come a time, without doubt, when the two theories of knowledge will confront one another in a final conflict. But today the cultural scientific tasks of Marxism are in the foreground, and the dialectical method does what is needed for these. In comparison, the problem of natural knowledge remains without urgency for Marxism.

Prof. Weber: Is there still such a thing as general validity or only the social standpoint as final arbiter? This is naturally not meant normatively, but only how things stand in fact.

Dr. Mannheim: *ad* (c): In his view, it is in fact the case that the different class standpoints also stand against one another as ultimate theoretical positions of knowledge, not immanently reducible to one another, provided that we neglect the refinements and mediations necessary in detailed study, as we shall do for now. This is not a happy state of affairs, but we must recognize the fact of the existential connectedness of thought. That there will be struggle among the different intellectual standpoints is ordained by fate, and it must be carried out (*vollzogen*) as such. The foundation of every existing standpoint forms and determines its wants and categorical designs, so that even the knowledge it gains possesses only a relative and particular validity. (He has, accordingly, attempted to lay out morphologically and historico-sociologically, the categorical determination by being in the case of conservative thought.) The stream of thought has in fact divided, but it is not the proletariat alone that has a chance of knowledge, as Lukács maintains, but every intellectual standpoint has such a one for its own part. Of course, always only up to the threshold of the concealments that it enacts in its thought, and this boundary always lies at the point of its own basic wants in the social process.

It is precisely research in sociology of knowledge, however, that is the way leading beyond the unmediated separation of the intellectual standpoints to something more inclusive—inasmuch as it recognizes the fact of the existential connectedness (*Seinsgebundenheit*) of knowledge and illuminates this in its analyses and supplies all knowledge with the requisite social equation. It represents the overcoming of the stage at which these intellectual standpoints confronted one another in ideological struggle, blind to one another and each [speaking] in the name of the only truth.

Prof. Weber: But is it really the *knowledge* that is variable and subject to relativization? Or is it only the basic aspirations, intentions and attitudes? Because the object to which they all refer, however different their ways, remains the same. The unity of the object of knowledge is not ruptured, its contents are the same.

Dr. Mannheim: This leads to the question of a sphere of truth-in-itself. But this does not exist in fact, and even if it were hypothesized, it could not be grasped in reality, but rather remain a fiction. No doubt, the unity of the object of knowledge is unruptured, but this unity is of no help since all the ways of knowing this object are different. And it is not only that the aspirations and attitudes are different, but rather that these aspirations at the same time form the entire categorical apparatus of thought and accordingly turn the knowledge itself into something connected to being and differentiated by standpoint. This conception is not however tantamount to mere relativism. In view of this factual connectedness of all knowledge to being, unlimited relativism is rather the outcome of clinging to an absolute conception of truth secluded from any connectedness to being, while, on the contrary, taking this fact as one's point of departure leads only to a *relationism* of knowledge. Without question, such a conception needs a new theory of knowledge which is not yet available. But this could not move back towards conception of truth of the earlier kind, but it must have first swallowed the fact of connectedness to being as presupposition and it must make just this to its starting point. This instance shows again how the growth of a problem to urgency is caused by the process of being, rather than being the unrolling of a previously existing chain of problems. The new theory of knowledge becomes urgent because we have in fact run against the fact of the connectedness of knowledge to being, and we have been forced, because the process of being itself has made it visible, to a confrontation with it.

But the connectedness of knowledge to being does not represent a source of error, but rather an opportunity for discovery. Marxism has thus discovered the element of struggle in thinking, while conservatism discovered the element of contemplation. But with its opportunity of knowing, every knowledge is just for this reason valid only in particular.

Prof. Weber: This is granted for historical knowledge. Although even here there is a progressive process of clarification and the possibility of progressive correction. But he cannot agree with this conception for natural-scientific knowledge.

Dr. Mannheim: There is such a thing as a consensus after the fact in history as well. What is discovered from a certain intellectual standpoint also enters into other intellectual standpoints during the confrontations of the ideological conflict, and it is recognized by tacit consensus as a correct fact—as, for example, the Marxist discovery of class and ideology has made its way.

Ad (d) and (e): Re: the question of meta-intellectualistic thought as against the dialectical. Several ways of thinking doubtless do exist side by side. But in the ideological struggle they conduct themselves in an imperialist manner towards one another as well as towards being.

So it is possible, for example, to proceed in a morphological manner and to put forward certain ultimate completions of form. But intellectualism asks, in protest, whether we must stop at this, and it overshadows the morphological view with its own agenda of questions. Or correspondingly, the obverse: morphology asks whether we must stop at the ultimate arbiter put forward by the intellectualistic view and overshadows intellectualism by comprehending reason as formation.

Marxism does not contest the possibility and the right of morphological parallelization and synopsis, but it asserts that this is not as far as we can go. It is possible to analyze and functionalize far beyond this. And with this, it goes as far as its possible. It must do this because it represents a fighting class that depends on the ability to master being. Because it is activist thought, it must be intellectualistic. And for this aspect it possesses maximal chances for truth—i.e., for knowledge of everything that is subject to rationalization and mastery in history. Dr. Mannheim acknowledges, on the other hand, that not everything has this character, and that, concomitantly, morphology also has its own chances of knowledge. Both attitudes represent only partial perspectives, like all intellectual standpoints. Morphology could not, e.g., ever become the proletarian science—or not, at most, until some later point— because the proletarian lacks, because of his social position, the "leisure" for such a view, as well as the adequate intellectual structure or means. Morphology is essentially connected in its standpoint to the "bourgeoisie," that assumes in this case all the postures of consciousness categorically built up by earlier upper strata with the opportunity for contemplation, and, as if it had a mission to do so, passes these on. When he uses the word "bourgeois," it does not mean the same as it does in the language of a fighting socialist, for whom it designates *eo ipso* a class condemned to go under, but rather an intellectual standpoint that has a function necessary for the future and not fulfillable by any other standpoint. But there is a struggle between the different cognitive standpoints, and such struggle is not only a persistent form but also a class struggle, above all, and to a greater extent than one might first think.

In the meantime, however, the different intellectual standpoints are today in the process of coming closer to one another, because they are all beginning to recognize one another as merely partial views and above all because their own particularity is beginning to become evident to them. And just this is the product of their struggles with one another and the attendant mutual shaking up.

Prof. Weber: But it seems inadequate to him that these problems of thought are formulated at all. It seems to him that something different, more decisive is lying behind this. It is not the polarity of thinking and being that is decisive, but other fundamental powers of existence. And these are here being left aside, or at most the aspirations continue to be included. (That is also what he had called intellectualism in Zurich.) But how did these aspirations come about? What is at issue here are the ultimate attitudes of soul, the ultimate attitudes of the soul towards existence.

Dr. Mannheim: And even if this is the case, he confesses his adherence to this intellectualism, not out of love of reason, but rather because it is without question the primary task of our time to carry intellectualism out to its end. Morphology has its justification over against this, without doubt, if only to protect against our losing what intellectualism does not comprehend. As complementary aspects, intellectualism and morphology are both justified.

Protocol
of the Second Meeting of the Joint Seminars of Prof. Weber and Dr. Mannheim. February 27, 1929.

Faced with the choice between departing from the basis of Thursday's discussion in the direction of problems of truth and ontology or remaining inside the framework of sociological questions, the decision is for the latter, and

Dr. Mannheim: introduces the discussion by raising the question of the fate and problem of the irrational in the present, and by giving it the following more precise form.

The rational and irrational can only be defined in correlation. Thinking that is rationally determined has achievement and the achievable as its paradigm, while the paradigm of the irrational, in contrast, is growth and the growing. This determination is not logically conceptual but oriented to function.

The reaction of the subject to the rational is cognition, while that to the irrational is to let it have a productive and formative effect on himself. What the irrational means to us is something with substantial being that we do not disturb in this quality when we encounter it. Take the example of pedagogy, where the teacher originally works on the student out of his own substantial being, in order to build education up out of the student's center, so that the student develops himself creatively. But in modern pedagogy, there has been a symptomatically significant change, since that which works creatively and substantively is retreating, as the orientation to the rationally achievable and controllable comes ever more to the fore. Thus psychoanalysis, above all, has worked out a rational method for treating things of the soul, where the attempt is made first to analyze things of the soul into certain basic elements and then purposefully to recompose the latter. And just as this trend increases in all fields, the case is the same for sociology, with Max Weber's methodology as paradigm.

We see thinking linked to the irrational in two ways. On the one hand, as thinking within the irrational and out of it (as something at work within the subject himself), and, on the other, as thinking about the irrational so as to rationalize it (with psychoanalysis as example). Dr. Mannheim views it as ever more the present-day fate of the irrational that it is increasingly subjected to the rationalization tendency. And it is a question of finding out just when it is that the field is clear for seeing the irrational in the guise of the achievable. For something has to happen in the realm of substance so that it is possible for this change in the fate of the irrational to commence and increasingly to take effect.

The rational enters at a breach in the enactment (*Vollzug*) of substance. Such a breach can occur, first, in the event of a relocation of the irrational, e.g., from art, where it was earlier alive, to a different layer of existence, where it has not yet been brought to consciousness. This seems at first like a disappearance of the irrational because it operates in its new place, as always, without being recognized. A breach in the enactment of the substantial takes place in a second way, when a social stratum that rests on an effectively irrational foundation is threatened in this foundation of being (through a change in function within the very process of being) and begins to feel this threat come close. Because in the first stage of the process—as we could observe in the history of the rise of conservatism—it reacts to this by rendering the irrational reflective, attempting to preserve it by concentrating on it, withdrawing to its core—and precisely the reflection on the irrational becomes a means to its defense. Here we have a becoming reflective of the irrational arising from vital causes and hence of the greatest existential durability.

Dr. Mannheim believes that he can also assess the morphological historical sociology of Professor Weber in this way. Because in this case too what is at issue is no longer the naive existence of the irrational but a reflection on it. The irrational contents are no longer preserved in their original form. But how? Here too there is a rationalization taking place, but of a different type than that which aims at the "achievable." There is a ratio, a rationalization, presented to us here that was invented and developed by a whole tradition, that is much more refined and supple than the mechanistic one, but that grew out of the same impulse, out of the compulsion to rationalization. Here too, the irrational is to be preserved not in life but only in thought. Morphology simultaneously expands and refines the fateful tendency of rationalization that dominates our age. Morphology addresses itself to the same present as any other rationalization, although from the polar extreme.

The question should not be stated, accordingly, as if thinking were on one side and the irrational on the other, but so that it is a matter of two kinds of rationality and rationalization. On the one side under the heading of the "achievable" and on the other with a dedication to rescuing the irrational. In this connection, Dr. Mannheim suspects that the tempo is set by of the functionalist rationalization process and that the other pole only follows this process, as it were, reactively.

Dr. Mannheim adds to the characterization of these two poles of thought that Marxist thought functionalizes in a manner that dissolves being itself into mere function and leaves nothing substantial intact; while, in contrast, thought that is morphological and oriented towards the irrational, functionalizes too, but functionally relates substantial elements to one another, in the course of which it interrupts the functionalization at certain places, "stops," permits itself to encounter things in their being, and, so to speak, "tastes." But it does not carry this tasting of things as essential entities fully through, because otherwise history would dissolve itself for it into a mere series of images.

After all this, the entire difference between the standpoints seems to him to lie in where one puts a halt to functionalization, and the problem therefore seems to lie in the question of where one stops.

Prof. Weber: He would have to confront Dr. Mannheim's expositions with two question marks. Above all, whether what he wants can be described as a preservation of the irrational, whether this is his actuating motive. Certain ultimate givens upon which he bases himself would have to be held in common with him by others because otherwise there could be no understanding between them. For this reason he had already pointed out in the discussion on Thursday that the questions addressed to history can only arise out of one's own will in the present. Although it goes without saying that instruments can only be rational, he is asking what the domain of the rational may be in history and how it may be embedded in history. Then one could also determine the bounds of the rational. But the preservation of the irrational was never the point of departure for him. His wants from the present aim in a completely active and practical direction, but they are highly complex. They contain rational things too, as well as the fate and standpoint of the working class, etc. Prof. Weber sharply rejects the imputation to himself of the Romantic posture of preserving the irrational. His position is rooted in certain "ideas," in ideal aspirations grounded in a certain posture of the soul, and on this basis he asks how the present looks from the standpoint of [actualizing] these things, about where we are situated in the totality, in history. The point of view of the "achievable" is included in this, since he asks, after all, where we can make changes and where not. It is possible to situate the objects of wants outside of the antithesis formulated by Dr. Mannheim.

Then too, the present is by no means the first [age] to be reflexive because, e.g., work was already done reflexively in Greek art as well as in the Renaissance. The discovery of perspective was completely a matter of reflection for the "experimenting masters." And this notwithstanding all their figurativeness. Moreover, there is reflection in productivity too, which is by no means only a "growing." For these reasons, he goes much further than Dr. Mannheim in overcoming the antithesis of rationality and irrationality. What remains to be ascertained is whether the rational can comprehend certain last things or whether it can at this point only express the authentic inauthentically. Without cavil, he concedes the developmental line of increasing rationalization in general history, but it always concerns only the stance of men towards things for purposes of control, that is only for the "achievable." He relativizes the rational through philosophy of history in a manner corresponding to what Bergson has done through theory of knowledge. Today's highest degree of rationalization simply indicates the usurpation of life by material questions of existence, to which we must practically subordinate everything else today.

Dr. Mannheim: But if Prof. Weber could dispute [Mannheim's] stand-point as "intellectualistic" in Zurich, we must have a clearly express-ible contradiction of positions put before us.

Prof. Weber views the spirit as something meta-intellectual and he limits the intellectual to the relationship with the natural. But [Mannheim thinks that the intellectual] increasingly stretches towards the things of the soul. Thus, the antithesis is not that nature is "achievable" and, over against this, spirit, soul, and man [are all] irrational. The align-ment of the poles is different. It runs diagonally through all the spheres. And he [Mannheim] sees it as the present task to extend the bound-aries of functionalization to the utmost.

Prof. Weber: What he meant by the reproach of intellectualism was that it is not possible still to designate certain things (which he would call "ideas") as types of thinking, because they are essentially different from [thinking]. [Instead, they are] ultimately acts of deportment of the soul, whereby a subject—an I-subject but perhaps a we-subject, also the proletariat, e.g., given the case—creatively unites itself with the object. This unification can appear anywhere, also in an intellec-tual garb. He would call it intellectualism if someone considers this still as thinking. Because in doing this one continues to move within the polarity of thinking and being that originated with the bourgeoisie and has dominated epistemology since Descartes. And he, for his part, wants finally to escape from this bourgeois antithesis.

Dr. Mannheim: Soul and thinking always belong together, in his view, and when he speaks of thinking, he does not limit it to pure "Ratio," to that which is matter for nothing but thought.

Dr. Weber: Dr. Mannheim stretches the concept of thought; and think-ing is identified with contents of consciousness given form under logi-cal categories.

Dr. Mannheim: But there are two such poles of quasi-irrationalist thinking. In the middle, lies the intellectualism of the bourgeois value philosophy, and on both right and left, there stands counterposed the irrationalist attitude of a kind of voluntaristic thinking. The Marxist dialectic is not in the least intellectualistic.

Dr. Sohn-Rethel: [Wonders] whether the opposition between Prof. Weber and Dr. Mannheim on the matter of intellectualism doesn't proceed on different levels. When Dr. Mannheim speaks about "thinking" and "standpoints in thought," he has in mind certain general attitudes towards history and being, which, for their parts, could equally well be rational or irrational in their own structures without thereby ceasing to be such standpoints of "thinking" or, better, simply of consciousness. And since they are different standpoints of consciousness, they are now first subjected to the real process of the historical totality of being, in which they are embedded in their existence. It is only in this relationship of all of these standpoints of consciousness or "thinking" to the historical process of being that enacts itself *through them* that the antithesis of thought and being plays itself out. For this purpose, then, it is properly posed, but it does not compete with contradictories that are located only within the standpoints of consciousness.

Prof. Weber: For him, the posture of consciousness toward being lies in a process different from the creative unification of the subject and object of which he has spoken. In this [process] the antithesis of thinking and being or of being and consciousness is empirically overcome. Admittedly he lacks a sufficient philosophical and epistemological answer to the question about ultimate values and "ideas" and about the inner nature of that creative unification. But if with regard to them a relationship with other men should arise, it would not only be a relationship with them, but a common relationship with being, and these values would have reality for him because he himself would belong to being. That is why, for example, he comprehends aesthetics only as an immanent aesthetics, which belongs to being itself. Although these values are always variable in the process of being, changing together with being, this does not amount to their relativity. Certainly he can only speak with those who share his aspiration to form, but with these values he feels himself connected to something objective and immanent in being, and when he speaks of "holy" and "sublime," and so forth, the attachment in these matters is a connectedness with being (*Seinsverbundenheit*). In this sense, he is very glad to speak of "connectedness with being."

Dr. Sohn-Rothel: But with just such an attitude, people today and people of other times—e.g.,the Renaissance, which was very close to such views—nevertheless remain subject to the functional operation of the enveloping process of historical being. In its totality, this process resembles a mill that absorbs all of these modes of conduct of men, with their postures of consciousness, as mere raw material for its processes, and subjects them to its laws. Marxism concerns itself precisely with recognizing the lawfulness of this process of the historical totality of being, in which, as was said before, all consciousness is caught up, together with its results, because for [Marxism] what is at issue is how it is possible to change this being—this historical total reality—in which we live, with effect and thus in accord with its own laws. Without this knowledge of the historical totality of being and its functional lawfulness, however, all action in the present must necessarily remain ultimately blind to its effects, while Marxism seeks, by way of this knowledge, the central lever within being itself, by means of which it is possible, in harmony with the law of the totality of being, to overturn this same totality of being, and to do so in a manner adequate to what is intended.

Prof. Weber: This standpoint presupposes an aprioristic conception of the totality of being, and in this respect it corresponds to the earlier type of philosophy of history. Here, the empirical world is approached from aprioristic categories and an aprioristic construction of totality. That is naturally possible, and if someone thinks that it will see him through, he should go ahead and try it. From a different layer of totality, however, one does not come first upon such a functional totality of being, but drives, passions, aspirations, postures of consciousness, creative acts. He himself, Prof. Weber, does not look for any philosophy-of-history explanation of the totality of being, but rather analyses the empirical totality available to him, and then comprehends it again synthetically. If in the course of this he notes three spheres (civilizational, social and cultural processes), this is not a construction of philosophy of history. It is merely in service of the effort so to grasp historical totality that anything confronting us empirically is illuminated so as to make it appear in its context of totality. And when one starts with the empirical in this manner, it is questionable whether everything is in fact drawn into the functionalization process of social being. In his view, this would mean that the "social process" had become all-consuming. Perhaps this is the case today, perhaps we really do have such a process of re-biologization or renaturalization today—indeed, of rebarbarization. Then everything would be swallowed up in an automatic process controlling life and what had earlier been a mere underlying support—i.e., that human beings have to eat—would become the ultimate question.

Dr. Sohn-Rothel: In comparison to Marxism, this offers an essentially different concept of the "social process." For Marxism, the social process does not have a natural and biological character; it is not, as for Prof. Weber, the "formation of the natural drives and impulses of will."

Prof. Weber: He calls the social process "natural" only in comparison to formation by the soul.

Dr. Mannheim: What is common to all of us is the determination not to let ourselves be swallowed up by capitalism. And for this reason, Marxism too wants above all to render everything subject to rule. It seeks to preserve the establishment of rule from capitalism. This is its irrational impulse.

While Marxism is constructivist, it is not speculative. And its constructivism is justified by the fact that it seeks to comprehend the totality of the historical process of being. This is impossible without proceeding in a constructivist way. Its points of departure for the construction of totality are grounded in reasons and not simply posited. It is necessary to approach history with expectations of structure and then to see whether these are fulfilled. But these expectations, the heuristic points of departure, are simply different.

Prof. Weber: His own posture towards history, as question, is the same as that of socialism: he does not want capitalism either. And if he has stopped thinking in a Marxist way, it is out of resignation and not on the basis of a different aspiration. Of course, one always approaches empirical materials with the expectation of a structural form, but whether or not one confirms it in one's research is a different matter. But the structural expectation must not be substantively specified, not colored. From his standpoint, he puts no obstacle in the way of analyzing the present situation materialistically. But that would not be enough for him. Earlier times, after all, cannot be comprehended in this way.

Moreover, such a view is insufficient if one wants to see the great continuous line of history. When he poses the question as to the powers to which we are subject today, he will make the attempt to go beyond the analysis of the present day.

Dr. Mannheim: What lessons for the present can one derive from a view of the forms of history? (This meant only as an inquiry.)

Prof. Weber: Above all, an insight into the absolute uniqueness of our contemporary capitalist situation. And from this it follows that all prophecy is nonsense. There is no point of talking of all the parallels with different times and historical developments attempted today (Spengler), or the predictions of decline derived from them. Infinite possibilities exist, as such, and no predetermination whatever. Granted all the arguments for evolution—as they apply to the process of civilization and capitalism—but the situations to which it brings us are always unique. So, for example, no one could have predicted that we would have communism in Russia today. The morphological sociology of history, however, lets us assess the things to which we are in fact subjected, which things must be viewed as irreversible, and how far that goes.

Dr. Eppstein: If one starts from the uniqueness of a historical situation and expands on the free play permitted by the possibilities it presents, the question is whether the two positions do not display a difference in the degree of activity, of aspirations for the present.

Essential for Marxism is where it derives the dialectic as the structure of meaning in the historical process. The freedom of a continuing historical conception sought by Prof. Weber may lead to variations in the level of functionalization in different epochs, corresponding to what is predominant when each gives itself to "vision." Prof. Weber's position rejects continuous historical structures along the lines of growth conceptions (in Scheler's sense), but this does not rule out the recognition of certain formal structural principles. The question is how far functionalization advances and whether this position has a different conception of historical totality, that proves compelling and communicable, to set against the Marxist dialectic. And if he attempts to provide such a conception, the question arises whether he does not hypostatize his structural scheme of history dogmatically, just as Scheler does.

Prof. Weber: He does not by any means hypostatize his structural scheme. He divides the three spheres only in thought, not in actuality. The totality of history comprises their unity. And if he attempts this mental division, the attempt is determined by his aspirations for the present. For anyone with different aspirations for the present—and thus with different questions for history—these categories are not decisive. But this scheme of the structure of totality is more than a mere heuristic value. This applies only to certain partial results. The conception of totality, however, is something essentially different, something completely bound up with a world-view. The questions he poses are shaped by a certain aspiration to a form for the present, which is, incidentally, not at all contemplative (this emphasized for Dr. Mannheim). Above all, he begins with the question of what is to become of the proletariat under capitalism. And he undertakes his whole analysis of history only on the basis of such activation of his aspiration for the present. If one starts out from a belief in the dialectical self-transcendence (*Aufhebung*) of capitalism, in contrast, all this is unnecessary. That is when one's relationship to history is altogether contemplative.

Dr. Mannheim: But how does the view of form in history escape determinism, the antinomy between determinism and freedom?
Prof. Weber: He is completely indifferent to freedom. When I think rationally, I must think deterministically. It is one thing to say that here we are subject to determination and there we are free, and quite different to say that we may always be subject to determination but unable to know it, to predict the future. This also touches on the difference between causal inquiry and evidentiary interpretation in history.

There are so infinitely many causal links in history that there can be no thought of grasping them all. Nor did Max Weber ever think of an all-encompassing causal inquiry. He always offered only "aspects," i.e., special causal analyses for specific individual problems of special importance (e.g., this was specifically noted in his study of the "Protestant Ethic and the Spirit of Capitalism"). He, Prof. [Alfred] Weber, does not engage in any causal investigation at all. Instead, he takes whole complexes of causal linkages as given, without analysis, and, in that condition, he incorporates them within a total inspection. His aim is always only interpretation, never causal explanation. For that reason, he is not subject to the antinomy of determinism and freedom.

Dr. Mannheim: For the proletariat, things stand different. It wants determinism because it affirms the determined goal, because its aspirations coincide with the determinations. The Marxist view appears as blind determinism only from the outside, while for the proletariat it means freedom itself. Here too, what counts as "freedom" and what as "determinism" is fixed perspectivistically. The proletarian view of history counts as blind determinism to the opposition because its aspirations go in the opposite direction. The opposition wants and needs indeterminacy; this means freedom for them, but just the reverse for the proletariat. That is why, in the last analysis, the proletariat sees and pursues structures, and the opposition emphasizes that which is freely formed and not structurally determined. Assume, however, that the proletariat's aspiration for freedom has been fulfilled, that socialism has been made reality, then both aspects have their justification, side by side and simultaneously, because then the structural view is no longer enough for the proletariat, it also needs form. Both in the name of its freedom.

Prof. Weber: If it was Dr. Mannheim's aim to "relationize" him [Weber] with this, he cannot expect that [Weber] will follow him in this, and if [Mannheim] is challenging him to "encapsulate" [Mannheim] in turn, he will decline, because that does not correspond to his attitude. The standpoint that he [Weber] represents offers no less a complete embrace of precisely the proletarian standpoint, because he grew up [in that standpoint] on the basis of an origin in [the proletarian standpoint] and a going beyond it.

Appendix
Karl Mannheim to Alfred Weber (July 25, 1938)[62]

My dear, greatly admired Mr. Weber:

From far away, I would like to be counted among those who are gathered around you on your 70th birthday, to offer you our thanks for the past and to wish you good courage for the future.

All of us imagined this day differently. Above all, it would have been self-evident to have proclaimed our affiliation with you through a publication as well as our personal presence. If this nevertheless fails to take place and if because of this your influence is not visible for all to see, I want to proclaim, just for this reason, that, according to my feelings, your living influence is among the greatest that teachers of social science in Germany were able to exert.

If this is not always so obvious as to be provable through citations, this is only because your influence was far too comprehensive and essential to be simply established and circumscribed. In my own case, thus, I can say that, quite apart from substantive matters, it is only from you that I learned what a seminar could be. For you, the meaning of this institution is as an arena for genuine spiritual contact and the awakening of the courage for free creative association. In your seminar, it was possible to learn how a magisterial teacher can avoid suppressing the originality of his students by his authority. Even the youngest beginner had the courage of his convictions because he had a person before him who had the strength, after lifelong study and struggle, to keep awake in himself the fruitful attitude of a beginner. I dare say that most of your students became somehow different simply through the fact of spiritual contact with you, and that each of your suggestions somehow arose fruitfully in us at some unexpected moment.

As an anecdote, I want to tell you something that I shall never forget. When a philosopher with a long beard wanted to force me, year after year, to think as he did, and when I then came to you to submit my work, I was struck by the fear that you would similarly control whether my thoughts reproduced yours. Then you said, to my great surprise: "I will read your work, but it has already been accepted, for you are an adult and must say what you think right."[63]

These sentences have had a lasting impact on me. It is only because of this experience that I overcame, from the outset, the teacher's dangerous inclination to attempt to form students in his own image. This attitude of yours is, however, simultaneously the explanation for the fact that you have spiritually independent students everywhere in the world, who, though they will always declare themselves for you in the depths of their souls, are much too independent to form a school in the usual sense, one that fights for one-sided principles or appears self-enclosed like a sect, unified by a dogma.

It is too bad that those of us who are far away hear so little about you personally. We only know that you work without respite; and we all wish to become acquainted with the new development of your thoughts. My wife and I can only imagine you in your perpetual youthfulness, and we hope that it will still be present today without interruption. Preserve it for us, since we all need the assurance of a center and a source of strength that unites people of the same spirit, beyond all boundaries.

In heartfelt memory and faithful loyalty,
Your, Karl Mannheim.

6

On Religious Experience
and Rationalization

Interventions in the "Frankfurt Discussions" with Paul Tillich, Max Horkheimer, Theodor Wiesengrund [Adorno] and others. June, 1931[64]

On June 27, 1931, the theologian Paul Tillich, recently appointed professor of social education in the unorthodox philosophy department in Frankfurt, organized a day long meeting between members of the informal Frankfurt discussion group who were his regular partners in intense talk about social and political questions and a number of Protestant theologians, several of whom were not a little skeptical of Tillich's secular involvements and social-philosophical religious thought. The immediate occasion was the soul-searching within the Church about the Christian mission in a secularized world, an inquiry given urgency by perplexity about the role of Protestantism in the face of the social and political conditions of the worldwide Depression. The participants included, in addition to "dialectical theologians" interested in Tillich, not only Karl Mannheim but also the classical humanist philosopher and university curator, Kurt Riezler, who brought most of these leftist thinkers to Frankfurt, and the three principals in the new Institut für Sozialforschung, Max Horkheimer, Theodore Wiesengrund [Adorno], and Friedrich Pollock. In his own first intervention Tillich defines the overall situation as one where the autonomization of culture and the rise of the proletariat critically challenge Christian thought and action. Mannheim concludes that he cannot accept the available religious formulations of this world, but he will also not accept the impoverishment of human encounters, their reduction to functional responses. He wishes for a restoration of deeper encounter experiences and must find a way of expressing this undertaking without denying his modernity or accepting the premature gratification offered by the old theology. Modernity and rationality and sociology belong together, in short, and Mannheim will not deny his calling to any of them. Somehow Mannheim wants to show that sociology is indispensable to that which sociology reveals to the sociologist it cannot do, just as the most complete rationality is inescapable for moderns who cannot live by rationality alone.

I would like to speak as an example of a person that you would have to convert, if you speak of a mission, specifically as one who does not know what he might gain from this conversion, and I would like to tell you what need this person would like to have met (*wofür er etwas haben möchte*). The word that has seized me (*das mich ergriffen hat*)[65] and that has joined me (*Anschluß*) to the presentations, is that primal religious impulses (*Urmotive*) are suddenly appearing in all circles, everywhere in the world, and that we are faced with a general situation in which this is going on. Interestingly, however, it is happening only in an atomized way. Everyone experiences it by himself. It has not yet merged in a movement but rather arises in everyone out of the common or similar situation.

First, an aside from the viewpoint of the sociologist: it is possible to think first of the political function of these things, and this question must be disposed of at some point. If the progressive currents we call the leftist political movement or enlightenment or industrialization— all the incursions that emanate from the new factors in universal history—drive towards polarization in a certain direction, then those circles which because of their location either do not want to go along or cannot do so must also collect themselves on the basis of a polarization. One could say that these primary religious impulses have only reactionary value. In a high percentage of cases, they undoubtedly arise from this impulse. Whenever this is the symptomology, I stand, as a person who desires a changed world, unequivocally on the other side. But these primal religious impulses do not spring only from this source. Politically, in any case, that is the function I see. I reject it, and do not want to discuss it further.

But I see an element that is independent of this locus, arising in individuals who do not want this element of vitality (*Lebenselement*) for anything politically retrograde, no restoration of a lost sanctuary but who, quite to the contrary, want to comprehend the new man from this point of view. The question is (and that is the question of the one who is yet to be converted) why should I not form these emerging primal religious impulses anew, out of my own situation? The answer would be that the spiritual and religious contents can only be stated in the traditional language. The positive sense of what you offer in response is to say that you cannot deal with these primal religious impulses without relying on conceptions that arose in earlier times, and this can be offered by a secularized religion that keeps itself very much independent of the church. What are these primal religious impulses, and what does tradition mean?

Every human being who has radically experienced rationalization, as I have done as a sociologist, tends to act like the vintner who smashed and demolished all about him as his vineyard was being destroyed by hail: "we'll soon see who first finishes it off." He wants to pursue rational thought to its conclusion, and he wants to get to the conclusion as quickly as possible. There is no doubt that the industrial, rational, sociological world causes the disappearance of certain forms of experience, certain forms of encounter, certain forms of self-explanation, certain kinds of possibilities; but the human being is more than this rationalized world, and these repressed elements are latently present in us and seek for a different form; and it is by no means a part of modern man that he represses these elements as well.

The distinctive way in which we gain insight into the other person cannot be grasped by psychoanalysis. But the old constructs by which a language of mythologization attempts to comprehend this are no longer tenable. When one has pushed rationalizing to its conclusion, one sees that the primal religious impulses are simply existentially there, and that they can also create problems for latter-day men. Is it really the case that things develop in men only in a forward direction? That side of the matter has been emphasized so often, that it is necessary to put emphasis on the other side as well. In the rediscovery of earlier elements, the point of orientation is never in the past, but in the new, in that which is emerging within us. This I call the utopian element in us. The forward orientation is already constitutive in viewing any individual object. Not the past determines what can be extracted from the past, but rather it is something present in us, out of the contemporary predicament of our life, *(Lebensnot)*, to drive us forward.

If I wanted to let the primal religious impulses that are present speak out, it would be a danger to take over the concepts formed by earlier religious experiences. I would rather stutter than to take over something that prematurely disposes of the phenomenon for me. When I ask, accordingly, what can be offered to me by a religious person, someone who stands somehow in the tradition (and this is said abstractly for the moment), or what can a Protestant theologian offer me, I would be afraid, in my suspicion and rejection, that what he can give me is the most dangerous thing, the words that originate in a different situation—and men of the present would do better to stutter. They get more when they wrestle with their errors than when they take over earlier formulations.

That is the first thing that may be said by way of objection.

*   *   *

Before we can even turn to substantive matters, it is necessary first to make some answer to the reproaches coming from the group that asked how it is even possible to occupy ourselves with primal religious impulses when men outside are hungry. I am in a difficult situation because I shall later have to talk about the primal religious impulses and in this context about the problem of God as well, and modern man is in the peculiar situation of shame that he speaks without inhibition about subjective matters but only with difficulty about God. A readiness to help and the solidarity with the proletariat is a matter of course, and it should be said. But one should not dispose of everything by this way of arguing. It is the most important thing, but there are limits to calling on it. And for me the matter becomes dangerous when the attempt is made to put a stop to every concrete set of problems with this, which goes without saying.

I want to say another thing in defense of the possibility of discussing primal religious impulses. If this set of problems is posed by my life, albeit in secular form, it is wrong to ask whether it is a *cura posterior*. I believe that unconditional evidence (*absolute Evidenz*) is available about the possibility of speaking about things, namely, if they are burning, if they occupy one, if they are set as a task.

The 7 percent (the terms elite and mass are wrong),[66] this small number, that has become fateful as a result of a sociological process, can legitimate itself. It lacks legitimation today if it does not understand itself on the basis of the others, if it does not recognize that it is living a representative life for others—whether one does this in an aristocratic manner through cultivation or through deepening of the soul, in the sense that one uses one's leisure not for dancing but to reach different layers of the soul—that is a representative function of which one need not be ashamed, in awareness that a humanity is forming itself by this means in which everyone, once they have a higher income, can join. If one thinks of it this way, it becomes clear that one is merely a vanguard, who has to deal earlier with certain problems that others will also reach. I can afford this good social conscience, if I also take serious part in the other. But it is simply the fact of the matter that I am brought into certain things sooner than the others. It is by no means necessary that the intelligentsia can only legitimate itself by a self-ironization as a spiritual canaille that can achieve nothing on its own for humanity. It should not degrade itself to this extreme. What I would rather hear and continue to contribute is what the intelligentsia can offer in return, so as to be able continue using it in the common struggle. One must have the courage of one's position, for it is a vanguard position.

All this as a prelude, so to speak, a *captatio benevolentiae* addressed to the one small group. Now it is the turn of the other group, with which I find it hard to speak in the same sense, if only because of terminological inhibitions. One ought to talk about God, and I do not want to evade this. I believe that the question of God must be posed here in a quite extreme form. Scheler has said, and I must go along with this: if there is a God and if he is supposed to matter to me, then, in view of the modes of experience, it can only be a personal God. Because the highest form in which I can be addressed is not spirit, machine, natural law, or anything altogether sublime, but the primal experience of personality. It must be possible for me to speak with him, he must be able to address me. That is the feeling I have unconditionally, perhaps from childhood, as a matter of genetic inheritance (*Erbgut*), on the basis of the modes of encounter that one has as a human being. Either a God or none—and if so, then a personal God. I must be able to beg his pardon, to pray to him; he must have this personal quality.

I cannot accept the intermediate stages that are placed between man and God, stages that are already installed by Protestantism. The development to the point of the Hegelian World Spirit arose out of this spirit of retreat. Spiritualization arose for the sake of the intellectuals, who found the simple personal conception hard to defend and who were able to arrange God for themselves only in this pantheistic form. This spiritualized God is of no use to me. On the one hand, it is the historical merit of Protestantism to have carried this process into effect, but on the other hand, it is a renunciation of much unconditional evidence and generative force.

If I return to the primal question of either a personal God or none, I cannot come to any conclusion but that I do not know. One thing I do know. A personal God has never addressed me. I have indeed have experiences that you would call religious. But to experience these as if I had encountered a personal God could only be done by a man from the middle ages. I can provide a phenomenological description of what I call self-encounter, but only as a being thrown back (*Zurückgeworfensein*) on my own loneliness, the innermost source that springs up within myself and that is ecstatic—and yet not so that a strange voice speaks into me, as a medieval mystic would say. Because I want to be just so exact (and modern man is like that) and because I have experienced it in this way, I cannot say that a personal God has spoken, and I remain silent about it. I have not had him directly, but that is not all right (*in Ordnung*). And things are not all right with the world, there is something wrong with the ever greater analytical breakdown (see [the earlier example of the vintner in the] hailstorm), something is lost. I also cannot see how my understanding could reach the point where it could say that there is nothing behind it all.

As I carry out the business of the hailstorm ever more radically, and penetrate the world with rational-functional thought, it is an exciting game to gain an immanent and sociological understanding of the world. But the more I drive the devil—or, as the case may be, God—out of the world, the more I discover that I have also driven out man. That is the first occasion upon which the primal religious impulses break out in me.

What I discover is that there is a certain schematic of thought at work in this whole mode of explanation, in accordance with which one attempts to investigate, of all the things in the world, only the apparatus of reactions. That is what modern man needs. Our relations become ever more superficial, they turn into practical reactions (*Handlungsreaktionen*) because we do not have time enough to pay more attention to others. This factor comes with industrialization. With this kind of thinking—being attuned to reactions and calculating them—everything becomes transparent to me, but I repress ever more—what we call modes of encounter.

These are incredibly plentiful in the religious world, and registered there, if only in a terminology that I cannot accept, i.e., with reference to a theological system. But it is clear that the modes of encounter—the ways in which another person presents himself to me—are becoming ever more impoverished. When we have finished driving God out by the method of the hail, we shall see how much has been excluded. The experience of encountering others in a certain mode of encounter is not merely reactive, and it was contained in the forms of religious experience of the world. I would like to wish its restoration. But I would like to find my own terms for this mode of encounter because I have the feeling that the old ones provide a premature gratification (*frühzeitige Befriedigung*).

*   *   *

NB: Mannheim's only other intervention comes at a point where the stenographic record breaks down. It comes after an intervention in which Horkheimer protests against Tillich's attempts to privilege sociology and to make sociology a support for religion. Dibelius says something and then Mannheim says, "The Communist theory can accomplish this too," whereupon Dibelius says: "I have not claimed that Christianity is the only possible allocation of meanings (Sinngebung); that is a different matter." In context, it seems that he is simply stating a sociological reservation, but the matter is uncertain. Horkheimer's statement, incidentally, includes: "The demonstration of connections between some ideology and world views with a social interest cannot in logic conclude anything about their truth."

7

On the Historical Character of Concepts

Letter of Karl Mannheim to Max Wertheimer[67]

In Mannheim's letter to his Frankfurt colleague Max Wertheimer, he offers an amplification of the themes of knowledge and distantiation from the 1930 lecture series. According to an apologetic note handwritten on the typed text by Mannheim, the letter was composed after a meeting of the Frankfurt "Kant-Gesellschaft," but mailed later. From the context, it seems that Mannheim may have been the presenter on the original occasion. The organization was evidently an important meeting ground for the academics introduced by Becker and Riezler. On July 15, 1931, for example, Max Horkheimer delivered a talk on Marx at the Kant-Gesellschaft, under the title, "History and Psychology." (MHA) Discussants included Mannheim, Riezler, Tillich, Solm-Rethel, Wiesengrund [Adorno], and Löwith. Wertheimer, who was also born into a Jewish family in the Habsburg Empire (Prague), is regarded as the most original member of the group responsible for the Gestalt theory of psychology, although he published very little. Without a university appointment after his doctorate in 1905, he engaged in private scholarship and secured his habilitation in 1912 at the Frankfurt Commercial Academy, which was the precursor of the university. As a Jew, he did not receive a regular university appointment until 1922. During the Republic he taught in Berlin until 1929, when he became a professor and co-director of the Psychological Institute and Philosophical Seminar in Frankfurt. He was dismissed by the Nazis in the Spring of 1933. He finished his career at the New School for Social Research in New York City. Like Mannheim, he was inter-

ested in the epistemological implications of his theory. In his own writings, Mannheim treated Gestalt theory as a continuator of romantic thought, a form of "organicist" and "morphological" method that he sharply distinguished from his own.[68]

2. May 1931

Dear Mr. Wertheimer,

With this letter I enclose a copy of "Conservative Thought"[69] for your friendly perusal. Unfortunately, I can give you only a proof, since I have no other copies left. I was very grateful for your interest and would be even more grateful for a talk about these problems when you have time. At the moment, I just want to emphasize that you should not let the tone of our discussion lead you to misunderstand that it is precisely the exchange with you that I find especially stimulating and interesting.

With regard to our last discussion, I want to note that my basic design (*Grundintention*) of depicting the spiritual in its distinctive [sociological] qualities is by no means governed by the aim of dispensing with the spiritual object as a standard of judgment for assertions. Nor is it my intent to exempt spiritual phenomena from the methodology of the natural sciences (in the broadest sense). With regard to the last point I would like to note that I am especially against the rift between the natural and human sciences that prevails in Germany, and that in almost every course I place emphasis on a sphere of calculability in the spiritual.

What keeps coming up in our discussion is, above all, [my] claim that, with historical-spiritual objectivities, one cannot simply project present phenomena into the past. Thus, for example, when Herr Riezler maintains that the Greeks also had the phenomenon of existence but did not articulate it as the separation of subject and object, I can only say that [in that event] the Greeks did not have the phenomenon of existence. For the phenomenon of existence constitutes itself only in a series of acts of distantiation, the most important of which are as follows:

a. One distances "things" and makes them into mere objects by taking from them the qualities imparted by their settings in place and time (*Umwelt-und Mitweltcharaktere*).

b. In the same way one objectifies ones own "experiences" by not remaining inside the performance of an act (*Aktvollzug*), but rather objectifying this act, as well, through distantiation.

c. One distances the "self" by not simply "being" it, but rather counterposing it to oneself.

Through this distantiation of everything that was ego, surrounding world and self-world, where one even keeps slipping out of the direct performance of one's own acts, a situation arises—not only on the level of theory, but also on the level of one's possession of self and world—in which bare existence and the "world in the position of object" stand counterposed. For existence to become a problem, one must have gone through all that (*vollzogen*); while its becoming a problem is then, on the other hand, an existential component of the experience of existence. This last sentence brings us to our specific disagreement. You assert in opposition to this conclusion that becoming conscious and "becoming a problem" are something secondary that does not belong to the object under investigation. In our example, this would mean that whether or not the experiencing subject thinks about the phenomenon of existence, interprets it, or becomes self—aware (*reflexiv*) about it could not affect the phenomenon in its modes of being, in its being-in—itself. It makes no difference for existence, then, whether its interpretation was mythic for the Greeks or becomes philosophical for moderns in the subject-object determination.

In general, I would say, what a person thinks about his experience, his self-interpretation, is [of course] not identical with what he actually experiences. On the other hand, however, I believe that one's self-interpretation of an experience, the meaning one gives it, is a constitutive element of the experience itself. This interpretation, moreover, is not to be taken at face value, i.e., not as *knowledge* of the actual content (*Wasgehalt*) of experience, but as a component of the same, as documentation of that which actually constitutes itself in experience. (See postscript).[70] What is specific to spiritual objects is precisely that they can constitute themselves only in experience, and that the foundations of their "actual contents" are the diverse modifications of the act of execution (*Vollzugsakt*), as well as the interpretive designs (*Sinngebungsintentionen*) contained in them, in all their possible variations. A stone remains a stone no matter what I may think about it, but my religious experience, for example, is no longer religious experience if I include my knowledge of this experiencing in the experience.

By means of this "inclusion" not only do I modify it, but also it is changed, its substance is transformed, and it becomes something else ontologically.

The object "experience of existence" cannot appear where thorough objectification has not come into effect (as perhaps with the Greeks); one can speak only of something that can be addressed as a historical precursor of this experience, or as an embryo out of which the experience of existence developed. Just as the fin-de-siècle mood registered by literary and intellectual history cannot be described as one of the invariant modalities of human psychic life (*Seelenleben*), since it does not appear in primitive groups, who lack the requisite self reflexivity and irony. The experience of existence is similarly a historical phenomenon. To reformulate this in over-pointed fashion: while the object in non-material history (*Geistesgeschichte*) is not identical with what the historical subject contributes by way of self interpretation, the manner of self-interpretation immediately changes the quality of this object's meaning and thereby makes it into a new object. As such, this object (in this case just like the natural object) can be understood rightly or wrongly by the researcher. The means of knowing are subject to objective criteria and, at this level of the problematic, the problem of relativism cannot arise.

I hope that I have expressed myself in writing with some degree of clarity about this somewhat difficult matter, and that we have at least arrived at a point where we can calmly discuss the matter at some time.

With the best regards, also to your wife, from the both of us,

K. MANNHEIM

P.S. Since you have already shown this generous interest in my writings, I will take the liberty of making available for you to read my other work relevant to our discussion. There I have attempted to distinguish the three phenomena that constantly overlap one another in these kinds of objects.

8

The Contemporary Tasks of Sociology: Cultivation and the Curriculum

Gegenwärtsaufgaben der Soziologie: 33–57[71]

The portion translated below represents about one-half of the bro-
chure published by Mannheim, containing the text of his presentation
to a meeting of all teachers of sociology in Germany on February 29,
1932. While the struggle over sociology had earlier been about the
recognition of the discipline and the appointment of new professors,
the economic conditions made the latter issue irrelevant and trans-
muted the former into a question of securing enough students when
cognate disciplines promised more vocational benefit and required
strict adherence to extensive requirements. Reluctantly, the sociology
teachers spoke of the need to come closer to the guild practices of
other disciplines, beginning with the delineation of examinable disci-
plinary boundaries and qualifications. The leading professors—nota-
bly von Wiese, Mannheim, and Freyer—agreed on certain common
formulas for transmitting their demands to the education authorities,
but Mannheim, as host, used the occasion to develop an expansive
rationale and program for the discipline. He says that his aim is not to
put forward the "sociology that can alone save our souls," but to
answer the questions about "the contents that should be offered to
university students and in what pedagogical-didactic form." (1)
The present selection covers the principles that should determine
the choice of subject matter. In the brochure, it is preceded by a
classification of sociological subjects, which marks some advance on

Mannheim's 1930 scheme. As "specialized discipline," sociology may be taught in an unhistorical-axiomatic manner (like von Wiese), in a comparative, typological form (like Max Weber), and in an historical-individualizing manner (which Mannheim says must "crown" the others (9)).[Sociology is also available as an approach to the subject matter of other disciplines, including not only literature and law but also knowledge as cultural objectification. The third grand category of sociology, according to Mannheim, is "sociology as a teaching about the total interconnectedness of social-spiritual happenings, or cultural sociology." (22) Sociography and current studies also belong to sociology. Mannheim's point is that all of these forms are legitimately parts of the discipline and that their integration should be governed by the principles discussed below.

The question is what should we select from the wealth of sociological materials available to us [as teachers]? What principles should govern our choice? We must pose this question with a full sense of our responsibility. As historians and sociologists, we realize that the original constellation of a science shapes its later form, and that its teaching form, above all, tends to work back on its scientific one. So, philosophy and the human sciences in Germany are strongly marked by the constellation of their origins, which was given form by romanticism and historicism at the beginning of the nineteenth century. Both the positive and negative qualities of the historicist-romantic approach still characterize the definition of problems in the human sciences. The limits placed on the formative questions of the human sciences, as well as on the concurrent philosophical design, still constrain today's fabric of inquiry, and, without anyone intending it, things have been left where the earlier generation too remained unable to advance. The conceptual forms that emerged then will still long determine what can penetrate these disciplines from the empirical realm and what these same concepts necessarily conceal. The simple fact that romanticism in Germany discovered history but not society, and the spirit but not the meaning of the concrete, empirical psyche—with all its hidden paths and evasions—continues to mark our human-scientific research, which even today, in keeping with this angle of approach, only knows two basic concepts: spirit and historicity. As a result it obscures all of the issues that French sociology has worked out ever more acutely for itself and for related disciplines as well, viz., the life of society and its significance for the psychological construction of concrete social human types, or, putting it a little simply, the power of conditions to shape human beings.

Even today almost all of the official German ontology and epistemology remains enthralled by this particular approach, for which "historicity" and "spirit" exist, but not concrete human beings in their social and natural situations, with empirically observable ways of behaving. Approaches of this kind are simply dismissed as shallow positivism and as belonging to the natural sciences. As much fruitful matter as this approach may have extracted from the historicity of all human happenings, as fruitfully synthetic as it is possible to operate with the concept of spirit, insofar as it is a question of working out interconnections that extend beyond the particular existence of the individual and that concern works and objectifications, just as much is this approach to problems blind, even today, when it comes to a question of ascertaining the most elementary state of the facts and of working out the significance of social group life for spirit and history. Interestingly, the gift for empirical observation fails at this point no less than do methodological reflection and the positing of ontological grounds. In so far as anything at all was said about such matters in the course of German development, it originated with the extra-academic opposition, which built upon French or English approaches to these problems, as was already the case with Lorenz v. Stein, Marx, and, later, Nietzsche. This shows how decisive the starting point and initial problem formulation can be for the future fate of a science.

If today there is an awakening of demand for the inclusion of the sociological point of view in the posing of problems in the human sciences, this too has a sociological cause. This desire does not simply emerge from the *immanent* development of human-scientific inquiry, but is rather a reflection of the fact that the extra-academic circles for whom the sociological approach first became urgent are encroaching ever more in the academic sphere. This is happening in proportion to the contacts and exchanges taking place in public life between them and the traditional representatives of official science. The categories and angles of observation of the two groups of thinkers are also ever more in the process of mutual penetration. This suffices to make it clear that more than methodological considerations are at issue, and that in this situation of a new beginning it is necessary to possess, as far as possible, express criteria for ruling and regulating the selection of subject matter. We are at present more concerned with a clear derivation of these criteria of selection than with their concrete implementation. The concrete program can always be modified in the light of experience and adjusted to situations, to the extent that one has first succeeded in developing points of view and guidelines. These points of view and guidelines, to which we now turn, do not simply express the purely theoretical requirements of sociology. They are gained, rather, from an analysis of the *general situation* whose needs sociology as teaching subject is supposed to satisfy in the present stage of development. In this sense, we distinguish three groups of demands affecting the selection of subject matter and the pedagogical shaping of sociology:

a. demands of the *present general state of society*;
b. demands from the *present condition of the academic teaching enterprise*; and
c. demands arising from the *present condition of the research enterprise*, from the general situation in science.

A. Demands from the State of Society

The rise of the sociological orientation to life appears to be obviously connected to the spread of the democratic social order. As the bourgeois citizen gains a right of co-determination in government, as compared to the political order of princely absolutism, it seems to become ever more important, in the same measure, to place him in a position to make an intelligent judgment of the political-social interconnections among events. What the bourgeoisie originally captured for itself alone gradually becomes common property of a spreading social democracy. The fact observable at the same time that dictatorships may very easily arise out of these democracies does not speak against this insight of an ever more radical democratization of politics. Modern dictatorship is itself democratic, if also only in this respect, because it too must be supported by the masses. It is not imposed from above by the prince or some oligarchy, but it has had to be at least tolerated, since its inception, by the masses. At our level of development, this tacit consensus of passivity arises on the basis of the inclusion in principle of all citizens in political life. What is new is exactly that in the modern age the integration of wills can be set in motion from below. Notably, the ruled are not originally passive in the modern age, but only through neutralization of their previously awakened activity. If one does not want this reality, this constitutive universal aliveness of modern society, to lead from a "democracy of reason" to a "democracy of feeling," in which the great majority acts only under the sway of momentary feelings, it is necessary that democracy must sooner or later be linked to mass enlightenment and schooling, which carries to the broad masses the forms of thinking and orientation that had hitherto been available only to very small ruling circles. The older ruling groups that ruled from on high always possessed some of the Machiavellian calculation that has the courage to consider even the processes of society as calculable sequences, by and large. If society is not to be swamped by anarchy as a result of the mere democracy of feeling, this view and this courage must percolate downward and govern the responsible citizen. What can naturally not be expected from such sociological orientation, from such capacity to reason social and political events through to their conclusions, is the disappearance of conflicts of interests. Much would already be achieved, however, if everyone were able promote his interests, properly understood, and, by virtue of the same reasoning with which he considers his advantage, to recognize the location of the boundary where his own partial interests are restricted at a given moment by the solidarity interests of the larger group. He must be able at each moment to consider carefully where the boundary lies, the transgressing of which by someone furthering his own demands threatens the existence of the framing group. People who think rationally are calculable; and it is always possible, where they are concerned, to move the frictions arising from a conflict of interests towards a dynamic, constantly renegotiated settlement and equilibrium. In the case of masses and hordes ruled only by feelings and "myths," in contrast, settlements will be achieved only in the manner of blind natural happenings, as happens with certain barbaric primitive people, through the destruction of the two contending sides. As far removed as we may still be from the universal dissemination of the sociological orientation, it has become much more widespread than it was a century ago. Social circles that had no entry to these spheres in earlier generations are now thinking in a political and sociological manner. It is necessary for this ever more widely distributed sociological orientation to become a common possession at a much different tempo than before. The refined social mechanism represented by industrial society cannot function if its operations are constantly interrupted by incursion from external irrationalities. The democratization of social life, in the widest sense, and especially the democratization of politics, in the sense of the potential co-participation of the broad masses, makes it imperative to subject the latter to sociological-civic schooling. This provides a basis for understanding French curricular efforts to create and teach a kind of sociological civics.

The more clear the need for a *political sociology* is shown to be in this context, the more energetically must one try to present these curricular contents to students in as value-free and non-agitational a way as possible. For it would be the death of sociology if it were to become nothing but the agitational instrument of one or more parties. It would be no less damaging, however, if sociology were fastidiously to avoid the political and social topics of life and our current existence from fear of giving offense, and if it were to withdraw, purely out of caution, to heights of abstraction where, in this respect at least, no harm could befall it. The art of the sociologist consists in talking about themes of the greatest relevance and urgency in a manner such that one communicates everything knowable needed to judge the materials realistically, while also presenting all possible alternative judgments in their proper contexts, so as to put one's own opinions as teacher equally in question. In this regard, the highly instructive dispute about value neutrality in the social sciences has pointed the way to a manner of teaching politics without suggestion and valuation of judgments. And even if the sociology of knowledge has called attention to several complications in this connection—complications that leave every account with a remainder of bondedness to social location, despite full self-denial in evaluation or "value-freedom"—it did this not to open the door to every kind of arbitrariness, but precisely for the sake of a still more complete self-regulation and objectivity. Interesting as we may find the attempts to extend our argument about the existential connectedness of thinking by tendencies employing the doctrine to legitimate their ever more questionable principles, we also consider certain conclusions that have been drawn from it to be dangerous. And when this theory goes so far as to give rise to the exaggerated notion that "a will that is true is a warrant for true knowledge," the door has been opened to every kind of arbitrariness in theory.[72] Who would not step into the intellectual arena armed with the conviction or pretense of a "will that is true?" And who in such a situation would not be pleased to be excused in future from having to make a properly substantiated case and to be permitted, instead, to invoke his inspiration and genuine conviction? Taken this way, the task imposed by insight into the reality of the existential connectedness of thinking is misdirected, because the insight no longer serves self-criticism and distantiation from existential bonds, as originally intended. Instead, it legitimates every conceivable kind of partisanship. On this point, the discussion will have to show the extent to which social-scientific knowledge is able ever more to master its existential connectedness the more critical it becomes and the more aware of its existential ties, thereby increasing its chances of escaping from propagandistic arbitrariness.

While sociology arose as an oppositional science and while it continues to gain its most fruitful insights from its critical posture, it is important to note, sociology does not identify with any of the points of view that are open to it, like socialism. Sociology as such is born out of the conflict among the various collectively asserted attitudes to society; and, if one insists on a common denominator to which all of its tendencies can be imputed, one would have to say that sociology is the life orientation appropriate for man in industrial society, leaving open the question whether this society is organized on capitalist or socialist foundations. The courage and the will to subject even lived social space to rational scrutiny first arises at this stage of society. For this society cannot maintain itself in the long term if the individuals comprising it are unable to exercise rational foresight, if they do not learn to act responsibly on the basis of factual diagnoses. (This "industrial" genesis says nothing, however, against the applicability and validity of a rational view for other ages.) A man of industrial society needs a sociological orientation just to make his way as an individual, if he wants to pursue a half-way complex "career." As early as a Balzac novel, one of the characters arrives at the insight that it is possible to rise in modern society only if one subjects to meticulous study the laws of the society in which one seeks to move upward. The Balzacian novels are themselves an attempt to work out such a sociological natural history of civil society. Their special charm, however— to stay with this point for a moment—consists in their sense for the fantastical that is in fact present in this society despite all rationality, or perhaps precisely within this very element of rationality. If it already true in the case of a problem of *individual* advancement in a somewhat complex situation that it is necessary to have accurate knowledge of the laws of that life space—the laws that produce the different human types and their ways of reacting, as well as the arenas in which upward mobility remains possible—then it is still less possible to master the fate of larger collectivities without more or less thoroughgoing knowledge of the total situation in which one is placed while acting. In these areas, one can make decisions only if one can at least calculate the prospects of an action's success. One can err and miscalculate in these diagnoses, and one will do so from time to time, but an action that takes real factors into account possesses a different dignity and, in the long run, a prospect of accomplishing its aims altogether differently from an abrupt action that proceeds planlessly, in a fog of myth-making, and that does not, in fact, comprehend reality even if chance should grant it an occasional success. The sociological life-orientation of modern man demands, in short, a theory of the total contexts against which the particular and accidental life-situation of the specific individual is set off.

Because of these most pressing requirements of individual and collective life-orientation, it is necessary to teach, alongside of general sociology—which is inevitably too abstract to reach individual and concrete life-situations—a sociological study of current issues. If it were not for the press of life and the sociological problem complex arising out of life situations and oriented to concrete needs, if the matter were viewed strictly from the standpoint of the purely immanent development of science, such current issues study would have to wait long for its emergence. Setting out from a theoretical general sociology, it would be a long way to the concretizations of problem statements that aspire to master unique historical constellations in their individuality from a grounding in the most general. Fortunately, however, the sciences do not develop solely on the basis of theoretical immanence. Rather, they generally receive their most fruitful impulses from the concrete tasks of the historically changing every-day affairs of a community and from the pedagogical requirements, taken in the broadest sense, of the concrete persons who are confronted with specific tasks and the solution of problems specific to collective situations. This manner of inquiry, setting out from two poles (from the needs of practice and the demands of theory), has already acquitted itself very well in the various disciplines of the human and social sciences. It has prevented, on the one hand, that elaboration of pure scholasticism towards which all "pure theory" tends, but, on the other, the elaboration no less of an empiricism devoid of all theory. The development of political economy, for example, is thus fruitfully advanced precisely by virtue of the fact that it moves forward in its tasks from the two poles of theory and practice, and that the two approaches come ever closer to one another. If it is the pedagogical situation above all that compels us to advocate, alongside of general sociology, the development of a sociological study of current issues for the sake of modern man's concrete life orientation, we nevertheless believe that this obligatory tie to the concrete also benefits sociological theory and protects it from excessive formalization and premature scholasticism.

B. Demands Arising from the Academic Teaching Enterprise[73]

In its original constellation, a new science must take into account not only the needs of life in the broadest sense, but also the acute needs of the concrete teaching enterprise within whose framework it is to be installed. At the present, sociology encounters an especially problematical situation in the university, which is just now undergoing radical change. The venerable humanistic cultivational institute of the *universitas* is in the process of breaking down *de facto* into an assortment of specialized schools. As sociologists, we cannot take an uncomprehending position towards this state of affairs, like that assumed by those who are unaccustomed to understanding phenomena on the basis of the total process, and who are in the habit of making judgments without any sense for the actual state of things, simply on the basis of their free-floating idealizations. For this reason, we also do not agree that the idea of the university is served if one simply laments from the standpoint of an inherited ideal of cultivation and condemns everything brought about by more recent developments. Putting it more strongly, we believe that we are placing ourselves at the service of the genuine ideal of an institution for cultivation precisely by attempting first of all to understand the original motives of the new developments on the basis of their own situation and by going along with the development insofar as it corresponds to the authentic needs of a new life.

We shall insert our corrections where the element of the new allows free play for the inherited tasks of cultivation still worth affirming.

Because we want at all costs to take new tasks and new necessities into account, we cannot line up with those who see only something lamentable in the extension of specialization. As sociologists, we know only too well that modern society, so advanced in differentiations, cannot manage without the specialist. In earlier times, when the stratum of property and cultivation could draw on its own cohort to fill administrative positions as they became vacant, when the tasks of office were still such that one could distribute them as honorific positions, a general arts education—one that abstained by and large from training for formal qualifications—still sufficed. Today, however, official duties or professional tasks generally make demands greater than the availability of a formal intelligentsia, of which it must be said that, however versatile it may have been and however capable of representing its own group, it will never be able, in the future, to take the place of specialized knowledge. The cultivated person today must thus be a specialist as well. The move in the direction of the specialized school cannot therefore be condemned, since it corresponds to authentic needs of the social process. What can and must properly be called into question, however—and this is the point on which the speakers for humanism must concentrate their attack—is that the advocates of specialized schooling overlook that the proposition that cultivation without specialized knowledge no longer suffices today cannot be equated with the proposition that the need of the day is specialized knowledge without cultivation.

When we oppose cultivational and specialized knowledge to one another in the present context, we cannot on this occasion provide systematic grounding for this contrast; nor can we present the sources of the distinction in intellectual history. We are forced to content ourselves with a provisional distinction. By specialized knowledge we shall understand all the forms and contents of knowledge necessary for the solution of a scientific-technical or organizational task. A knowledge whose advantage consists in its pure applicability and in its capacity of being separated from the purely personal is in essence always addressed to distinctively differentiated tasks in the social process, in a manner that is both particularistic and specialist. By cultivational knowledge, in contrast, we shall understand the tendency towards a coherent life-orientation, with a bearing upon the overall personality as well as upon the totality of the objective life-situation insofar as it can be surveyed at the time. Nor will there be, on the present occasion, a closer consideration of the detailed ways in which an age or a representative social stratum within it arrives at such a life-orientation and attempts simultaneously to form a picture of the world and to awaken a certain conviction in the subject.

All decisive culturally representative groups have until now achieved this one task in a variety of ways. The humanistic form of cultivational knowledge was itself only one of many possible outcomes. It is therefore impossible simply to equate cultivational knowledge with humanism. While it is of decisive importance that in the western line of development the cultivated stratum derived its life-orientation, self-expansion and shaping forms largely from the substructures of the classics of antiquity, this cannot by any means be made the criterion of cultivation and of all future cultivation as such. Not to be forgotten in this connection—and this has been correctly pointed out by others—is that the Greeks themselves were cultivated without having enjoyed any kind of humanistic-aesthetic education. It may well be that the form in which alone cultivation appeared to us to be realizable will in the future only be within reach of a very small group of intellectuals. What is meant by this is the cultivation that was determined by the study of classical languages and of the works and paradigmatic careers transmitted in them, as well as by a philosophy that laid the basis for the aesthetic-contemplative, deferential attitude appropriate to this study. Viewed from the overall perspective, its representatives will in the future be assigned at most a function as carriers of one pole—to be sure, a vital one—in the overall structure of tensions in spiritual life. But it is very likely that altogether different groups in the intelligentsia, and especially the groups that originate in the directly active sectors of social reality, will spark their cultivational knowledge on different substructures. The essential thing is whether this kind of experience arises in them at all and whether this experience is not only kept awake but also called forth and satisfied by the university as an institution. The distinctive self-expansion of the breadth of personality, together with the deepening of experiential dimensions, that was in large measure the meaning of the experience of humanistic cultivation for earlier generations, may very well arise today for other groups from other substructures.

The humanistic form of cultivation (insofar as it actually achieved its goal) shaped a new human type in the cultivated person, as against the vulgar one, first of all by virtue of the fact that through knowledge

and appropriation of history he gained distance from his own accidental activities and his own accidental circumstances of life. He was
more than his mere activities and more than his mere situation because
he was not simply reduced to them, but rather, through cultivation,
attained to a fruitful distance from immediacy. But such distantiation
does not by any means have to be kindled exclusively through the
reading of classical authors in a certain frame of mind or through
traditional questions of philosophy. The groups that today, unchanged,
still feel their greatest powers awakened and fostered by humanistic
contents should continue to uphold these values and by all means
continue along the path they have chosen. The question is only whether
it is right to close oneself to the possibility that certain life situations
with completely unclassical contents might also lead to such
distantiation from life and to self-expansion. Is it not possible that for
other persons the ever deepening understanding of life and society
might lead to a new type of cultivational experience?

We can see that, without our having contributed much to it, a new
type of genuine intelligentsia is arising spontaneously by virtue of the
fact that there are ever more persons who are discovering, while wres-
tling with social problems, the problems of socialization and the social
character of being human, and that this insight is leading them to just
such a deeper understanding of self and expanded understanding of
the world as quite differently situated themes of life did at an earlier
time. Is it not the responsibility of a university that cares for genuine
cultivational knowledge to incorporate these spontaneous and organic
impulses and to build these new forms of cultivational experience into
its plans of education and cultivation?

When one takes these psychic needs of modern man into account,
the social study of current issues will also be seen to make a consider-
able contribution in this respect. To the extent that it springs from a
genuine and radical need for self-orientation, it will inadvertently widen
into historical sociology, cultural sociology. For it is clear that the
human being gains more radical insight into his own most immediate
situation if he is able to see it from the standpoint of contemporary
society as totality and no longer from that of the circles accidentally
made available to him by his own milieu. Once he has broken through
the limits of his immediate milieu, this drive towards ever broader
vision for the sake of orientation to his own situation will lead him to

the past, and, in this way, he will arrive on his own at the point of letting his cultivational experience be enriched by history.

Modern man seems at the moment to be losing his sense of history. He appears to be so much pressed by the new tasks of the present that he has nothing left for a backward look. There is no longer any interest for history to be found in wide circles, unless one can succeed in elucidating through history the social problem that concerns us so much, the social aspect of events. Pedagogical experience shows that a lively interest emerges as soon as one can present history as a natural widening of the horizon from the place where we all stand. If we think over the course pursued by broad strata of our academic youth, we must in the end conclude that it is impossible to deny any epoch its aspiration newly to plot its own route to the past, and that it is more important to keep the interest in history among cultivated men alive by any means than to make the effort to rescue at all costs a historical consciousness of a certain sort, preshaped in the past. From this point of view, sociology has it as its task—even its mission—to collaborate in rejuvenating the historical sense through the line of approach of a generation that has grown up amid social tensions.

Our duty is done even if we have not conserved and shaped the sense of the past as such but only the form of understanding by means of which access is easiest for modern man. Such a historical sociology, that aspires first of all to extract the general structures of historical change, is not intended as a substitute for historical research, which must continue on its own way and which will at most let itself be enriched by sociology, but as an attempt by sociology, beginning with its own characteristic themes, to make the historical horizon its own and to offer a historical account of the rise of social formations and their cultural emanations. Sociology becomes historical at this point in order to clarify its own problems through the materials of history.

The cultural aspect of the sociological problem complex becomes especially prominent if, in addition to the contributions of the specialized science, one wishes also to include in the educational enterprise something for the cultivational dimension of modernity. In itself, sociology has neither the possibility nor the function of offering, all by itself, the cultivational matter that goes beyond the specialized. It does, however, have a special opportunity of moving, beginning with the modern problem complex, towards the solution of the problem of cultivation, as well as of satisfying, in a modern form, the traditional need that aspires to cultivational knowledge. This is why it is desirable from the standpoint of the demands that the new situation of the university makes of it, that sociology in its future development equip itself *not only as a specialized subject but also as a cultivational one.* The mission that it must perform in the cultivation of modern man and the university graduate, the central core of the teaching to which it must constantly recur, is to show that the individual, viewed in isolation, is an artificially abstracted fragment of a context and that he understands himself falsely if he is not capable in every situation of constantly restoring himself, in his thought and sense of life, to the context to which he belongs. It must similarly teach the individual that the present is ultimately not a fragment, separable from the past, to be examined by itself, but that the social situation that is put before us at any time and that we call the present can be fully conceived and derived, in its condition of having become what it is, only from the past.

Appendix
Lectures on Method

After the introductory course, Mannheim's lecture courses in Frankfurt followed a sequence of historical periods, each used as the occasion for highlighting a distinct complex of institutional concepts largely derived from Max Weber's systematizations. The Summer 1931 course that covered the time period from antiquity to feudalism, for example, developed the concepts of family, tribe, and patrimonial rule; the Summer 1932 course on the high middle ages and early modern period brought out themes of upward mobility, classes, women and the educated strata. Each course was paralleled by a proseminar (Übung) focused on a more narrowly defined body of literature, notably in the history of political thought. In a retrospect prepared as he was planning his English classes, Mannheim lists:

1. *Forms of the family*
2. *The interaction between family and tribes*
3. *Dissolution of the tribe (Rome)*
4. *Local territorial rule. Patrimonialism. (Germans)*
5. *Development of the agrarian world. Peasantry. Feudalism.*
6. *The rise of the urban world. The bourgeois.*

7. *The rise of state organization (absolutism). Officialdom.*
8. *Democratization of state and society.*
9. *The new integration of central powers. Fascism. Communism.*

In line with the argument he spelled out in his 1932 lecture on the curriculum, the historical-conceptual units originated in a discussion of current questions and returned to them. The attached excerpts from the 1931 and 1932 courses present this "life-based" method.

Mannheim prepared detailed, handwritten lecture outlines for his courses, and many of these are preserved in the archives of Keele University in North Staffordshire, England. There are notes not only for his Frankfurt classes, but also for courses he taught at the London School of Economics and the University of London. These materials have barely been utilized as yet, not least because it would be necessary to have a thorough familiarity with the standard topics of German historical sociology in order to identify Mannheim's distinctive contributions. (Cp. Kettler and Meja 1993) The present selection is designed to supplement the discussions of sociology as (political) cultivation.

Introduction to "The Social Forms of the Present and their History." April 20, 1931

At first, about the *How*, and then about the *What*.

1. *The How*
   a. After I have offered a preliminary exhibition of the basic design, I shall want to explicate it.[74]
   b. There are two kinds of presentation: (i) the scholastic, (ii) the life-based. (The latter is the new aspiration that is just now emerging.)
      i. *The scholastic presentation* is one that lays out its materials while governed by a prescribed architectonic, led by an abstract principle (and neglecting the dynamic of life's problem complex). Model: The structure of a reference book. A more or less mechanical location of the basic themes.
      ii. *The life-based presentation* has two major features.
         (1) It does not want to destroy the original interconnect-

edness of its subject matter.

Example: Methodologically it is possible to partition off the points of view of sociology and social psychology. The abstract isolation of points of view.

(a) Social psychology: psychic processes viewed as endowments of the individual, together with their regularities.

(b) Sociology: psychic processes as component of interhuman relations and formations.

(c) In material reality, these are so closely bound together that the unity of the subject matter could be destroyed by the unity of scientific objectification. The difference can maintain itself only as a guideline.

(2) It does not want to destroy the original life-problem-complex that leads to the themes:

(a) Things become problematical in a distinctive, living concatenation (and only something that has become problematical in life is a problem). It is our task to track these concatenations, not to break them apart.

(b) Only in this way do we learn to think *productively*, to think *creatively*, to make the discovery of problems our own.

c. *Scholastic* thinking presupposes recollection of dead items of knowledge (memorization). *Life-based* thinking is intended to enhance two capacities:

i. To find one's way. Orientation.

ii. To have a direction in thinking and seeing. To be able to follow a direction.

iii. To see where the heart of the matter lies.

d. This does not only instruct us in intellectual matters of knowledge; sociology today has the task of *self-clarification* and *clarification of the situation*. To answer the question, what am I about.

i. No other discipline is fitted for achieving this task today to the same extent as *sociology*. It is today the organ for breaking through horizons.

ii. We see ever more clearly that we live in a shrouded world.

      iii. Precisely in the interpretation of the world most immediate to us, we drag along misinterpretations, intentional and unintentional misrepresentations—a false mythology.

      iv. Sociology brushes these things aside with ease. Matters seem to take a 180–degree turn. The new self feels itself lifted above itself. Whoever lacks the courage for this, should get out of the way.

   e. [It does not by any means follow from this that one must fall into *planlessness*.[75]

      i. The *method of feeling one's way* has a direction, a guiding thread, even if it lacks a scholastic scaffolding.

      ii. Although one permits everything that belongs to a subject matter to resonate fully, as well as everything that pertains to the original life—problematic, one finds one's way back to the theme and picks up the thread.

      iii. In this setting, one learns

         (1) subject matter

         (2) method

         (3) self-discipline

         (4) opinion

         (5) the opinion of others]

2. *The What*

   a. Next we want to analyze sociologically the basic social forms undergoing transformation in the present situation.

   b. We begin with the most basic social form, the family. How far we get is less important than it is to offer a paradigm of how such a thing must be viewed.

   c. An overview of the theme:

      i. Everyone knows that *the upheavals of the times* have not seized upon the political sphere alone; (The political must not be overvalued)

         (1) And not only the problems of the spirit;

         (2) And not only the realm of feeling and psychological construction;

         (3) But that the basic forms of society are in the same state of upheaval.

      ii. Every one knows, because everybody is always talking about the facts that

         (1) the family is in crisis,

(2) sexual morality is in crisis,

(3) the frequency of divorce is a problem,

(4) people speak of an uprising of woman, an uprising of youth,

(5) there are experiments with new forms of marriage and child rearing,

(6) one can speak of a strike in new births,

(7) psychological impairments are uncovered that emanate from the family (psychoanalysis),

(8) there is hope of shaping a completely new human being.

d. To be entitled to take part in such discussions—to pass judgments—one must know many facts, one must be able to distinguish the basic facts from incidental phenomena, and one must in general have given the matter much thought.

i. So it will be necessary to know, on the one hand, in what measure and in what shape the change has in fact set in:

(1) in which strata is the family in dissolution,

(2) which of the factors in the family are dissolving, and

(3) which of the factors are simply undergoing change.

(4) In short, whether it is the family as such or only a specific form of the family that is in crisis.

ii. To be able to make decisions in these matters, it is not enough to acquire information about the current state of things. It is necessary to have an idea, a concept of the family, to work it out. I speak of working it out because it is obvious that if one posits the previous state of the family as a basis it can easily happen that one will elevate an accidental phenomenon to the status of essence, that one will postulate as constant something that is most variable. In order to discover the essence, the concept of the family, it is necessary to reconstruct the historical stages of variability in the family (Intution of essence [*Wesensschau*]).

iii. That takes us to the history of the family. But once one has the historically variable phenomenon in view, the question arises right away whether the phenomenon changes by itself, immanently, or do other phenomena have an effect on this change. The following relations and correlations, for example:

(1) economy and family; division of labor
(2) property, law and family
(3) state and family
(4) human types and family
(5) Instinctual underpinning: Is instinct variable?
(6) Construction of the soul and family
(a) Ideals: asceticism, celibacy, jealousy, sexual morality
(b) Individualization
(7) Effects of the family structure on the next generation
(a) family feelings
(b) processes of intimacy
e.   Only when one knows something about these things can one really take a position.

Introduction to "Theory and History of Social Classes, Problems of Upward Mobility and the Cultivated Stratum." Summer Semester 1932

A Life-Based Method

1. *Elimination* of historically-socially presented misinterpretations.
2. *Concomitant Phenomena: a) Clarification of situation, b) Clarification of self.*
    a.   *Clarification of situation*: Most of the time, we live in a situation that is presented to us in a false rendering.
         Examples [of such false renderings].
    i.   The *destructive*. Actually that which lays bare.
    ii. The *irrational*. As counter-movement to glorification of the Understanding ("shallow Enlightenment"). Those who could not or would not go along still called it the *unreasonable*. J. Möser and Hugo. In the next generation it is already the *supra-reasonable*. Schelling. Savigny. Privileges as well as man's dark areas are elevated to this level.
    iii. The *idea of progress*. As if things were so unambiguous.
    b.   *Self-Clarification*: Every individual understands himself on the basis of the situation and the meaning ascribed to it. That is why sociology is always simultaneously self-clarification. When Jaspers speaks of a spirit as such and a self as such, in his book, *The Spiritual Situation of our Time*,[76] the emptiness of

such talk is clearly evident.

i. We do not stand in a situation as such, with man as such and his self (in a vacuum) quite separate, but rather man can extricate himself only with great labor from one concrete form of his self-existence into another.

ii. It is the unique vanity of modern man to seek his essence only where he is different from the others. The genesis of idiosyncracy.

iii. Modern man suffers first of all from no longer finding himself in tune with his situation. His actual situation overtakes its supposed interpretations. Those are the real ideologies. That is why we need a historical sociology.

Examples [of such discrepancies].

(1) The wife of the Biedemeier Period, the woman embedded and built into the household economy, provided the model for the insight into the essence of womanliness. Her properties:

(a) Woman's proper place is inside; and man's proper place is outside. She proves herself in domesticity. Thucydides: The best woman is the one of whom one hears neither good not bad.

(b) Foundation of intimacy and privacy.

(c) Renunciation of spiritual stimulus. (Petty bourgeois woman)

(d) Dispensing with an outer sphere of validation. Prohibition of competition with the man.

(2) The woman employed in outside occupations: The norms do not fit. They cannot actually be implemented. And yet *she explains herself on their basis*. Origin of conflicts—for much that is individual is nevertheless typical.

(a) Sexual anxiety of virginity. Frigidity.

(b) Inferiority complexes fit here.[77]

iv. Sociology begins with a new stratum understanding itself on the basis of its own situation.

v. Methods of Self-Clarification

(1) It is part of the supporting apparatus of the competitive society—and it is important to know—that ambition and self-consciousness possess certain structures

that are simply bred in the mechanisms of upward mobility. Mechanism of competition.

(2) But this self-clarification is not superficial. It penetrates from the outside into the deepest regions of the self.

    (a) The sterility of the hypothesis of a tension between outer and inner.

    (b) It is not a superficialization when the inside is brought into view on the outside.

(3) [Steps]

    (a) Eliminating misinterpretations.

    (b) Laying bare the material social linkages. The approach to the material. (Not obstruction, but courage for reality.) *Who speaks?*

    (c) Sociological self-clarification can only succeed, however, *if one has found the way to sociology in one's own life, drawing from the most fundamental experiential linkages of one's life.*

        (i) That is why one must not merely narrate the fundamental social facts in a matter of fact way, as in a compendium, but must instead avoid dismantling the original vital problematic that leads to the themes of life.

        (ii) One has to understand history in the instance of one's self, but for an understanding of history one needs one's own life and its tensions even more.

        (iii) The laying bare of the real phenomena takes place at the moment of *crisis*, as things become problematic through an antinomic situation.

        (iv) One of the antinomies is the discrepancy between the self-explication of the situation and the situation as it is altered in fact (the discrepancy between the level of the forces of production and the relations of production).

        (v) One must accordingly always start from the antinomies that one has experienced in one's own body, in one's own soul—and one must also learn how to interpret these sociologically and not to see them simply as one's own, to see as from the social situation of mankind.

3. Life-based Method: From the rise of the problematical to the actual matter.

    a. Anyone who has not as yet been perplexed by his own situation has no genuine access to sociology and should not pursue it.

        i. Anyone who is psychically too young, too satisfied, or too anxious.

        ii. Anyone who has not experienced, as a *youth*, the tensions with the older generation (parents' loss of authority)—who has not had the youth movement experience—does not understand the problem of generations.

        iii. Only someone who has experienced, as a *woman* or *girl*, how society gives her no room for effectiveness—how it enlightens and cultivates her, on the one hand, but provides no room for action—is afflicted with nostalgia and certain psychic illnesses that we will study in the history of the *lady*.

        iv. Only someone who has experienced, as a *woman*, how one is received once as lady (a reminiscence of yesterday) and then again as colleague or competitor begins to recognize that this is a social situation and not a destiny of her sex. (Disproportionality in the development of the forces of production: the spiritual foresight of the practical effectiveness of functional embeddedness)

        v. Only someone who notices, as *intellectual*, that he is, on the one hand, elevated above everything as someone who is educated, but that he is, on the other hand, nothing as bourgeois and worker,[78] that he knows everything and does not know how to do anything, that everyone needs him and that he is nevertheless rejected,—such a person comes not only to a general theory of the powerlessness of the spirit[79] but also recognizes it as the fate of a social layer and understands himself on the basis of the social situation.

    b. Life-based method is thus where one takes one's life situation as starting point.

4. Stages of Sociological Comprehension
   a. Elimination of received misinterpretations
   b. Laying bare the phenomenon as social happening
      i. Clarification of the situation
      ii. Clarification of the self
   c. Starting out from the experience of crisis, because that is where the discrepancy between the transformed situation and the old, received misconstruction comes into view. (Example: the employed woman and the ethos of the woman embedded in the household.)
   d. But that still only gives you the phenomenon (family, asceticism, woman) as a fragment that is detached in several senses, a source of errors that no one wants. The phenomenon must be sought out in its enmeshment.
      [Aspects of Fragmentation:]
      i. Only at a single historical stage. [Overcome by] *a reconstruction of the historical stages of variation*
      ii. Only as it appears in one's own milieu. [Overcome by] *a reconstruction of social differentiation.*
         (The human being does not understand the things of his life on the basis of his own life alone, or on the basis of his milieu. A prejudice of the liberal age and its philosophy.) As a historical matter, the original situation has after-effects.
      iii. As a stable phenomenon, resting on itself and not as part of a historical cycle.[80]
   e. Example: (a) The problem of enmeshment; (b) interlinkage
      i. The family can be presented as solution of the sexual problem only as a phenomenon correlative to prostitution, because prostitution solves all of the problems of sexuality that the family has not solved.
      ii. Prostitution is an extrapolation [of the family].
      iii. [The family] stands in a similar reciprocal relationship to the other power and legal formations. The struggle between the family, the kinship group, the status group. The kinship group as center of power and law.
      iv. Similarly in the economy. Economies tied to family, kin-

ship group, city, territory, and state.
- v. Similarly in education. Extrapolation of the educational function in male lodge, church, monastery, boarding school.
- vi. But not only formations and institutions are interwoven in this way
    - (1) Variability of social human types in the element of variability in social formations. Housewife. Concubine. Prostitute. Hetœra. Old Woman. Lady. The working Woman.
    - (2) Variability in forms of experience.
        - (a) Sexuality, first of all = Eroticism (sensuously charged experience).
        - (b) Then the fullness of experience = Culture. Sublimation. (Extrapolation of the unmastered drive: repression or sublimation.)
        - (c) We become acquainted with the drive being given form:
            - (i) Cultivation of sexuality.
            - (ii) Sublimation of sexuality.
            - (iii) Rise of asceticism. Its significance for the forming of the soul, total consciousness, and the formation of culture.
        - (d) Variability of valuations, morality, male ideology.
        - (e) Reflexive effects. Forms of self-possession.

9

The Spiritual Crisis in the
Light of Sociology

Mannheim published this short article in the Stuttgarter Neues Tagblatt
*on December 31, 1932. A week later, January 7, 1933, a slightly
shorter version was published in the* Hamburger Fremdenblatt *under
the title "The Roots of the Spiritual Crisis." Written halfway between
the Reichstag elections of November, 1932 and Hitler's coming to
power (January 30, 1933), the article illustrates some characteristics
of Mannheim's thought at the time. The shift from an emphasis primarily on the intellectual elite to one that included the ordinary person is
demonstrated here, as are Mannheim's pedagogical concerns. Both of
these characteristics would carry over into his English writings. In
addition, Mannheim continued to believe, even at this late date, in the
transformative promise of the crisis. More than a week after the second version of this article appeared, he urged Oscar Jászi's son to
study in Frankfurt rather than Berlin, because the opportunities for
political reflection would be greater.*

A great deal is written and philosophized about the spiritual crisis;
it is viewed in a moralizing fashion, and those affected by it are
patronized, warned and directed onto the right path, all in a preaching
tone. In all this, it never occurs to the high and mighty rescuers, in
their observation posts remote from the struggle for existence, to ask
about the natural grounds of the spiritual crisis, to regard it not only as
a problem of morality, but also as a problem of struggling life, seeking
to form itself anew. One can change only what one really knows. To
really know, however, means to understand the thing in terms of its

actual conditions. But in this context, grandiose surveys based on intellectual history provide as little access to real happenings as do philosophical analyses of the essence of the phenomenon "crisis in general." For the crisis is one of contemporary people in their instant, contemporary situation; and this can only be comprehended if one puts oneself in their situation and understands their actions and sufferings on these terms.

But anyone who has ever experienced the crisis for himself and who has observed his own conduct in the situation gradually realizes that the phenomenon of crisis is misunderstood from the outset because it has become habitual to view it exclusively as an evil. For the course and development of vital psychic processes, however, what is decisive is how we bear ourselves towards them, the stand we take towards our own crisis, towards the crisis in our closest environs and society. The malformations, rigidifications, and entanglements that can hardly be eliminated once they have become matter of habits are first wrought by the wrong attitudes (*Verhaltensweisen*) to the crisis.

A man's fate as a whole is decisively affected by the way he conducts himself towards his crises, conflicts and occasional failures. Crises and conflicts in personal and social life are not meant to be magically banned or repressed. Instead, the forces of life erupting in them demand to be properly grasped and understood. In this correct understanding, it is decisive to recognize that spiritual crisis, seen as social processes, are usually nothing but readjustment efforts by the drives, the understanding, the whole psychic attitude in general.

A radical change in the situation of individuals and groups must necessarily dissolve, loosen, and smash old modes of conduct, so as to be able to carry out the most advantageous adjustments and attitudes in the new situation. In the general spiritual and psychic crisis that characterizes Germany today, the unknown soldiers of life contend for a reorientation, a readjustment, in the course of which they reform themselves into new men through a vast number of small, invisible processes. With the ruin of old, obsolete modes of conduct necessarily comes the ruin of old ideals (*Ideale*).

Ideals (*Ideen*) are not something independent of situations, something inspired in us and sublime, but they come into being and grow with new situations. They emerge out of these gradually, as directive energies, and they are freshly won through countless small confrontations and clashes. Only a norm and ideal that is won in this way has a real relationship to life, is itself life. Every pedagogue knows—or at least should know—that the ideals of the parental home and school must often fall apart with the entry into life, if the individual is to have a chance of finding himself. What applies to the individual also applies to many individuals; and what are group fates but the interconnected fates of many who are placed in the same position. What we encounter as a crisis of ideals from a spiritual point of view is in reality nothing but a reflection of the many spiritual-psychic readjustment processes of people who have ended up in a new life position. In this condition of being catapulted out of their stability, they are thrown back on themselves, and from this they may perhaps become able to identify tasks for themselves where earlier everything had been veiled. Or in these adjustment struggles it may be a matter of those who have lost not only their minimal livelihood through the dreadful process of unemployment but also their arenas of validation, and who now labor, in their inactivity, to achieve a feeling of self regard.

The insight that the process of the spiritual crisis is not a process of the "spirit as such," but that it must be linked to the concrete change in the situation of the individual and that one can help only if one has more or less appreciated these most elementary connections, brought me to the idea of gathering some sample survey data in this connection, by means of a questionnaire, at first within narrow limits. I was not concerned with acquiring indicators of the extent of the spiritual crisis, but with observing the ways in which the individual copes with the spiritual problems posed by life. Accordingly, the questions went as follows: in which spheres of life has the belief in ideals and values been lost, which values remain steadfast, and, in case of a change in valuation, which values are now preferred,. A second group of questions addressed the most important forms of situational change in the life of the individual. Finally the question was raised about the form and manner in which the individual after a spiritual reorientation now gives form to his life, how he coped with the "spiritual crisis."

Without exaggerating the reliability of the information gained in this manner, the survey nevertheless had the value of bringing phenomena that are much discussed considerably closer. It became clear that the experiences which the individual in his psychic isolation cell believes to be altogether personal and his alone are common to many. The sociological surmise with which I started, that spiritual crises and revaluations are called forth above all by changes in situation, was also confirmed. For it is clear from the responses of those who have not experienced an essential disruption in this respect that they are basically little affected by the spiritual crisis. They remain true to their established beliefs because their closest surroundings, their family, and their standing in their family or profession have remained undisturbed. It does not by any means represent a rare extreme when a woman writes, for example, "Because I have been married for 22 years, I have not, in the last years, had any experiences or changes of the kind mentioned by your questionnaire." From this and similar reports it emerges clearly that a person who has once effected his adjustment within a situation, who fulfills his concrete duties and assignments, has no real sense (*Organ*) for crises occurring outside of his most immediate environment, however violent they may be. On the average, he remains in this secure, imperturbable attitude until the wave of general events actually takes him in its immediate grasp.

In contrast to this, there is also, to be sure, a comprehension of events, crises, and disruptions of value, by way of cultivation and empathy. But until now we have overestimated the significance of such reactions. The scattered answers that point towards this type of merely spiritual reception of values confirm the surmise that only the values and contents that have been won in struggle with the difficulties of one's own situation, as a result of the external threat to existence, penetrate to the depths of personality and remain fixed there. The "external" and the "depths" are thus fundamentally interconnected,. This is also how to understand the words of another response, in which it is asserted that the most essential inner transformation of the last years in this individual consists in the fact that since his reorientation (*Umbruch*) he is against all ideals that are offered to him and henceforth values only "self-won ideals."

For the present, only these few samples, but they suffice to show, despite their patchiness, that it is wrong to see in the spiritual crisis nothing but an evil that must somehow be eliminated. In the case of a spiritual crisis, what is at issue is not merely getting rid of it, putting it behind us, but rather finding how it can be worthily carried through (*ausgetragen*). As wrong as it would be to fall into the opposite extreme and to cover up the dangers entailed by the crisis, it is no less in error to adopt the wrong attitude from the outset towards the crises presented by personal and collective life.

Whoever wants to be really of help is not therefore required to elevate the crisis into something uplifting and to speak of a fading of ideals. Because it is quite possible that precisely in the place where a false assessment sees only a destruction of values, many small costly struggles are bringing into being a new man.

10

In Defense of Functional Reason

Correspondence between Eduard Heimann and Karl Mannheim about Mannheim's *Mensch und Gesellschaft in Zeitalter des Umbaus*

Eduard Heimann earned his doctorate under Alfred Weber. In the Weimar period, he was best known for his studies of the welfare state and his close collaboration with Paul Tillich. He retained his ties with Tillich during his American exile, when he taught social policy at the New School. Mannheim probably knew him in Heidelberg, as well as in Christian Socialist circle around Tillich in Frankfurt. The exchange with Heimann is Mannheim's only contribution to a set of letters that Tillich and his associates circulated among themselves, evidently in the hope of generating a periodical out of this traffic. Other participants included Mannheim's close friend, Adolph Loewe, Alexander Rüstow, and Arnold Wolfers. Extant letters cover topics in macrosocial theory notably the questions posed by Oppenheimer about the role of force in primal social organization, as well as the planning problems addressed in the Mannheim—Heimann correspondence. Although these letters date from Mannheim's English period, they focus specifically on unfinished business from the Weimar years. The short German core of the book that later appeared in English much expanded was addressed specifically to his German peers in exile.

Prof. E. Heimann
3536 Cambridge Avenue
New York City
Tel. Halifax 5–0996
NewYork, 1.31.1935

Dear Mannheim,

It moved me deeply that you did not spare the effort and expense of dedicating a copy of your book to me. I take it as an important sign of the bond between us, and I am profoundly grateful. I wish that I could also thank you with comparable joy in the matter of substance. But the affair is too serious and you are too serious for me to content myself with an expression of the admiration and gratitude for which the reading provides ample occasion. In fact, I do find the reflections and analyses mostly surprising, remarkable, and persuasive, insofar as I can presume to make a judgment in the field that is most your own. But I am all the less convinced by the overall view, within which the analyses seem to stand and which they are presumably supposed to serve, if I understand the book correctly.

I believe that I can best explain this by following along the line of your concept of the "rational," and I shall do this in two stages. First, I was extremely surprised at the self-evidence with which you equate the contradictory pair of the rational and irrational with the pair of the salutary and destructive (You qualify this in only one place, to the effect that the irrational is not necessarily evil (p. 40 [62])[81] and may even be the most valuable thing about humankind. But the connection suggested here between the two poles is altogether left out of your systematic construction.) You naturally have good reason nowadays to emphasize the positive value of the rational, but it is just as important not to overlook the demonic possibilities in all human capacities, including the rational; and precisely the undeveloped reservation on p. 40 should have pointed you, in my opinion, towards the danger always present in the rational, the danger of making things empty—something that you do not touch on at all. I am convinced that the sudden eruption of the irrational is retribution for the fact that no irrationality was put down as the foundation for the rational democratic form. You worked so closely with Tillich that this obvious objection cannot have escaped you. I am therefore not sure how to interpret your overall vision in this regard.

Or rather, to be quite forthright, I think I see that your concept of the rational suffers just this emptying out, and that it can therefore serve as an instrument of immediate utility for any dictatorship, whatever its aims or its degree of irrationality. You construe the word rational in a purely positivistic way, and positivism in turn as pure pan-sociologism. In the beginning stands a self-movement of the social process whose decisive component is the process of production. This process is a mystical entity to which the human being is in part adapted and to which, in part, he ought to be adapted. It molds the human being according to its needs. The aim of this process is the purely formal one of maintaining its operation, although one can also give it the apparently more attractive and richer name of integration.

First, I want to say that this is not in any case Marx's conception, however little I want to swear by Marx. For Marx, as for you, the apparatus itself rebels in a crisis and forces to reconstruction. But Marx also has a second rebellious force, the proletariat, and that is missing in you. While it is doubtless correct that proletarian rebellion draws its prime nourishment from the experience of crisis, the ground of its rebellion is more comprehensive. It is exploitation. And however much the crisis is linked to exploitation—because purchasing power is weakened through exploitation and does not suffice to repurchase the product—it would be fundamentally wrong to link the phenomena of exploitation and proletarian rebellion only through the crisis, and thus to derive the human uprising from the explosion of the apparatus. Please do not misunderstand me. I do not want to commit either Marx or myself to a premature anthropology, as if some eternal human nature would rebel against capitalism. My argument is much more modest. No sociology can exclude the possibility that the human being reacts to pressure with counter-pressure instead of being, to use your recurrent self-betraying expression, remolded. The fact is, however, at least according to Marx's theory, that the proletariat simply does not adapt itself to the necessities of capitalism, and that it conducts itself even more negatively towards capitalism in times that are more or less free of crisis than at the moment when the apparatus of production rebels. The whole world of negative reactions—in short, logically, one half of the world—is pushed aside into the irrational, in your work, and branded as something that should not be. The more perfect human being, as you describe him once, is the one who is integrated more without friction into the social process.

Now it is obvious that the concept of the rational is supposed to serve you as a weapon against fascism—which you give a negative evaluation, as you do the groups that uphold it—so that your unclearly qualified negative assessment of the irrational has this as its source. But your formalized concept of the rational does not suffice for this purpose. The rational is the means appropriate to the end—to any end. That is why you are quite wrong to call on the Enlightenment, for which the rational meant not only reason but also freedom for reason, as well as the community of human beings in reason and freedom as precondition. The Enlightenment had a very decided, luminous image of man, in which it believed. Fascism too believes in something. What you believe in is not clear, at least from your book, and what you may credit to yourself as a self-denying attitude opens your book to very ambiguous effects.

Since Marxism, in its communist as in its social-democratic variety, has abandoned the pathos of the freedom struggle, it has retreated to the formal rationality of planning; and it has fallen prey as a result to the emptying out against which we fought in vain during the last years and that became plain to everyone in its sorry end in Germany. But the Marxists could retreat to this limited position only because they believed themselves to have a monopoly in it, because they hoped to triumph over their opponents by virtue of it. Most recently, Löwe again expressed his surprise that in my November article I did not include the unconditional socialization of at least the strategic points among the prerequisites of planning. If planning has become an indubitable life necessity at the present stage of production, it should be achievable by the proletariat alone. I consider this idea—the latest version of the Marxist two-class schema—not only fundamentally wrong in theory (I have already indicated as much in my article and attempt to show this more precisely in the version in print) but also as already empirically refuted.

There is, in my opinion, no reason for thinking that it is possible to plan, fashion, and maintain only an egalitarian cycle, and not just as well an inegalitarian one. If no purpose is stated, no dedication to an ultimate value, if, in short, rationality is made into a mere means, then all of the techniques you describe can as easily serve fascism as communism or the authoritarian democracy that you sketch so vaguely. They not only can, but they are already doing so. War economy or not, one cannot in any case deny the reality of economic steering in Germany. And the intensive leadership training that you describe has been successively under way for many years in the Brown House in Munich. Only in one place do you attempt to shield yourself against this possibility of fascist planning, in your polemic against Freyer.[82] You are of course right that power alone does not in itself provide the correct plan, but one could answer immediately that at the stage of the struggle Freyer was right to overemphasize the first step to power rather than the second step to planning. And you do not deny the fundamental possibility of fascist planning because it cannot be denied. Once one has grasped that national socialism is the emancipation of the pre-capitalist domain of the petty bourgeois sphere from the bourgeoisie, it follows directly that there are no inner inhibitions to keep them from incursions into the sphere of the bourgeoisie and proletariat. Why shouldn't people learn to think if it is useful to them—and insofar as it is useful to them? Just this is after all your thesis. The demarcation from fascism cannot be discovered by denying it the capacity for solving the intellectual tasks entailed in its rule. The actual demarcation lies in belief in spiritual values—belief in truth, justice, and love. Whether this belief can triumph is a different question, one that does not in any way concern me in this letter or otherwise.

To summarize. Your rationalism is not opposed to fascism, but rather, because of its reduction to the social-technical, politically neutral—and therefore supportive of the prevailing power. I do not know whether you intended this neutrality. If not, as I believe, your book would fail to match your intentions. If yes, however, you will understand why you cannot persuade me, since my principles are quite different.

I think that I must try to make my criticism at least somewhat more understandable by indicating my own standpoint. Löwe wrote me, without further interpretation or explanation, that my article on socialism and democracy is obsolete in his own opinion and in the opinion of all of you. I understand this to mean that you view fascism as an accomplished fact, with perhaps a weak possibility of an alternative (*sic*) to an equally gruesome communism, a fact to which the sense of reality and science must adjust itself and against which it is meaningless to seek for other ways out. If this is your opinion, then I gladly accept the judgment of "obsolete" and give it an altogether positive evaluation. I do not take part in any Marxism or sociology that require me always to go along. Not everything that exists is rational; it can rather be demonic to an extent that simply forbids my going along.

Then nothing would be left to me except to describe the right solution to the indicated problem as clearly as possible, and to leave it to God or History to do what they want with it, since it too ultimately comes from them. It is not altogether impossible that some parallel situation in the historical future may occasion a reconsideration of the ways that could be taken today. I have no illusions. It is not very likely, and it becomes altogether unlikely if I am more or less left in this to my own doubtless insufficient personal strength and do not have the support of those to whom I feel closest in substance and idea. But this cannot change anything in the subjective necessity of the attempt. I do not aim at positive truth in your sense, but the genuinely intended truth in place of the truth of the lie and violation.

I do not write this letter with pleasure, and I remain, with the most faithful wishes for you and your wife,
Your,

*   *   *

Dear Mannheim,

The letter has already been waiting for two and a half weeks to be mailed. I have held it back, however, because I, as well as several of our friends here, wished to check everything once more very carefully and to talk it over. The importance of the book demands that. Then I also spent eight days in bed, and so I get around only today to finishing up and mailing.

In the main, I want to add two points. 1. What I called pan-sociologism is perhaps most evident in the formulation on p. 110 [161], where, in the absence of a still sufficient medieval or an already sufficient modern totalitarian organization, the division of spheres is interpreted so that the human being simply follows the functional laws of the environing sphere in which he happens to be active. The primacy of the sociological over the human is most clearly expressed here. And on p. 169 [204–205][83] the ideal is even construed out of the social function. 2. My first letter undoubtedly did you an injustice when it asserted that you make no effort to subject the social process to any norms whatever. This assertion is contradicted above all by the very strong formulation on p. 91, where planning for the whole rather than planning for a one-sided violent rule is demanded. Indeed, there is to be found there even a formulation of the creative life—and thus of the religious in life—of which one cannot however say where else in the context of the book one could put it. The whole thing is most nearly reminiscent of the synthetic role that you claimed for the intelligentsia at the conclusion of *Ideologie und Utopie*, without however showing, here or there, the sociological location of their power. Then follows on p. 159 [197] the important passage where you introduce a kind of dialectic in order to show that a one-sided coercive planning (which is possible, after all!) cannot sustain itself in the long run. Without doubt, your true personal objective becomes visible here once more, your belief that there cannot—and should not—be a lasting satisfaction through force. To this extent, my earlier letter is again in error. But there is still no extra-sociological criterion for this more perfect course; one could still equate perfection with lack of friction and thus reduce it to the technical level. It would be a most pallid, pre-sociological democratism to recognize as a solution that planning is now to be on behalf of the "whole" instead of a one-sided partial rule. This whole is structured somehow, and it is necessary to reveal the structural principle towards which one plans. This structural principle, one that would offer a genuine solution and not simply a wiping away of the conflicts, was the object of my efforts in that obsolete August article. And I do not see how your attempted solution, as long as it does not announce such a principle, precludes in any way the fascist possibility. That is valid in a very practical sense. Hitler has such a principle and claims in its name to represent and to plan the whole, and so he would not be hit by your polemic against planning in the interest of a partial rule. By a detour, then, I return to my earlier conclusion that the sociological offers no criterion to distinguish a genuine fomative activity from an overpowering that would bring things technically to the loss of all corporeality.

I am your and your wife's faithful

    *   *   *

Dear Heimann,

It hardly seems possible that I am responding only now to the letter you sent me about my book. Anyone who shares in the struggle to master the tasks set for us abroad, however, will know that it is not until the vacation that one can achieve anything comprehensive and address challenges that are of long term significance. This letter was also delayed by the fact that I originally wanted to answer collectively to all those who gave me their opinions in extensive letters. But this task proved unmanageable in this all-encompassing and so I prefer to answer you directly.

First of all, I want to express my thanks that the distance and the fact that we landed in fundamentally different situations have not estranged you from me, as is shown best by the vehemence of your disputation. I am just as well pleased that you become aware of this commonality between us more through a refusal to go along than through agreement. I should be glad if the discussion were to lead to a further strengthening of the awareness of commonality because I crave above all exchanges about the problems that arise for us through the fact that we once experienced common things in a common way and now, by virtue of simultaneous encounters with new worlds, experience both past and present as problems in different ways.

Before I address your arguments individually, I want to complain about something, as author, notwithstanding my gratitude for your stimulation, because I consider it necessary in view of future discussions. As interesting and thought-provoking as your objections may be, they do not, in my opinion, reach the intentions of the author but only certain premises of the book, which were not by any means at the focus of his inquiries. Put briefly, I wanted to write a book about two issues. First, the question why the present liberal social order has ceased to function productively in most spheres, especially in culture. And second, about a development in the history of thought that I see as leading from discovery through invention to planning, whereby I then attempted to uncover the distinctive characteristics of this planning in modern methodology as well as the most important intellectual currents of the time.

Over against this, you demand a book from me about the difference between communism and fascism, a book about freedom rather than planning, and finally a sociology that does not offer causal explanations but rather produces goals for the future purely on the basis of its own method. I am ever more of the opinion that, especially when authors criticize one another, they would like them to write exactly those books that they are themselves in the process of writing, although they would of course really be mad if one did in fact preempt their books.

Joking aside, however, I have in the meantime read your essay on planning in *Social Research*.[84] It is excellent and contains many very important stimulating ideas, but you could surely not have expected me to voice my opinion about the difference between desirable and harmful planning when I was talking about a stage in the history of thought and especially emphasizing the converging element in modern tendencies of thought (viz., that, despite all differences, the situation in all dominant groups drives towards planning). An author will always believe himself to be treated unfairly as long as he is not judged by his primary intention and as long as what is most essential to him is obscured by his being taken on terms external to his own, even if this external reading brings to light a number of important new objections.

Now I can proceed to the objections, which are important to me, one at a time.

A. *"The Emptied Ratio"*

I must confess to you that the more I think over the word "irrational," the more inexplicable do I find it that it could have been made into a positive slogan. The word has a negative-positional content, but no positive one. When someone says "rational," one can understand something by it that is positively and substantively graspable, namely thinking—the ability to describe in thought something experienced, encountered, existing, to explain causally, to subject to structural analysis or to reconstruct synthetically. In contrast, "irrational" is an entity only in a negative and positional sense, because it points to everything in the world that is not thought. It thus comprehends such heterogeneous entities as, e.g., a stone, the as yet unknown in nature, sense impressions, feelings, sleep, God—in a word, everything that is not thought. What there is about this heterogeneous entity to merit a positive evaluation, for the sake of which one marshals youth movements, philosophies, etc. is a puzzle to me.

Now there is a second possible way of interpreting the enthusiasm for the "irrational," if one does take the word not in a literal sense (for you will concede to me that it has no inner unity but represents a functional entity only in certain situations, where that which is not thought through and that which is not organized[85] are taken as problematical) but uses it for the experience that it is more beautiful not to think things over or not to think them through to the bottom, or that certain things are denatured for experience if one thinks about them. That is what religious people, the Romantics, and the youth movement appear to have in mind.

If one takes this use of irrational, it is indeed an entity with content, but I must confess myself its opponent. The lowest form of this enthusiasm for irrationality has been turned into a program by the Nazis, inasmuch as they attach higher value to the inability to think, the unrational (in contrast to the irrational), and blind submission than to tenacity in thinking, given that one has begun to think.[86] But I am also against the higher forms of this kind of enthusiasm for irrationalism that think that certain contents of the soul or cosmic substances are destroyed by being thought about. It has always been my experience that real thinking enhances the capacity for experience and that faiths can only be elevated by the courage to think. Even when it comes to "the religious," I agree with Guardini, who spoke the following true word about Pascal, "He is far from the new-fashioned weakness of nerve that considers 'the religious' threatened whenever concepts are brought into play. He is not in the modern sense a believer in experience." (R. Guardini, *Christian Consciousness. Studies on Pascal*).[87] I believe that thinking is one of the highest gifts of the human species, the most radical instrument for penetrating the world—directed towards the outer world no less than the world of experience—and emptying out results not from the fact that man thinks but from the fact that empty men think. Thus the collapse of the social democracy did not happen because it thought rationally but because all of its original beliefs were gradually abandoned.

B. "Instrumentalist thinking"

If we are agreed that thinking as such is no sin but rather, properly applied, an enhancement of human penetration of the world and self-realization, I am left with the task of feeling out just what it is about my thinking that disturbs you. I believe I can see it. Let me identify my way of thinking in this book as the instrumental form of thinking, in contrast to ethical-existential-political thought. There are many forms of thinking, according to the achievement goals they are supposed to meet in the life process. At times it makes sense to connect them with one other, but at other times what is called for is to keep them strictly apart. If I may formulate your reproach in my language. What is at issue is that you want to see my instrumentalist way of thinking turned into a political-ethical-existential one. My answer is that—although I believe that we must think in life and politics in a manner shaped by our convictions, and that we must in fact make our convictions themselves topics of thinking—there must nevertheless be a sphere in science where evaluations are postponed as long as possible, in order to see the purely causal and functional relationships the more clearly. In this range, I believe, the social sciences can follow quite a way along with the physical sciences, where the greatest progress has been achieved by substituting a functional way of experiencing nature for the substantialist and conviction-laden one. The physician must decide whether a kidney operation is necessary in a given case. He does this on the basis of an observation of the kidney's function for the life of the organism. It is not up to him to decide whether it is better to live or whether it would not be better to let people die, instead of healing them. If he were already to raise this evaluative and existential question in the observation of reality, he would never carry the functionalist attitude through to its conclusion. Yet it would be wrong to say that the physician is evading the existential question, since he affirms the value of life by his very deeds, inasmuch as he dedicates his whole life to healing, and it is in its interest that he closely observes all functional relations. That is why, precisely from the standpoint of existentiality, I have always given a higher rating to productions that spoke as little as possible in the course of inquiry about conviction and existence, but made their existential intentionality apparent in the manner of their implementation. Against this example, it could be objected that the analogy to the physician cannot be transferred to social observation inasmuch we do not simply want to preserve an existing "social organism" but to rebuild it, and must therefore know which society is right. But even conceding this point, the separation between instrumentalism and goal-setting must be strictly maintained. Let us suppose that biology has advanced to the point of being able to rebuild organs, to build them anew. Even in that case it would not be the task of biology to decide whether it would be better to have men grow wings in order to become a mobile being, with all the spiritual consequences of the separation from groundedness that would follow as a result. Its task would only be to decide how this new organism would have to be reconstructed in all its parts to fit the new objective of bringing into the world a flying being, together with the new mentality appropriate to it.

With this, I have conceded to you, on the one hand, that there must be a place somewhere in the science of society—and a method too—

where one comes to agreements about norms and goals, about the form of society that one considers desirable. This would be the place to decide, for example, whether one wants freedom, and, quite concretely, what kind of freedom. On the other hand, I must emphasize that instrumentalist analysis cannot of itself, as is well known, arrive at such decisions about norms, and that it should therefore not make them. You are completely right that instrumentalist analysis has only a quasi-norm: the correct or incorrect functioning of a given organism, the adaptation or maladaptation of the parts to one another, the appropriateness or inappropriateness of human actions as gauged by the ideals and functions that the whole and the individual have to fulfill in this case. Its means do not enable it to decide the purpose for which a society must exist or which principle of construction among possible social situations is the "most just." Once a value is established, however, let's say "planning connected to freedom," then it is necessary sooner or later to be able to show exactly, by means of instrumental analysis, the forms of institutions, pedagogical influence, and so forth by means of which one aims to guarantee socially the possibility of such freedom reconciled with planning. It is just in this sense that I find a lack in your otherwise very important essay of an instrumental answer to the profound philosophical challenge of a "self-realization of men after their self-alienation." What is the institutional solution by means of which you prevent officialdom in a communist society from expropriating the possibilities of choice, if also not individually (like capitalists) but in a collectivist way on behalf of their estate. In short, I believe that with the proposition about the alienation of man we have only brought forward an ideological moment in the socialist movement, as long as we do not achieve the institutional equivalent by means of an instrumental analysis. As ideology, National Socialism also wants to liberate man from the machine, just like Christian socialism. I do not have to emphasize to you that what counts is not ideology and what men say, but rather what can be actualized through the configuration of their deeds, and how it can be actualized. That is the reason why, although I consider existential and political normative clarification to be essential, I have been attempting to concentrate at the moment far more on the instrumental task. I believe that it is the next task of sociology to be able to transform general ideas into instrumental proposals. But one can do this for the future only if one has first learned to see the functioning of society at the instance of the past and the immediate present. For myself, I am not yet far enough along to be able to say instrumentally how a society that is planned and yet does not oppress freedom might look. I believe, however, that I will be able to discover it in time, or, at least, I hope that others will discover it after me, if we all make the effort to become aware why—by virtue of what functional causes—liberalism failed, by virtue of what functional causes dictatorships suddenly became possible today, what functional errors are operative in these dictatorships themselves, where they could be most easily undermined, which functional forms in past societies achieved an equilibrium between regulation and individual freedom. It is this lack of knowledge that causes my book to be written in an expressly exploratory attitude, one that allows wished-for goals to shine through only from time to time, but that otherwise single-mindedly applies the theme of functioning to the historical phenomena it treats. It is not through false modesty, then, that I impose this limit on myself, nor emptied-out rationalism, but because of the conviction that our normative wishes will find the social means to their fulfillment at the stage of planning only if we carry instrumental thinking through as rigorously as possible. That immediately raises two further questions. How is the apparently absolutely deterministic and very strongly simplifying method of sociological thinking to be understood? (The problem of pan-sociologism) And the second, what can instrumentalist-functionalist method contribute to the specification of possible norms.

C. The Problem of so-called "Pan-sociologism"

First of all, I would like to ask you to avoid in our discussion such expressions as "pan-sociologism," emanating from the atmosphere of German world-views. They damage our ability to bring the state of affairs directly before us and obstruct the way to looking at the relationships in themselves instead of their consequences in world views. If man were determined 100 percent by society, no scolding of the person who diagnosed this condition would help us. But that is by no means the opinion of sociological analysis; it asserts only that there is nothing but a sociological explication of the human. I hasten to add that this does not mean that man cannot also be explained and understood on the basis of biology or from his ideas, but only that it is senseless to abstract either the biological or the intellectual from the fact that both the biological and the intellectual have to prove themselves in concrete situations of the social and that no one has ever seen a human-biological reaction in which the relationship to the relevant situation was not present, just as there have never been ideas that were not spoken by someone to someone or against someone, or that were not thought or experienced in the current of others or against the current of others. That does not mean univocal determination in the sense that every social situation prescribes only one solution for everyone, but it does mean that—by virtue of the relatedness to the situation—this situation, the social, does enter in biological behavior, as in ideas, in some sense (and precisely this sense must be specified from case to case). If you should agree with me up to this point, you will understand that I cannot go along with the sentence cited in your second letter (where you speak of an unacceptable primacy of the social over the "human"), from its formulation alone. It is pointless, and we create needless problems for ourselves if we construct a "human-as-such" in opposition to the "social." I have never seen a human expression—I must say it again—in which the fact of being oriented to society is not somehow present. In its essence, the human is simply determined by its being existence oriented towards society.[88] That does not mean—to reformulate the point—univocal determinacy, first, because every situation leaves open many kinds of possibilities for responding, and, second, because every living being may react differently to one and the same situation, by virtue of its inner organization, its bio-physiological primal force, and its previous history. Yet neither is there an infinity of possible reactions to a situation or reactions possible for a living being formed by its history, but rather a limited number. And our tracing of a social situation in the course of understanding and explaining it consists of painstakingly laying bare which of the possibilities of a situation were responded to by a given person in accordance with his own possibilities. So you see that there is a third alternative between completely thinking the situation out of the way (as philosophers love to do), in order to arrive by this path at a "man as such" and a "spirit as such," and a mechanical determinism, that considers only one specific reaction to a specific stimulus as possible. Now if I had to analyze an individual case sociologically (your development in the new country, perhaps, or mine), I would endeavor to work with this refined analysis of situations, in which I would have to relate two sets of factors to one another, the relative multiformity of possible responses to the new situation and the relative multiformity of our spiritual forms for dealing with situations, which latter are, in turn, shaped by our biological-psychic constitution and our previous history. If I would proceed in this manner, I would write a biographical-sociological analysis which would give utterance to the whole multiformity of fitting in. (By the way, adaptation and fitting in do not, in my word-use, mean the same as compromising, abandoning oneself to the situation, but rather acting with reference to the situation, so that even a revolutionary group makes itself fit in, in this sense, because it conducts its rebellion with reference to the situation, and its function is to shift and change the situation. There is no phase of a rebellion that is not formed as much by the situation as is the manner in which the obedient and submissive conduct themselves. Only the psychopath acts without reference to the situation, since his illness consists precisely in his loss of the means for grasping situations. He would be a good example of the "human as such" of the philosophers, insofar as it exists without society.)

Since I pursue structural sociology in my book and do not concern myself with the biographical-sociological analysis of individual cases, the book does not extend to the presentation of the full wealth of encounters between individual character and situation but only to the deliberately simplified presentation of the operation of block-factors in certain historical-typical situations. (Such as liberalism, age of guilds, etc.) The guideline controlling the simplification is the problem of the functioning of society and the functional value of typical modes of conduct. The hypothesis underlying this is that when one distances oneself from biographical uniqueness and considers the average reactions of the greatest number of cases that become relevant for social happenings in general, these eventually tend in the direction of a functional fit. The individual may be "extravagant" and may degenerate from the multitude of possible actions relevant to the situation, doing something that corresponds more closely to his peculiar makeup, and he may possibly go to his destruction because of his excessive deviation, i.e., he may be eventually rejected by the social process that selects among actions.[89] The average will, however, in the typical situation of a dominant social structure, execute the actions that are *decisive*, in the sense of an optimal fulfilling of functions. This is the sense I intend when, in the sentence to which you object, derive the liberal division of spheres from the fact that the man of that time heeded the functional systems of the various environing spheres (p. 110 [161]). It is not possible to write a complete biography of a specific liberal person on the basis of this principle, because not all of his transactions are situated in the direction of fulfilling functions and it is unlikely that he invariably adapts himself in the direction of the average typical fulfillment of function, but it is only on the basis of this principle that it is possible fruitfully to discover the typical forms of reacting to typical structural situations of a social order by the greatest number. When one has this level of human action in view, however, society is much more deterministic than one likes to imagine or than it appears to someone in the biographical attitude of our everyday private forms of encounter. (The resistance to sociological functional observation originates unconsciously out of this biographical-privatizing observation of the world of ours in our everyday life, by means of which we also hide from ourselves the adaptation in the direction of the typical at work in ourselves.) Or is it perhaps not the case that the typical manner of conduct that we are bound to observe as consumers or as owners of stock tends in the direction of the average? Not to limit myself to economic examples alone, doesn't the average mode of conduct we acquired from the living models of our generation and social stratum tend in the direction of a type? Something that becomes immediately evident when we compare ourselves with the next generation or with a different stratum in our own country or with the same stratum in a different country. If, accordingly, one interprets average cases on the level of structural sociology, not biography, in functional analysis, the picture naturally becomes far more deterministic. Then it becomes evident that, looking at great numbers, much more adaptation takes place as a result of selection than one could surmise from a close biographical view. It is only at this level that there exists something like (what you object to in my method of presentation) a self-movement of the social process in which the individual is in part integrated and in which in part he ought to be integrated. (By which I naturally do not mean a society moving towards a secret goal but only a trend resulting from causality and adaptation.) At this level of the average and block factors, there has always been an almost mechanical seeming determinism in history, something that we very much dislike to admit. From this point of view, even the ideas and self-interpretations of man were best explained on the basis of social functions. (Consider, for example, the "idea" arising "spontaneously" in almost all patriarchal religions—China, Greece, Rome, the Christian realm—that it belongs to the essence of woman's nature that she must prove herself in the home, but the man in public.) Whether the observation that the average modes of conduct of men tend in the direction of fulfilling functions in a given society is valid or not can be settled neither by philosophical doctrines of freedom nor by the slogan "pan-sociologism." It is a question of fact whether this can be proved or not. Admittedly, this extensive deterministic sociologism applies only, as should have become clear, to the structural—sociological way of seeing, to the observation of the average and the great number.

Now I will tell you why I am so insistent about observing men and society first of all at the distance of structural analysis and not at the level of biographical encounter, which is so much more capable of nuance. Because, in my opinion, it was precisely the sin of the German intellectuals that they did not look first at the fundamental general contours of things (as is naturally done by people who are impelled to action in public), but rather (corresponding to the conditions of privacy and intimacy characteristic of their existence) fled directly into nuances, and dissipated themselves there. We must now come to the insight that nuances gain meaning and significance only against the background of the coarser outline. The so-called "natural-scientific" manner of thinking is not ontologically tied to nature. It is rather correct in every object domain to look first at the general, the block-like (to reduce everything until the depiction becomes "mechanical") and only later constructivistically to interpolate the individual. A second reason why I want to become ever more simple in sociology, in the sense of resorting to the structural and to the functionally average, arises from the fact that I consider the emancipation of men from the alienated compulsion of a society at the level of planning possible only if one brings the efficient laws of block factors to consciousness, in order to make precisely these laws subject to steering through interventions. Just as the consumer, shareholder, or worker can do little as an individual against the pressure upon their activities, up to the point of compulsion, exerted by society and must therefore join together, as an individual, with all the others participating in his situation in order to steer the social determinacy as a whole in the direction of being influenced in a more favorable way, and just as, in this connection, if he is to act correctly and to be free, he must study the large determinants in history, so must someone who really wishes to free men from

the unwanted compulsion of a badly organized society study the interconnections precisely in the place where the core of the large-scale
false determination lies. Or have you never been struck by the paradox
that those who wanted to get rid of determination were the ones with a
materialist-determinist world view, while, on the contrary, the ruling
strata, for whom it was not a vital necessity to get rid of the existing
form of society, spoke of human freedom much more often than the
oppressed? Only one who wants freedom sinks his teeth in the task of
tracking the determinations that exist. One who is comfortable with
existing determinations lays out the world for himself as achieved
freedom. The will to freedom engaged in its genuine actualization
dedicates itself to exposing the present bonds,—someone who is really
artistically endowed does not talk about art (which he needs in any
case) but only about the means by which he could carry it out.

D. "The instrumental-functionalist method" and its contribution to the existential-political-normative attitude

After all this it must nevertheless be conceded once again that instrumental analysis imposes a certain asceticism on itself and that it is
not possible to deduce from it the norms for society as it should be. I
hope that this deliberate limitation can no longer be interpreted as a
hollowed-out reason. If it is impossible to deduce values from an
instrumental analysis, it can nevertheless contribute two things to the
discovery of values. First, it can show negatively which values, though
they can be proclaimed at a certain stage of society (*flatus vocis*), are
incapable of precipitating themselves in this reality as an actuality of
practice. So, it is, for example, demonstrable that the form of liberal
permission to let things go and grow without restraint that we have
hitherto known as "freedom" was tied to a certain stage of economic
technology, a certain stage of the deficient centralizability of the technology of war and the influencing of opinion. The form of freedom
that was the flip side of a defective social integration, that arose through
the possibility of getting out of the way, not planning, will no longer
be possible today.

That does not mean that one abandons the demand for freedom, but
that one thinks through the conception of freedom that is reconcilable
with planning. The ideal that does not correct itself by instrumental
possibilities is fated to become an ideology. Second, we must recog-

nize as sociologists that an instrumentalist thinking through of the situation can be highly productive not only in the sense of a negative limitation (according to which certain ideals are no longer possible in the old sense), but also in the sense of positive discovery. For if one makes oneself a picture of the way in which humanity actually arrived at its norms, these did not fall from heaven, they are not visionary anticipations, as the prophets present themselves, but they got there by searching, groping, in constant tension with situations.[90] The norms that become real do not usually arise in a manner such that someone sets out to found a liberal, fascist, or communist society and constructs everything according to prepared ideals, an anthropological system in his hands, but rather one comes to new wishes in part through the operations of society, in part because one sits in precisely that corner where the negativities of the social process affect one most strongly or most noticeably, and in part by figuring out counter norms in defiance of the norms in place.

These small, searching acts of suffering and ressentiment coalesce in a faith that runs against the stream. Rebellious interventions and formulations emerge from time to time out of the conflicting faiths, and these impose, sometimes with success and sometimes without, the new counter-norms upon segments of the process. If they fail, the norms modify themselves. If the opposition succeeds in something, one listens for the secret of their effectuality. This attitude towards the world of norms is an aggravation to the philosophers. The politician too, as long as he is a prophet or a propagandist, has to pretend that he knew beforehand, through revelation, how things stood with the absolute. The sociologist is the only one who has to take on himself, in this too, the uncomfortable task of showing men how they actually think and how they arrive at their norms. In acts of discovery, step by step, in interaction between revulsion and accommodation. Viewed from this point of view, even an ambivalent attitude towards values in a time of transition and reconstruction has a certain justification. I am fully aware of the fact that my book is supported by antitheses. I uphold with full conviction, for example, the superiority of liberal values, the incredible importance of human freedom, the spontaneity left to the individual in his circles, the superiority of the liberal period in the field of cultural creation, and yet I cannot avoid seeing that this period is over. I hate bureaucratic planning, but I cannot avoid thinking all the more intensively about it. The reason is that I am of the opinion that these tensions are constitutively apportioned to us as children of the age of transition. (On the one hand, through our past, on the other, by the possibility of looking , nevertheless, into the world that is taking on new structural forms before our eyes.) But very few of us have the courage to admit to ourselves that such antinomous tensions are actually motivating us. Who among us would not want both? Planning, order and free initiative, democracy and yet no massification of taste and spirit. The fewest admit to the antitheses of their normative world because they are afraid of being inconsistent and believe that one has to stand firm in ethical matters. In the face of this, it is quite good, I think, if it is at least recognized as the task of sociology to assume the position of the searcher with regard to norms as well. With the sociological method alone, as noted, it will neither produce nor discover them. But it will be helpful in the concretization of norms, initially by applying criticism to existing norms from the standpoint of their realizability, and then by showing, by means of instrumental analysis, where the society could be levered out of its foundations. At the stage of planning, there is a gradual supersession of the old division by which both the norms and the transformative interventions were only found by accident, and thinking must shape the norm more apt for the change in prospect, and concretize instrumentally the change of norms brought to consciousness.

You see, the major reason for the delay in answering rested in the feeling that one would have to reach very far into the sphere of premises in order to rise to your questions and to follow up the stimulus you offered. This is only a fraction of an adequate reply, but I hope that it contributes either to showing our differences very clearly or gradually to our finding together what unites us. And perhaps I may even hope, now that the differences in premises that disturbed you have been discussed, that you will tell me your opinion about the material questions of the book, for the sake of which it was actually written. I am convinced that there too I will learn much from your approval as well as from your disapproval, as was the case now with regard to methodological-anthropological questions.

Yours faithfully,

Notes

1. Dirk Kaesler, ed., *Klassiker der Soziologie* (Munich: C.H. Beck, 1999). Other sociologists included in the first of two volumes are Robert Michels, Marcel Mauss and Maurice Halbwachs, Theodor Geiger, Karl Mannheim, Norbert Elias, and Alfred Schütz, to whom the observations in the text apply almost as well, although they are at least one generation younger. The contrast with the careers of most authors covered in the second volume brings out the point: Lazarsfeld, Parsons, Adorno, Freyer, Aron, Homans, Merton, Mills, Goffman, Luhmann, Habermas, and Bourdieu. A majority could count on an institutionalized frame to constitute their work as an academic science, and even those among them who chose to make the relationship to politics a major theme enjoyed the backing of a recognized academic status.
2. See Colin Loader and David Kettler, *Sociology as Political Education: Mannheim in the University*. New Brunswick and London: Transaction Publishers, 2000.
3. Karl Mannheim, "On the Nature of Economic Ambition and Its Significance for the Social Education of Man." In *Essays in the Sociology of Knowledge*. Ed. and trans. Paul Kecskemeti. London: Routledge & Kegan Paul, pp. 230–275; Karl Mannheim, "The Sociology of Knowledge." In *Ideology and Utopia*. London: Routledge & Kegan Paul, pp. 237–280.
4. David Kettler, "Marxism and Culture. Lukács in the Hungarian Revolutions of 1918/19." *Telos*, 10: 35–92.1971; Eva Karádi and Erzsébet Vezér,.,eds. *Georg Lukács, Karl Mannheim und der Sonntagskreis*. Frankfurt/Main: Sendler 1985; Mary Gluck, *Georg Lukács and his Generation, 1900–1918*. Cambridge, MA: Harvard University Press ,1985.
5. Endreß, Martin and Srubar, Ilya, eds. *Karl Mannheims Analyse der Moderne. Mannheims erste Frankfurter Vorlesung von 1930. Edition und Studien (Jahrbuch für Soziologiegeschichte 1996)*. Opladen: Leske und Budrich.
6. Loader and Kettler, *Sociology as Political Education: Mannheim in the University*.
7. The following are the notes for a more schematic opening drawn from the Kurt Wolff Lecture notes discussed in the Preface. There is no explanation for the discrepancy. Perhaps there was an introductory session of some sort before the start of the formal series for which stenography was wanted. Then too, as noted, the physical evidence by no means precludes this as a transcription of Mannheim's own lecture notes, which the text resembles in form, and which Mannheim may have superceded.

   Sociology. Larger research context. A center [is] necessary. Systematic location. Orientation, answering the most urgent questions. What is sociology? What are its sub-divisions? Its critique, etc. This endless task is to be solved only in fragments. But taking our departure from the whole, in order to be able to classify the individual elements. Task: (1) Discovering the systematic problems. (2) Linking the systematic problems, expanding the horizon.

Formal Sociology. Open to attack if it claims to be all of sociology. Good as a sub-field.

Field: Research into formal social occurrences. (1) Mass and group. Mass-psychology. (2) Significance of the differentiation of society, for the individual as well. (3) Sociological construction of the consciousness of self (*Ichbewusstseins*); viewed from three sides: how the "controlling ego" ("*Kontrollich*") constitutes itself, as viewed from childhood, the primitive, and history (*die Historie*). Philosophy, psychoanalysis, etc.

Where does man stand? Sociology makes us conscious that it is not a question of the world, of every human being; we are not in a state of being, but on the move. *Sociology of the Primitive.* It suffices us to see the beginning clearly, the original situation, insofar as we can gain access to it. *Political Sociology*: Of immediate concern to us. Research strongly takes its start from here. Sociology of the family, state, nation, economy, property. All this can be discussed only from a historical-sociological distance. *Cultural Sociology*: [. . . .]

Material Sociology (Realsoziologie). = Formal, Primitive, and Political Sociology.

Problem of a *Sociology of the Spirit (Soziologie des Geistes).*

What could sociology mean to the other sciences?

In America, France, and England, sociology is indisputably the center of the sciences. All the human sciences are strongly influenced by sociology there. Destruction or enrichment of what was formerly Philosophy (*der früheren Philosophie*).

8. Except in cases where there are standardized English equivalents, such as *Geisteswissenschaften* and *Geistesgeschichte*, we use "spirit" and its derivations for "*Geist.*" Mannheim's struggle with the legacy of Hegel's *Phenomenologie des Geistes* requires this translation, despite occasional awkwardness.

9. Johann Wolfgang von Goethe, "Bedeutende Förderniß durch ein einziges Wort," in *Goethes Werke* (Weimar: Böhlau, 1893), div. 2, v. 11, p. 59. Goethe believed that even the formation of "physical" organs is due to external stimuli. In the introduction to his *Theory of Colours*, he writes: "The eye may be said to owe its existence to light, which calls forth, as it were, a sense that is akin to itself; the eye in short, is formed with reference to light, to be fit for the action of light; the light it contains corresponding with the light without." *Theory of Colours*, trans, Charles Lock Eastlake (Cambridge, MA: The MIT Press, 1970), p. liii.

10. Cp. Mannheim's letter to Max Wertheimer (below).

11. A direct reply to the opinion of Leopold von Wiese, widely broadcast before its formulation in von Wiese, *Soziologie. Geschichte und Hauptprobleme* (Berlin: De Gruyter, [1931] 1960), 38f.

12. In German, "*Attitude*" has more the connotation of a psychological term, while "*Einstellung*" is an expressly non-psychological term in phenomenology for a mode of addressing an object.

13. Max Scheler, *On the Eternal in Man*, trans. Bernard Noble (New York: Harper & Row, 1961).

14. Edmund Husserl, *Ideas: General Introduction to Pure Phenomenology*, trans. W.R. Boyce Gibson (New York: Collier, 1962).

15. Karl Jaspers, *Psychologie der Weltanschauungen* (Berlin: Springer, 1919).

16. Mannheim, *From Karl Mannheim*, ed. Kurt H. Wolff (New Brunswick & London: Transaction Publishers, 1993), pp. 136–187, 244–260.

17. Compare Mannheim's concept of "conjunctive knowledge" in Mannheim, *Structures of Thinking*, trans. David Kettler,Volker Meja and Nico Stehr (London: Routledge and Kegan Paul, 1982), pp. 191–194.

18. There follows a reminder, presumably by Mannheim: "Indicate the impossibility of such an experimental attitude to life within a religious consciousness."

19. The translation of *seelisch* as "psychic" is an unhappy necessity. There is first a consistent distinction to be upheld between *Geist* and *Seele* so that neither "spiritual" nor "mental" can be made to work. Cp. Mannheim's *"Seele und Kultur,"* In Karl Mannheim, *Wissenssoziologie*, ed. Kurt H. Wolff (Berlin and Neuwied: Luchterhand Verlag, 1964), pp. 66—84. Second, an unsteady but important distinction is introduced later between a *seelische Einstellung* and a *psychologisches Phänomen*, so that "psychological" would be misleading. So we will go with the "Soul" as the noun and "psychic" as the adjective. We have discussed this further in Loader and Kettler, *Sociology as Political Education*, p.xxx.

20. There is no satisfactory translation of the Hegelian term. The technical philosophical term "sublation," coined expressly for this purpose, would obscure Mannheim's design more thoroughly than retaining the very ordinary German word. Mannheim's threefold definition corresponds not only to Hegel's usage but also to the three ordinary language meanings of the core term, "aufgehoben." In context, Mannheim does not use Hegel in a technical way, as witness his mix of concepts quite incompatible with Hegel's thought. *"Augehoben,"* in Mannheim's present appropriation of Hegel's coinage, serves in effect as a metaphor superior to the geological metaphor it qualifies.

21. Mannheim omitted this phrase from his quotation of the passage in the previous lecture.

22. *Vollzug* and *vollziehen* are among Mannheim's most frequently used technical terms in this text, and they are the most difficult to translate. They highlight the vitalist element in activities of the most diverse sort, from the *Vollzug* of an individual act to the *Vollzug* of a norm to the *Vollzug* of life itself. The most likely source is Heidegger. A decisive conception below is the idea of a person "becoming separated" (*herausfallen*) from an enactment (*Vollzug*) , which presumably refers to the paradox of the devitalization of a vital act. We have translated the root word variously as enactment, carrying out (or through), effectuating or executing, depending on the location of the specific use on the spectrum of connotations we believe to be intended by the term.

23. Mannheim explores this theme in his unpublished play, *Die Dame aus Biarritz*. See David Kettler and Volker Meja, "Their 'Own Peculiar': Karl Mannheim and the Rise of Women," *International Sociology*, 8 (1993), pp.5–7.

24. Mannheim, *Ideology and Utopia* (London: Routledge & Kegan Paul [1929] 1936).

25. Examples evidently omitted from manuscript.

26. Cp. Note 11 and Mannheim's attempt, below, to defend his *Ideology and Utopia* against the charge of abandoning sociology for psychology.

27. We read *Werdungen* as a misprint for *Wertungen*: see a few lines below.

28. The existentialist concept of *Umbruch* was very important in Mannheim's teaching. It is among those highlighted in the acutely focused parody written by Norbert Elias and others at the time of Mannheim's departure from Heidelberg. Soziologischer Kollektiv 1930, *"Die Wolke," oder "Politik also Wissenschaft,"* in Henk S. Woldring, *Karl Mannheim* (New York: St. Martin's Press, 1986), pp. 391–403. His doctoral student, Nina Rubinstein, made it central to her dissertation on the French *emigrés*. See Nina Rubinstein, *Die französische Emigration*

nach 1789. Ein Beitrag zur Soziologie der politischen Emigration, ed. Dirk Raith (Graz: Nausner & Nausner, 2000). Cp. Kettler and Meja, "Own Peculiar Way," pp. 17, 21, where the term is riskily translated as "regenerative transition."

29. This term literally means "screwed back" or "ratcheted back" and implies the application of force.

30. This is a response to critics of *Ideology and Utopia* such as Ernst Robert Curtius and Eduard Spranger. See Loader and Kettler, *Sociology as Political Education.*

31. This is the note on which he ended the essay on Utopia which concluded the original edition of *Ideology and Utopia,* published the preceding year. Cp. Colin Loader, *The Intellectual Development of Karl Mannheim* (Cambridge: Cambridge University Press, 1985), p. 111.

32. Sigmund Freud, *Group Psychology and the Analysis of the Ego,* trans. James Strachey (New York: Bantam Books, 1960), p. 80.

33. The topic of the *Übung* mentioned by Mannheim suggests that he worked through materials from his study of nineteenth-century conservatism in the class exercises. For parallels between Mannheim's explication of sociology in the sense of an attitude in the present lectures and a coded undercurrent in the *Habilitationsschrift,* see David Kettler and VolkerMeja, "The Design of Conservatism." in pp.1–26 Mannheim, *Conservatism:A Contribution to the Sociology of Knowledge,* ed. David Kettler, Volker Meja, and Nico Stehr. London and New York: Routledge & Kegan Paul, 1986. Sociology as specialized science dominates the surface appearance of the earlier work, but not its underlying point. These lectures clarify the multiple levels.

34. Mannheim gives Adam Müller an important place in his earlier study of conservatism. This interest brings him close to Carl Schmitt and other anti-liberal writers. See Mannheim, *Conservatism*; Schmitt, *Political Romanticism,* trans. Guy Oakes (Cambridge, MA: The MIT Press, 1986).

35. Sigmund Freud, "Thoughts for the Times on War and Death," pp. 288–317 in *Collected Papers,* trans. and ed. James Strachey (London: Hogarth Press, 1956).

36. From Freud, "Thoughts for the Times," 316. The authorized translation uses "civilized" for Freud's *"kulturellen,"* here as elsewhere. We have left the former term intact in the quotation, but revert to culture and its adjectival forms in the Mannheim paraphrases, since "culture" and the "cultural" are important terms of art in his writings, used in a way that presupposes Alfred Weber's contrast between culture and civilization.

37. Mannheim may be making an unusually personal reference here, since at least one of his intimates in the Lukács circle in Budapest, the writer Emma Ritook, allied herself with fascist currents.

38. Reading *legt vor* instead of *liegt vor.*

39. For Mannheim's family circumstances, see Mary Gluck, *Georg Lukács and his Generation, 1900–1918* (Cambridge, MA: Harvard University Press, 1985). The personal nature of this comment, as well as his earlier references to Hungarian acquaintances who gravitated towards fascism, are unique in Mannheim's writings or lecture notes. This increases the likelihood that the main topic of the present lecture, Marxist orthodoxy, represents a settling of accounts with Georg Lukács. The lead essay in Lukács' *History and Class-Consciousness,* (Cambridge, MA: The MIT Press, 1968), is entitled "What is Orthodox Marxism?" and Lukács treats the designation as a binding norm. For Lukács' submission to his degradation within the Communist movement during these years, see Loader and Kettler, *Sociology as Political Education.*

40. Mannheim's caution at this point is a fresh indication of his awareness of the

politics of the day. The Center Party was critical to all the coalitions of the Weimar years. During the months of Mannheim's course, a split between the Social Democrats and the Center precipitated the election that ushered in the final agonies of the Republic. Whether its right wing or center left would control the Center Party, accordingly was an immediate and urgent question.

41. Reading *Aufforderungen* for *Forderungen*.

42. Mannheim's word is *"primitiv."* But that is inconsistent with Mannheim's other uses of the term, even in this paragraph. These cannot be reconciled with this instance, where the context shows that the reference is to thinking in its original structure and function (*ursprüngliche Struktur des Denkens*), a conception that is the antithesis of what he calls primitive in the context of "reprimitivization."43.

The text reads "psychological" here, but that is certainly a misprint, because it would flatly contradict the argument Mannheim is making. On the distinction between sociology and psychology, see also below. It is striking that Mannheim turns from critics of *Ideology and Utopia*, who are addressed throughout this lecture, to critics of the lecture course itself. Both the fact of criticism and Mannheim's responsiveness to it are worth noting.

44. Mannheim may be referring to a specific incident since his arrival in Frankfurt. See Loader and Kettler, *Sociology as Political Education* for Mannheim's settling of accounts with Marxism and his disagreements with Max Horkheimer and Theodore Wiesengrund [Adorno].

45. In the discussion below, Mannheim speaks repeatedly—and seemingly as insider—of *"die Partei"* ("the Party") when referring to the political articulation(s) of Marxism, although he expressly distinguishes between communism and socialism whenever the occasion calls for it. In our opinion, Mannheim's term normally refers to the "party of socialism" in a sense broad enough to encompass the religious socialism of Tillich, to which he was close, as well as both the Social Democratic and Communist parties. This usage abruptly ceases below when he abruptly slides from "orthodoxy" as a tendency within the presumably socialist "party" to the "orthodox party" as the expression of fascism. In this context, then, there is also a surprising affirmation of the possible "necessity" of a fascist party of the deed.

46. For the concept of *"Realdiskussion,"* see Mannheim, *Ideology and Utopia*, where he credits it to the Marxist conception of theory and practice. The term cannot be simply translated as "realistic discussion" because the realism encompasses the limits of discussion, too, so that there is a strong element of bargaining. The concept is expressly developed against the liberal conception of parliament as a "platform" for rational discussion. See Kettler and Meja, *Mannheim and the Crisis of Liberalism*, pp. 101–102, 171.

47. In Mannheim's usage, in general, the "political doctrine of theory and practice" refers to Georg Lukács' version of Marxism. Mannheim's rather one-sided dialogue with Lukács in his Marxist phase dates to his first semester as tutor in Heidelberg, when he conducted a workshop on *History and Class-Consciousness*. See the discussion of Lukács on theory and practice in *Ideology and Utopia*, pp. 110–111. See below the Protocol of a seminar on Lukács that Mannheim conducted jointly with Alfred Weber.

48. The syntax is awkward here, and it is impossible to be certain that Mannheim imputes the "second solution" to Nietzsche as well. The whole paragraph is remarkable because Mannheim shifts without notice from the discussion of the activist and orthodox moment in socialism to fascism, perhaps in reprise of his earlier characterization of Mussolini's shift. This discussion should be read not

only in light of Mannheim's struggle with Marxist colleagues, students and models, but also in view of his complex relationship to Hans Freyer. See Loader and Kettler, *Sociology as Political Education.*

49. Friedrich Nietzsche, *Beyond Good and Evil; Prelude to a Philosophy of the Future,* trans. Walter Kaufmann (New York: Vintage, 1966), pp. 11–12. On the margin, Mannheim notes that the quotation is not literally correct, but the italicized words represent his only noteworthy revision of Nietzsche's language. The original is *"gewohnten Wertgefühlen,"* which is correctly translated by Kaufmann as "accustomed value feelings." We follow Kaufmann in the rest, inserting ellipses where necessary.

50. Ludwig Binswanger, "Lebensfunktion und innere Lebensgeschichte," *Monatschrift für Psychiatrie und Neurologie,* 48 (1928).

51. Georg Misch, *A History of Autobiography in Antiquity,* trans. E.W. Dickes (London: Routledge & Kegan Paul, 1950).

52. Mannheim is probably playing a German allusion off against a Hungarian one, in line with the general litrerary design of the article. "The Broken Jug" is a humorous piece by the classical dramatist, Heinrich von Kleist, whose work Mannheim cited, for example, in his Hungarian lectures on cultural philosophy. The Hungarian reference would be to a proverb about the jug breaking if it is taken to the well too often. While Kleist's jug stands for virginity, the Hungarian one evokes experience to excess.

53. Endre Ady (1877–1919) was the Hungarian poet most admired by Mannheim's generation of social and cultural reformers. His premature death in the early days of the Hungarian Revolution made his funeral a highly dramatic occasion in the capital and fixed his symbolic status as the politically uncompromised voice of renewal.

54. All of these "prophets" had connections to trends such as vitalism, Nietzscheanism and the Youth Movement that were scorned by many academics as "dilettantish." The author of a study on Nietzsche, Rudolf Steiner preached "anthroposophy," which presented spiritualism in a "democratized" form. Oswald Spengler's popular book, *The Decline of the West,* offered a pessimistic study in which cyclical biological analogies were "morphologically" applied to history. Hans Blüher and Gustav Wyneken were both important leaders of the Youth Movement. Blüher, who was critical of bourgeois home life, schooling and the church, interpreted the Youth Movement as a homo-erotic phenomenon. Wynecken, the leader of the Free German Youth, rejected nationalist themes to place an emphasis on achieving the highest individual creativity. Hermann Keyserling, a friend of Mannheim's mentor Alfred Weber, wrote popular philosophy with a strong vitalistic emphasis on spiritual creativity. Weber also had strong ties to Wynecken. The circle of the poet Stefan George is discussed by Mannheim below.

55. The earliest letter from Mannheim to Kracauer uncovered in archives dates from 1928, but Mannheim regrets that they have not been meeting as often as before, when Ernst Bloch brought them together (Éva Gábor, *Mannheim Károly levelezéze. 1911–1946.* [Budapest: Argumentum Kiad—. MTA Lukács Archivum, 1996]: 33). That leaves the dates quite uncertain. While Mannheim's additional letters to Kracauer in Germany contained requests by Mannheim for Kracauer's help in publication matters, a letter in 1933 hints that Mannheim may be able to help Kracauer out of his desperate condition, an allusion to Mannheim's unsuccessful Rockefeller plan, for which he hoped to employ Kracauer (Gábor, *Mannheim*: 63; see above).

56. After a first visit in Frankfurt in November 1930 by Louis Wirth, the American

sociologist who was to be responsible for the English translation of *Ideology and Utopia,* Mannheim wrote him: "Since I have experienced in my own case and in that of others how difficult it is for a mere examination to do full justice to an investigation which emerges in a different setting, I would ask you, in the spirit of our conversation, not to take a final position on our sociological efforts until you have a chance of living with us for a while and seeing how we pose scientific problems in the immediate problem context of our life here." (Mannheim to Wirth, November 17th, 1930. Louis Wirth Papers, Regenstein Library, University of Chicago, 7:11). Mannheim's interest in American sociology, in turn, is more than casual. See Mannheim, "American Sociology," in *Essays on Sociology and Social Psychology,* ed. and trans. Paul Kecskemeti (London: Routledge & Kegan Paul, [1931]1953), pp. 193–194; cp. Kettler and Meja, *Mannheim and the Crisis of Liberalism.*

57. In our view, the collegial mood of this seminar casts substantial doubt on Norbert Elias' recollection that there were harsh feelings between Alfred Weber and Mannheim in their dispute. Cp. Norbert Elias, *Norbert Elias über sich selbst.* Frankfurt: Suhrkamp, 1990, and Reinhard Blomert, *Intellektuelle im Aufbruch: Karl Mannheim, Alfred Weber, Norbert Elias und die Heidelberger Sozialwissenschaften der Zwischenkriegszeit.* (Munich: Hanser, 1999), pp. 242—243.

58. Ibid., pp. 202–203; Mathias Greffrath. *Die Zerstörung einer Zukunft: Gespräche mit emigrierten Sozialwissenschaftlern* (Hamburg: Rowohlt, 1979); David Kettler and Volker Meja, *Karl Mannheim and the Crisis of Liberalism. The Secret of the New Times* (New Brunswick & London: Transaction, 1995). Ibid., pp. 202–203; Mathias Greffrath. *Die Zerstörung einer Zukunft: Gespräche mit emigrierten Sozialwissenschaftlern* (Hamburg: Rowohlt, 1979); David Kettler and Volker Meja, *Karl Mannheim and the Crisis of Liberalism. The Secret of the New Times* (New Brunswick & London: Transaction, 1995).

59. Walther Killy and Rudolf Vierhaus, eds. *Deutsche Biographische Enzyklopädie* (Munich, 1998), p. 362.Walther Killy and Rudolf Vierhaus, eds. *Deutsche Biographische Enzyklopädie* (Munich, 1998), p. 362.

60. Blomert, *Intellektuelle,* p 429.

61. Eberhard Demm, *Von der Weimarer Republik zur Bundesrepublik. Der politische Weg Alfred Webers 1920–1958* (Düsseldorf: Droste, 1999), pp. 443f.

62. Alfred Weber Papers, Deutsche Bundesarchiv, Koblenz, Germany.

63. The bearded professor is Heinrich Rickert, Professor of Philosophy. Weber may have said what Mannheim reports, but the matter did not go quite so smoothly. Mannheim wrote a second, more sociological treatise to replace the one that he evidently had available when he first came to Weber, but his actual habilitation work was a third work, a case study of conservative thought, and his prime sponsor was Emil Lederer, not Alfred Weber, even though Lederer was serving as a guest professor in Tokyo during the time of composition. Weber's extraordinary tolerance of opposition from his students is documented in the protocols of several seminars reproduced in Demm 1999: 462–470. The audacity of the Jewish Menshevik student, Boris Goldenberg, is especially remarkable. Demm, *Von der Weimarer Republik,* pp 462 f. Cp. pp. 81f. See above.

64. Paul Tillich, "Das Frankfurter Gespräch," in *Briefwechsel und Streitschriften* (Frankfurt/Main: Evangelisches Verlagswerk, 1983), pp. 314–369.

65. Note Mannheim's use of evangelical language.

66. Reference is to a comment by Pollock belittling the tiny proportion of people who can concern themselves with the topic under discussion, compared to the great mass of people in material misery.

67. Max Horkheimer Archive, Frankfurt Municipal Library IX, 210.
68. Karl Mannheim, "The Democratization of Culture," in *Essays on the Sociology of Culture*, ed. and trans. Ernest Mannheim und Paul Kecskemeti (London: Routledge & Kegan Paul, 1956), pp. 171–246; Mannheim, *Man and Society in an Age of Reconstruction* (London: Routledge & Kegan Paul, 1940).
69. Karl Mannheim, "Das konservative Denken," *Archiv für Sozialwissenschaft und Sozialpolitik* 57, 1:68–142, 2: 470–395. Mannheim, "Conservative Thought," in *From Karl Mannheim*, pp. 260–350, is a later version, with different contents. But are derived from Mannheim, *Conservatism*.
70. There is no substantive postscript fitting this context in the document preserved in the archives. See below.
71. Tübingen: J.C.B. Mohr (Paul Siebeck).Tübingen: J.C.B. Mohr (Paul Siebeck), 1932. See Colin Loader and David Kettler, *Sociology as Political Education*.
72. This quotation comes from Hans Freyer, *Soziologie als Wirklichkeitswissenschaft: Logische Grundlegung des Systems der Soziologie* (Leipzig: B.G. Teubner, 1930), p. 307. For Mannheim's critique of Freyer, see Loader and Kettler, *Sociology as Political Education*.
73. Paragraph breaks in this section have been inserted by the translators.
74. Mannheim opens with a defensive remark, which he strikes: "It might sometimes appear as if the presentation might exhibit planlessness."
75. In his notes, Mannheim crossed out section (e). We are restoring it because there is no conflict between this part of the analsysis and the rest.
76. Karl Jaspers, *Man in the Modern Age*, trans. Eden and Cedar Paul (Garden City, NY: Doubleday Anchor, 1957).
77. In a preliminary sketch of the lecture, Mannheim adds: "If she becomes educated but functionless, she sickens from it."
78. Since *Bürger* is ambiguous, the phrase could be read as "citizen and worker," and this reading would better fit the copula. Yet it would suggest a social equation that Mannheim consistently rejects. Intellectuals are either bourgeois or proletarians, depending on their social location—from which they are only *relatively* detached.
79. Mannheim's reference is to Max Scheler's concept of the *"Ohnmacht des Geistes."*
80. In a preliminary note, Mannheim lists the following senses of fragmentation: (1) quantitative: one is only one person and does not know everything; (2) qualitative: one has one—sided interests; (3) in the division of labor, only one part of reality falls in our purview; (4) we see things only at the historical stage at which we stand.
81. Heimann refers to Karl Mannheim, *Mensch und Gesellschaft im Zeitalter des Umbaus*. Leiden: Sijtoff, 1935. We have inserted in brackets the appropriate page numbers of the expanded English version, *Man and Society in an Age of Reconstruction*, trans. Edward Shils (New York: Harcourt, Brace, 1940).
82. This "polemic" against a work by Freyer on planning occurs on p.194 of *Man and Society*. Mannheim identifies a "fascist element" in Freyer's book that contains an "over-emphasis on power."
83. Interestingly, it is here that Mannheim brings pedagogical concerns of many of the Frankfurt writings into *Man and Society*. He speaks of a "new human type" who is able to deal with the changing modern world. The school, he says, must become "an experimental community." Cp. Loader, "Kann ein experimentelles Leben geplant werden? Mannheims zweite Übergangsperiode," in Endreß/Srubar, *Mannheims Analyse der Moderne*.
84. Eduard Heimann, "Types and Potentialities of Economic Planning," *Social Re-*

search, 2 (1935).

85. This is the only sense in which I made use of the word irrational in my book. I did not mean to comprehend anything substantial in the sociological analysis, but merely to indicate the role of the unorganized in psychic and social life. [Marginal note by KM]

86. That is the glorification not so much of the irrational as of the inability to think—the *ressentiment* typical of backward strata unable to meet the intellectual requirements of modernity. [Marginal note by KM]

87. Romano Guardini, *Pascal for Our Time*, trans. Brian Thompson (New York: Herder & Herder, 1966).

88. The entire precedent social cultural stream, with its language of thought and feeling, is present even in a monk's cell or in Meister Eckehardt's state of "inner departedness," and the retreat retains society within itself inasmuch as it is society from which one turns away. Solitude too is a sociological phenomenon. [Marginal note by KM]

89. Or he may make become a model, because he happens to be the one who accidentally reacts in a manner appropriate to the new situation. (As in the case of Hitler, the psychopath, who would have been sent to a psychiatric clinic for assessment in a period of social consolidation but becomes "Führer" in a time social dissolution.) [Marginal note by KM]

90. In the prophets, the experimenting life of many individuals coalesces to public visibility. [Partially illegible marginal insert by KM]

Index